735

MAN AND SOCIETY IN CALAMITY

Man and Society in Calamity

THE EFFECTS OF WAR, REVOLUTION, FAMINE,
PESTILENCE UPON HUMAN MIND, BEHAVIOR,
SOCIAL ORGANIZATION AND CULTURAL LIFE

BY

PITIRIM A. SOROKIN

36679

GREENWOOD PRESS, PUBLISHERS
NEW YORK   1968

Printed in the United States of America

CONTENTS

[5]

ACKNOWLEDGMENTS

The author is grateful to the following publishers for permission to quote from the books mentioned:

Allen and Unwin, Ltd., J. Burckhardt, *The Civilization of the Renaissance in Italy*, and J. Nohl, *The Black Death*.

American Book Company, Pitirim A. Sorokin, *Social and Cultural Dynamics*.

British Medical Journal, F. Dillon, *Neuroses among Combatant Troups in the Great War*, and E. Wittkower and J. B. Spillane, *Neuroses in War*.

Cambridge University Press, C. Creighton, *History of Epidemics in Britain*.

Columbia University Press, E. K. Nottingham, *Methodism and the Frontier*, and S. H. Prince, *Catastrophe and Social Change*.

Gerald Duckworth, Ltd., K. Humsun, *Hunger*.

Harvard University Press, A. Lawrence Lowell, *Public Opinion in War and Peace*.

William Heinemann, Ltd., E. Mikkelsen, *Lost in the Arctic*.

Johns Hopkins University Press, W. F. Albright, *From the Stone Age to Christianity*.

Oxford University Press, M. I. Rostovtzeff, *Social and Economic History of the Hellenistic World*.

Charles Scribner's Sons, James H. Breasted, *The Dawn of Conscience*.

PREFACE

We live and act in an age of great calamities. War and revolution, famine and pestilence, are again rampant on this planet. Again they exact their deadly toll from suffering humanity. Again they influence every moment of our existence: our mentality and behavior, our social life and cultural processes. Like a fell demon, they cast their shadow upon every thought we think and every action we perform.

This book attempts to account for the effects these calamities exert on the mental processes, behavior, social organization, and cultural life of the population involved. In what way do famine and pestilence, war and revolution, tend to modify our mind and conduct, our social organization and cultural life? To what extent do they succeed in this, and when and why do they prove less effective? What are the causes of these calamities, and what are the ways out?

In dealing with these problems the book tries to give not a detailed description of all the unique effects of this or that specific calamity but the *typical* effects of famine and pestilence, war and revolution, such as have repeatedly occurred in all major catastrophes of this kind. To use academic language, it attempts to formulate the principal uniformities regularly manifested during such calamities.

The study opens with a concise characterization of the influence of disasters upon the simplest mental processes and upon mental life as a whole. It proceeds to an analysis of the typical effects upon human behavior and vital processes—deaths, births, marriages. From this it passes to an investigation of how calamities modify economic, political, and social organizations, social migration and mobility; and how they influence the ethical and religious, scientific and artistic, and philosophical and ideological activities of

[9]

society. The last part deals with the causes of calamities and the methods of effectually coping with them. The volume ends with a concise application of the conclusions reached to the crisis of our age.

From the comparative simplicity of the problems of the first few chapters the study proceeds to the increasingly more complex and more significant problems of theoretical science and practical conduct. In the last three parts of the work the generalizations and conclusions rise to the level of the broadest inductive generalizations of social science, throwing considerable light upon the basic changes in social structure and mobility, in ethics and religion, in science and the fine arts. Here the sociology of calamities becomes a general sociology, as well as an inductive philosophy of history. One of its conclusions is that calamities are not an unmixed evil: side by side with their destructive and pernicious functions they play also a constructive and positive rôle in the history of culture and man's creative activities. With human beings as they are, catastrophes are great educators of mankind.

The bibliography is reduced to the necessary minimum and is placed at the end of the volume.

The author is indebted to the Harvard Committee for Research in the Social Sciences for financial help in the typographical preparation of the manuscript, and to Mrs. Marjorie Noble for the typing. He takes this opportunity to express his thanks to the numerous persons and organizations who, finding something valuable in his previous works, have generously encouraged him in a continuation of his studies.

PITIRIM A. SOROKIN.

Harvard University
September, 1942

PART ONE

THE INFLUENCE OF CALAMITIES
UPON OUR MIND

Chapter One

How Calamities Influence Our Affective and Emotional Life

1. *Introductory Remarks*

The life history of any society is an incessant fluctuation between periods of comparative well-being and those of calamity. For a given period the society enjoys peace, order, prosperity, and freedom from notable catastrophes. Again, its life is darkened by calamities which, singly or en masse, assail it and destroy its previous well-being. Sooner or later this catastrophic phase is succeeded by a new stretch of well-being, which is replaced, in turn, by a further period of calamity. And so this alternation goes on, throughout the entire duration of the society in question.

The relative duration of each of these stretches of the historical road differs for different societies. Now the era of well-being is longer than the catastrophic; now the calamitous phase is more permanent. The historical road of some societies is made up mainly of stretches of well-being, punctuated by bumpy portions of misery. The road traveled by other societies consists principally of dreary stretches interspersed here and there by short sections of good pavements.

Among the manifold and diverse calamities that have befallen mankind, four have probably proved the most frequent, most destructive, most terrible, and, at the same time, most instructive and significant—namely, war and revolution, famine, and pestilence. These four monsters are the subject of this investigation, in so far as they affect our minds and behavior, our social organization, and our cultural life. Let us now address ourselves to this task, beginning with the study of their influence upon our basic mental processes, and then passing to their effects upon our conduct, social organization, and culture.

Before undertaking an analysis of how calamities modify our emotional and affective experience, I would stress the general principle of the *diversification and polarization of these effects* in different parts of the population. By this principle is meant that *the effects of a given calamity are not identical—indeed, often are opposite—for different individuals and groups of the society concerned*, since individuals and groups differ from one another biologically and psychosocially. Thus, a person who is immune to a given disease is naturally not affected by it in the same way as one who is not immune. One possessed of robust courage and morale conducts himself on a battlefield in a way very different from the behavior of a person lacking in morale and courage. One becomes like well-tempered steel,—a moral hero,—whereas another turns into a coward, a nervous wreck, or a criminal. This diversification and polarization of the effects of the same calamity is attributable also to the fact that not all the members of the society are equally exposed to its dangers and hardships. Even in war, as a rule, only a part of the population, the combatants, are directly subjected to the danger of death and to other hardships. The rest of the population is less exposed, and some groups are only remotely affected. During famines not all suffer equally: some die of starvation, others suffer less, and still others are fairly well nourished and even derive profit from the tragedy of the victims.

To sum up, owing to biological and psychosocial differences and to the varying incidence of a given calamity, some persons emerge as moral heroes, others as criminals and profligates; some prove highly religious, others atheistic. Subsequently we shall develop this *law of the diversifica-*

tion and polarization of the effects of calamity in more detail. For the present we shall be concerned primarily with the effects which calamities tend to produce when unopposed by other sociocultural forces. When they are so opposed, their consequences are frequently very different from those which arise when they are the sole factors that control human behavior. In the next two chapters we shall describe chiefly the effects that calamities tend to produce. In subsequent chapters this one-sidedness will be corrected by a study of the actual effects of calamities in conjunction with the many other forces that determine the life of society and of its members.

2. The Change in Emotions and Feelings Induced by Physiological and Psychosocial Starvation

We must distinguish between *complete, physiological starvation*, where the quantity and quality of food consumed are below the physiological minimum necessary to meet the needs of the organism, and the *partial or comparative, psychosocial starvation* due to our habits of eating certain kinds and amounts of food at certain times, to our preference for finer and more appetizing foods, to the contrast between the luxurious and inferior diets of the upper and lower classes, respectively, or to other psychosocial conditions. Though no physiological food deficiency exists in psychosocial starvation, we insist, in addition, on eating our meals at the habitual time, and we feel either "hungry" or dissatisfied if we miss a meal and its gustatory pleasures. When we are forced to forego foods of finer quality, we resent such a degradation or else accept it grudgingly when it proves inevitable. If we seek for food when we are hungry physiologically, we also seek for superior food in preference to a more primitive fare. This point should not be overlooked, because many an individual action and many a social process has been stimulated not only by physiological but also by psychosocial starvation. If, for instance, biological hunger plays a tangible rôle in generating social conflicts, no less important is the rôle played by psychosocial starvation. The same is true of many other social phenomena. Physiological starvation is either *absolute*, when the organism is totally deprived of food, or *relative*, when the food is insufficient either quantitatively or qualitatively. Likewise, psychosocial starvation assumes many different degrees and forms.

Let us now pass to a consideration of the effects of starvation in the field of our feelings and emotional experiences. If we refrain from eating for a number of hours, or if we see, smell, or taste a particularly tempting dish, we experience an access of "appetite." In its pure form it is a pleasant rather than a painful emotion,[1] as suggested, for instance, by the Continental greeting "Good Appetite!" The complex of experiences covered by this term is not something uniform and identical but represents a group of passive-active emotions differing from one another both quantitatively and qualitatively. Quantitatively we experience different degrees of appetite, beginning with the slightest and ending with the most intense "wolf's appetite." Qualitatively the appetite for meat differs somewhat from that for sweets or fruit. The emergence of appetite in our inner experience is the first radical change, generated not so much by physiological as by psychosocial starvation. It is experienced daily by all healthy organisms not suffering from physiological starvation. After a few minutes or an hour (depending upon the person) it disappears, even if we do not take any nourishment. It can be killed momentarily by the sight of a worm or by the mere mention of unappetizing objects such as worms and dirt. With the onset of physiological starvation it becomes intermittent, until, in the more pronounced phases of this phenomenon, it disappears entirely. Its main physiological function consists in reminding one of the advisability of "refueling" at the habitual time in order to avoid possible complications.[2]

When psychosocial starvation gives place to physiological starvation, appetite tends to disappear and is replaced by a very different experience—that of *hunger*. While appetite is a rather pleasant experience, hunger is definitely painful. The only similarity between the two consists in an urge for food. Whereas appetite can be dispelled by any disagreeable external stimulus, hunger is not extinguished by such stimuli and often impels one to eat nauseating food—in exceptional cases even human corpses.

Like appetite, hunger is not a constant emotion, nor does it progressively grow with an increase of physiological starvation. It is, rather, an intermittent phenomenon. If physiological starvation is not absolute, hunger appears and disappears intermittently. But if physiological starvation is absolute, after the first few days the sense of hunger disappears as a special emotion being replaced by a complex of diversified painful feelings, sensations, and emotions. Besides the craving for food it ordinarily involves a dull gnawing sensation, fatigue and weakness, a feeling of emptiness and apathy, difficulty in concentrating on anything except food, nausea, irritability, and the like. The imagination flares up, only a moment later to die down. Instability, erratic change, jumps and jerkiness pervade the victim's affective and emotional processes, though his prevailing mood is one of depression and apathy.[3]

It is to be noted that hunger in artificial laboratory conditions and in actual life are two different things. In the laboratory, starvation is induced for scientific purposes, under the supervision of doctors, without any danger to life, without any undue exertion. As such it is something very different from the imposed starvation of actual life, which involves the uncertainty of procuring food, as well as serious danger to health and life, and physical and mental exertion. Under laboratory conditions persons like Succi or Tanner "starved" for a period of 30 or 40, even up to 80 days. In actual life, they would have succumbed, long before this to absolute starvation. In the laboratory the subjects do not experience any particularly painful feelings or sensations, whereas in actual life starvation is very painful. In the former case the specific emotion of hunger disappears after the first two or three days of absolute starvation; in actual life it intermittently appears, disappears, and reappears, followed by other painful experiences. In laboratory conditions persons can maintain a cheerful disposition; in actual life this is hardly possible. Hence the investigator of the social effects of starvation has to deal with the phenomena of real life in distinction from controlled conditions.

A few factual self-observations will illustrate the foregoing characteristics of the emotions aroused by starvation. "I am empty," observe several psychology instructors who starved for scientific purposes.[4] With the growth of physiological starvation there appears "the painfully distinct sensation of growing more and more empty inside, until at last it seems as if the internal organs themselves had disappeared entirely," notes E. Mikkelsen, who underwent two and a half months' starvation in his Arctic wanderings.[5] Many other Arctic explorers and persons who have passed through the ordeal of prolonged and serious starvation testify to the same emptiness, lightness, and similar experiences. Apathy, quickly replaced by irritability, is again uniformly noted by most of the observers or self-observers of starvation in actual life. Mikkelsen refers to his and his companion's "growing apathy";[6] K. Hamsun excellently describes the alternation of apathy and of sudden attacks of irritability in the autobiographical hero of his *Hunger*. His starving hero is now apathetic, now kind, and now highly irritable, apparently without any reason. Sudden and sharp emotional changes permeate his whole conduct.[7] "Dull and hopeless apathy was the main characteristic of the masses in the famine years of the Middle Ages," declares a historian.[8] Similar observations are made by many an observer of famines in Russia, India, China, Persia, and Europe.[9]

An increase of unreasonable irritability and anger on a mass scale has been observed in many a mass famine. Speaking of the Russian famine of 1840, N. Lesskoff writes: "Among the peasants there began to grow an ominous grouch. Without any reason husbands began to beat their wives, the older persons assailed the children, and everyone reproached the others because of the lack of bread and invoked upon all damnation."[10] During the famine of 1918-1921 in Russia "the neurosis of inanition manifested itself among the children in a combination of unusual vindictiveness, extraordinary irritability, and chronic crying. Many children quite frequently suffered spells of extraordinary rage, animosity, and irritability."[11] Similar traits were exhibited by the surviving members of a wrecked ship, *Medusa*, after prolonged starvation. "Irritability and despondency" marked their psychology.[12]

Apathy and lifelessness are noted again and again by Marsh and his wife, who lent themselves as subjects.[13]

These and many other testify further more to the feelings of weakness, jerkiness, and fatigue, and especially to the depressive mood and to the sudden sense of cheerfulness after a good meal.

"It is a remarkable fact that, let things be as bad as they may, once in the [sleeping] bag, and with food in prospect, all one's troubles sink into oblivion. The human being becomes a happy animal, which eats as long as it can keep its eyes open, and goes to sleep with the food in its mouth. Oh, blissful state of heedlessness," writes F. Nansen during his "hard struggle" with starvation in the Arctic.[14]

Likewise, E. Mikkelsen and his companion were depressed again and again each time they suffered from extreme starvation in their Arctic wanderings and were overjoyed each time when they found food.

"Indeed, it is horrible in a way to see how overjoyed we are over the food. [This they had found in a depot.] . . . It is a sight for the gods; we cannot tear ourselves away [from the food], and as we lie there by the depot we feel amply repaid for all the hardship of the last long months."[15]

Similar self-observations are made repeatedly by other Arctic explorers, including Peary, Scott. The days of starvation were periods of depression for the explorers as well as for their dogs, whose drooping tails served as a barometer of their mood. The days of good meals, per contra, were uniformly cheerful. As soon as they either got to a food depot or killed a bear or muskcow, the pessimism evaporated; jokes, songs, and laughter ensued, and they were at peace with themselves and the world at large. The same was experienced in Soviet Russia by millions of people in the hungry years of 1918-1922.

Other factual illustrations will be given later on. Meanwhile the above gives a concise account of the profound change in the emotional and affective life of human beings wrought by starvation. Incidentally, it should be added that not all persons lose their emotional control under such circumstances. Save perhaps during the period immediately prior to death, some persons remain masters of their mind and their conduct while suffering from the acutest starvation. Such persons, as we shall see, successfully resist the mental, moral, and social disintegration induced by starvation. What forces and factors are responsible for such polarity will be analyzed at a later stage.

3. Change of Emotions and Affections Induced by Pestilence

That bubonic plague, typhus, fever, influenza, smallpox, and other serious diseases alter the sensations, emotions, and feelings of their victims need not be demonstrated. The general characteristic of the change induced by all these diseases is the pain, fear of death, delirium, and sense of weakness experienced by the victim. Apart from this common trait, each of the main epidemics discloses its own pattern of transformation of the victim's sensations, feelings, and emotions. For our purposes it is unnecessary to characterize the specific changes produced by each of these diseases. It suffices to say that all the important pestilences profoundly transform the emotional and affective life of the patient. This transformation is due not only to the biological forces of the sickness itself but also to the profound change in the social relationships of the victim. He suddenly finds himself isolated from almost all his fellow men, often even the members of his family. His condition plunges him into a sort of social vacuum. Hundreds of persons with whom he was linked by the ties of friendship and attachment, business, and common interests now try to avoid him. The victim is in the position of a spider whose web has been torn asunder. The former subject—or active participant in social life—is turned into a helpless object, avoided, forsaken, and repellent. He ceases to form a part of society. Socially he is already dead though he is still alive biologically.

Regardless of the biological factors, this abrupt psychosocial lonesomeness, this social death, is alone sufficient to create the profoundest change in the victim's affective and emotional life. Even gradual psychosocial isolation alters the whole mental life of persons so profoundly that often it drives people to commit suicide. As a matter of fact, psychosocial isolation is the primary cause of so-called "egotistic" suicide. Vastly more profound is the change created by the psychosocial isolation due to pestilence. It comes abruptly; it isolates the victim suddenly. It effects a thoroughgoing revolution in the mental life of the victim.

Pestilence affects also the emotional life of all those who are in contact with the sick. Their emotional tone is also profoundly disturbed. Anxiety, sorrow, and fear, sympathy for the sick and egoistic concern for their own safety, hope and despair, mounting depression alternating with outbursts of macabre exhilaration, irritability, and fatalistic resignation, emotional excitation and dullness, a reckless "devil may care" attitude and intense religiosity—these and similar waves of emotion sweep over the society ravaged by a pestilence. As in famine, its emotional life becomes unstable, jumpy, and uneven, subject to contrasting moods and violent changes. This instability and these contrasting emotional changes are probably the most important characteristics of such a society from the sociological standpoint.

4. The Disturbance of Emotional Life by War and Revolution

Here we must distinguish between the population as a whole and those who are directly exposed to the danger of death and of wounds and other injuries. Soldiers on the battlefield, revolutionaries and counter-revolutionaries facing the possibility of the firing squad, guillotine, gallows, and the like—these are directly exposed to the most serious dangers. Hence *fear* as the all-pervading and dominant emotion in their psychology. Being one of the most painful and powerful emotions, fear disturbs profoundly the whole emotional life of these groups and plays havoc with it. Many succumb to it; others resist through the pressure of such counter-forces as the sense of duty, courage, shame, and the fear of being shot in the back. But even these are placed between the hammer of fear and the anvil of the counter-forces. The result, even in the most courageous persons, is an abnormal, high-voltage emotionality. A study of the notes, memoirs, and other statements of those who have actually participated in an international or civil war or have faced the danger of execution during a revolution leaves no doubt as to the dominant rôle of fear in these situations.

This is clearly stated, for example, by Karl von Clause-vitz, in his famous *Vom Krieg:*

"Battle generates the atmosphere of danger in which all military activities proceed like fish in water or birds in the air. . . . The immediate consequence of this is the tendency to avoid the danger; when this is impossible, [there arise] fear and horror."

Only through the most potent counter-forces can fear be somewhat neutralized. A great Russian general, Skobe-leff,—famous not only for his victories but also for his personal courage on the battlefield,—when asked by a friend whether he was afraid of being killed, answered: "There is none who is not afraid of death; and if any one says so, spit at him: he lies. I am also afraid of death no less than others. But there are persons who have sufficiently strong willpower not to show this, whereas others do not have it and therefore flee from danger. Though I possess this willpower, it means a terrible inner struggle which potently affects my heart, subjecting it to a heavy burden every minute."[16] Here General Skobeleff excellently stresses the high-voltage emotionality and its enormous cost to the organism on the part of those who do not succumb to fear in the face of immediate danger.

"As a matter of fact soldiers are always afraid," declares Bessières, who participated throughout the campaign of 1914-1918 in the French army.[17] In this, Major Ardan du Pic concurs in his classical work on battle psychology.[18] It is stressed by practically all the active participants in the war of 1914-1918 whose notes and memoirs are published by J. Norton-Cru in his remarkable collection.[19] Perhaps the most penetrating analysis of the rôle of fear in battle is given by General N. Golovin, on the basis of his own experiences and the testimony of first-hand participants in battle. "The line separating you from the enemy is the line of death. Nobody likes to approach it, and the servile intellect looks for thousands of pretexts to avoid a closer contact with the enemy."[20]

Finally, this is well corroborated by the actual behavior of soldiers in many battles. They are caught between the conflicting impulse to conquer and the impulse to avoid the danger. If before the battle the first tendency is strong, with the opening of the battle there appears a growing tendency to avoid the danger—which practically means to avoid battle. As a result of this tormenting situation many soldiers become cowards. Not infrequently they commit suicide; more frequent are the cases of self-inflicted wounds or self-mutilation; finally, a multitude of soldiers try to avoid danger by simulating death in an attack, by lying down behind any protection they find, or by any other means available. In the battle of Wagram, of 22,000 of Napoleon's soldiers only 3,000 reached the position they had been ordered to occupy. About 7,000 were killed or wounded; the remaining 12,000 disappeared. How? By lying down, simulating death, and so on, in order not to go forward as they were ordered. And these were the glorious soldiers of Napoleon! Still greater is the proportion of such cowards (the victims of fear) in other battles.[21]

Facts of this kind, together with other evidences, leave

no doubt as to the dominant character of fear that pervades active soldiers and revolutionaries at situations of imminent danger. They also show how tormenting and chaotic is the emotional tone of both the cowardly and the courageous in such situations, and how drastically the affective and emotional life is altered under the impact of war and revolution.

However, the acute transformation of emotional life in war and revolution is not limited to the forces of fear and counter-fear. *Many other emotions* are aroused, such as *intense compassion for and commiseration* with killed and wounded companions, *rage and hatred* toward the enemy; *exaltation* in victory and utter *despair* in defeat; *admiration* for heroism and *reprobation* of cowardice; *indignation* at ignoble actions and *approbation* of noble ones; *satisfaction* with the faithful discharge of duty and *repentance* for failure. These and many other emotions are incessantly aroused by war and revolutionary situations. They all attain high-voltage intensity; they all rapidly come and go, rendering the whole emotional life highly turbulent and unstable. The disturbance is further reinforced by hundreds of trying conditions inseparable from war and revolution: the lack of necessities and elementary comforts; dirt and filth; the sight of ruin and destruction, including the corpses of the victims; pain from wounds and privations; the environment of prison and concentration camps; anxiety for the safety of dear ones; and the like.

The civil population, which ordinarily is not so directly exposed to danger, is in a somewhat different position from that of the other groups. Nevertheless, war and revolution create many conditions which disturb its emotional and affective life deeply. Here also fear plays its part.

"War arouses in individuals fear concerning the nation, the local community, and the family circle. The main sources of fear are (1) the risk of attack and injury, (2) economic changes, (3) the threat of family separation, and (4) the threat of shortage of food and deprivation of luxuries and pleasures."[22]

All in all the disturbing emotions and feelings are about the same as those that sweep over the emotional and affective life of the more exposed groups: fear, worry, compassion, depression, exaltation in success, rage, hatred, and kindred emotions. Likewise, the material and other conditions of this less exposed part are again somewhat similar to those that surround the more exposed groups. The chief difference is that these emotions and conditions are somewhat less extreme in the former case than in the latter.

Summary. The calamities in question call forth a sudden, sharp, and profound transformation of the emotional and affective life. The changes effected by famine and pestilence, war and revolution, differ in many ways from one another. Nevertheless, they all cause an increase of emotional instability; they all generate emotional intensity of a high voltage; finally, they all elicit painful or depressed feelings at the expense of the pleasurable and cheerful ones.

This does not mean that 100 per cent of the population involved experiences these changes. On the contrary, as we shall presently see, a part of the population either fails to experience them or it is affected in a very different way.

Like Skobeleff, they may fear the dangers of battle, revolution, or pestilence. But instead of cowardly flight, they overcome their sense of danger and display courage; instead of trying to save their life at the cost of others, they sacrifice it; instead of avoiding dangerous posts, they deliberately seek them; instead of losing their control over their emotions, they become cooler and more self-possessed. Such opposite effects of war, revolution, or pestilence upon the emotional and affective life have always been present in certain elements of every great society.

Chapter Two

How Calamities Affect Our Cognitive Processes, Desires and Volitions

1. First Basic Change

Since calamities disturb acutely our emotional and affective life, they cannot fail to influence the cognitive processes, beginning with the simplest, such as sensation and perception, memory and imagination, and ending with the most complex processes of creative thought. Each of the four calamities enumerated in Chapter One modifies our cognitive processes in many ways, which differ for each disaster. Nevertheless, these effects present many factors which are essentially similar. In the present chapter we shall concentrate upon these similarities.

We shall waive discussion of the numerous changes in the most elementary cognitive processes brought about by famine and pestilence, war and revolution, since these modifications are too abundant and too diverse for specific consideration, and since, so far, hardly any uniformity in this field has been discovered. For instance, some of the investigators of the influence of starvation upon such mental operations as addition or subtraction, upon the number of errors in calculations, and upon the sensitivity and rapidity of sensation, and the like found that starvation somewhat facilitates mental work, whereas others arrived at different results. Instead of a detailed analysis of these and similar problems, let us point out two fundamental changes of our cognitive processes induced by calamities. When these central uniformities are understood, a host of specific, concrete phenomena become readily comprehensible.

The first of these effects consists in the *tendency of all the cognitive processes to be concentrated more and more upon the calamity and the phenomena that are directly and indirectly connected with it, together with increasing insensitivity (beginning with sensation and perception) toward extraneous elements.*[1]

Our mind in all its main cognitive processes tends to be increasingly monopolized by the calamity, which tends to drive out of the field of consciousness (and even out of the sphere of subconscious activities—for instance, dreams) all topics unrelated to it. Such is the first general effect.

When a calamity enters our life, our *sensation and perception*, or our sense organs, tend to become exceedingly sensitive toward all the phenomena of the calamity and all the objects and events connected with it. When we are hungry, our sense organs seize upon and register anything connected with food: its appearance, its odor, its place, its bulk, and so forth. Many aspects of food—more especially its odor—which in a state of satiety we overlook are now easily discerned by our sense organs. Even such incidental phenomena as the clattering of dishes, the appearance of a tablecloth, the sign over an eating-place, etc. are sharply perceived when one experiences a sense of hunger and even a keen appetite. Conversely, in a state of starvation our sensations and perceptions relating to phenomena not connected with food become less intense, even dull.

The same is true of our *attention*. Starvation "has a tendency to direct . . . our attention toward food phenomena and to distract it from everything unconnected therewith."[2]

Likewise, starvation quite definitely conditions the *association of images and the flow of ideas*. "It disrupts the previous associational flow of ideas or the sequence of images and introduces such images and ideas (or a chain of these) as have no relationship with the preceding ideas and images and concern mainly food . . . and anything associatively or logically connected with food—for instance, the length of time that remains before dinner, and so on."[3]

Food images and ideas forcibly obtrude themselves upon the field of consciousness, driving out all neutral ideas and images, regardless of, and often in spite of, our desire and volition. During prolonged and intensive starvation this intrusion becomes so powerful that the strongest effort of the will is sometimes insufficient to suppress it. Indeed, the food images and ideas sometimes grow so intense, clear, and vivid that they acquire a hallucinatory character, leading to the so-called *delirium of inanition.*

Even in subconscious activities—for instance, *in dreams* —the same intrusion occurs: the dreams of the hungry are preoccupied primarily with various food phenomena.

Finally, the same effect manifests itself in our *memory and reproductive imagination.* Except during the last stages of starvation (shortly before the death of the victim), in hunger, our memory preserves and readily reproduces the phenomena connected with food and weakens in regard to most of the things unconnected with it. As a rule, prolonged and intense starvation serves to weaken our memory, apart from the images relating to food, which are retained and reproduced more clearly and vividly than under normal conditions.

Since the whole field of consciousness is thus occupied by food topics, it is natural that starving persons should *speak* (orally or in written form) *mainly of food and related topics.* However different may be the initial topic, they very quickly—and often to their own annoyance— find themselves discussing food. Even though they try deliberately to change the subject, very soon they revert to the same unescapable point. *Thus, in a starving society not only do its members talk principally of food, but its newspapers, magazines, books, sermons, lectures, fine arts, philosophy and religion, science, and public meetings (including those of government bodies) are dominated by food topics, which occupy ever-increasing space and time, to the detriment of other considerations.* In written and printed works this may be measured by the increase in the number of publications, articles, or inches of space devoted to the topics in question; in oral speech, by the increase in the number of meetings, the length of time consumed, and similar factors.

What has been said of famine may be said (with the proper qualifications) of pestilence, war, or revolution. These calamities similarly modify our cognitive processes, which they monopolize making the given calamity the central point of the conscious and the subconscious mind.

A few typical factual observations and self-observations will serve to illustrate the point. From personal observation we know that food shown to a hungry dog fairly hypnotizes it. Its sensations, attention, and entire consciousness are concentrated on the food, to the exclusion of everything else. If you move the food to the right or the left, the dog's head or body moves correspondingly. In such a situation if you kick the dog, the blow is likely to pass unnoticed. Every effort to distract its attention proves futile.

E. Mikkelsen, speaking of the behavior of his dog during his wanderings in the Arctic, remarks:

"The best time of the day is when we are cooking a meal. . . . She takes no notice of our patting or kind words, but sits as quiet as a mouse, staring at the wonderful [gas] stove with a saucepan on top; only her tongue cannot keep still, but moves in and out of her mouth, which literally waters at the sight."[4]

Similar observations are noted by Nansen and other Arctic explorers.

In a still more detailed form these facts are reported by I. Pavlov and his pupils in their experimental studies of dogs.[5]

As to human beings, the recent mass starvation in Soviet Russia and the present famine in Poland, in Greece, and many other countries afford unlimited corroboration of the changes described. Among the children of Soviet Russia in 1918-1922 "food topics incessantly occupied the whole consciousness of the preschool and school children. Conversation about meals was the only possible approach to them. To everything else they reacted either irritably or negatively."[6] The grown-ups were inattentive to most things except food rations and other food phenomena, to which they gave extraordinary attention. In spite of the difficulty of obtaining information, owing to the chaotic conditions which prevailed, they were excellently informed as to where, when and what food was given by the government, as to the possibilities of obtaining bootlegged rations, and scarcely ever overlooked even the chance of buying a chunk of horse meat. Soviet newspapers and other publications of the years 1918-1922 devoted a disproportionately large space to food topics. Those who lived there during those years, as the author did, know that food topics were the all-absorbing theme of individual conversation, as well as of public and private meetings. Annoyed by the persistence and monotony of the theme, people often deliberately attempted to drop the subject and to talk about something else; yet after a few moments the conversation usually drifted back to the same topic—food!

A similar picture is presented at the present time by the conditions that prevail in Greece and the Balkans, Poland,

France, and other countries suffering from abnormal malnutrition.

The individual experiences of starving explorers and experimental investigators furnish further testimony to the same effect. Scientific self-experiments with hunger and thirst stress the insistent and persevering character of food and thirst topics. One self-observer, after 20 hours of thirst, notes that in the process of work he automatically stopped, going to a caraffe of water without realizing what he was doing. Once he even took a gulp of water before he realized it. After 23 hours of thirst a vague visual image of a glass of water became persistent. Similar experiences are reported by other experimenters with hunger. The idea of food becomes ineradicable and tends to drive out other images and ideas.[7] Still more clearly is this stressed by starving Arctic explorers.

"The pangs of hunger are worse, increasing every minute and causing us physical pain. For my own part, I can think of nothing but food. At first my thoughts dwell upon all sorts of dishes, but gradually they concentrate themselves upon Danish sandwiches. . . . Otherwise I have for the last few days dreamed chiefly of enormous juicy steaks . . .—treasures that I would give years of my life to buy. . . . We do not say much [to one another], and what we have to say is of food—food in any shape or form. . . . One's whole consciousness becomes concentrated on one importunate demand for food—food—food."[8]

It absorbs so exclusively the mind of the explorers that they pay little attention to fatigue, dangers, or other considerations.

"Fatigue is forgotten, our aches are no longer felt, hunger is all we feel, and food, food, our only thought."[9]

Finally come hallucinations and the delirium of inanition. Mikkelsen and Iversen take stones for sandwiches, imagine themselves in Copenhagen cafés, and rush to grab the imaginary sandwiches.

"So great was the force of the hallucination that I have actually turned out of my course. . . . But the little food packages still haunt me, and before long I catch myself again running off after little white stones, quite certain this time that there is no mistake. . . . The semi-delirium of starvation aids the illusion."[10]

When they *eat*, they can at last talk of something else than food. Finally, in their dreams they see

"enormous quantities of food, huge smoking joints, mountains of bread and butter. . . . But it is all moving and shifting, just out of reach. I run and run; it is always there, a little farther on. . . . Then I wake, bathed in sweat."[11]

In a famished society, *in the total stream of its oral and written speech reactions the share of food topics invariably increases in proportion to the duration and intensity of the famine.* If a given society is in a state of chronic starvation or is faced with such an emergency, its government will set up permanent committees to deal with it, many decrees will be enacted to cope with it, and the population will incessantly discuss the issue. Examples are afforded by the government and society of ancient Sparta or Athens.[12]

The victims of a pestilence, as well as those who surround them, cannot help perceiving, reflecting upon, and discussing the calamity and all the phenomena connected with it. The same applies to those who are directly or indirectly involved in a war or revolution.

In war, not only is the normal mental life of the combatants and, in less degree, of the civilians dominated by the phenomena of war and related topics, but even abnormal mental processes, including numerous psychoneuroses, become definitely "colored."

"War can exert different influences upon different varieties of mental troubles. Now it simply colors them, giving the content of its topics to a mentally sick person. Now war works in a deeper way, directly and indirectly inducing or reinforcing certain mental troubles. . . . [Among the forms assumed by the coloring of mental troubles by war] one form consists in the mentally sick person's becoming obsessed by military events, which he explains in his own way, and which enter his delirium and dominate it. . . . In other cases the mental patient orients his delirium in such a way that war becomes incompatible with his habitual preoccupations. Finding himself unable to interpret war in a systematic way, he does not hesitate to deny its very existence [and behaves accordingly]."[13]

There are many other varieties of this coloring of the content and form of mental disease by war. Suffice it to say that in many abnormal processes war becomes the central topic, monopolizing (positively or negatively) the field of consciousness of the patient. This applies with even greater force to the mental troubles directly caused by the horrors, shocks, and similar phenomena of war.[14]

The same is true of any other calamity, be it earthquake, volcanic eruption, flood, or what not. Each of these cataclysms becomes the most vital and dangerous phenomenon in the life of the population concerned. It imperatively focuses attention upon efforts to cope with it and, if possible, to avert its consequences. Hence our sensations and perceptions, attention and memory, association of ideas and images, and the like all tend to concentrate upon the calamity and to ignore matters unrelated to it.

No special measurement is necessary and no exact statistical data are required in order to see that with the outbreak of the present war in 1939—and especially after the entry of the United States in December, 1941—the majority of newspapers and magazines devoted themselves to war topics and related themes. The same is true of the radio and other means of written or oral communication.

These topics are uppermost and central in our minds. They incessantly intrude upon our mental processes. It is futile to try to banish them from our thoughts or conversation. They obsess even our dreams. Conversely, other topics, unrelated to the war, are progressively neglected, tending increasingly to fall into oblivion.

The foregoing discussion reveals the first uniformity of change of our cognitive processes induced by calamity of any kind. The greater the disaster the greater the change. The phenomenon reveals itself in the past history of the most diverse societies; it is repeating itself in present societies; and it will recurr in future societies.

2. *Second Basic Change*

The second fundamental effect of calamities upon the cognitive processes consists in a *tendency toward disintegration of the unity of our "self" and of mental functioning. It manifests itself in an increasing incapacity to concentrate on objects unrelated to the calamity, in a growing dependence of our thinking upon fortuitous external influences; in a decreasing autonomy and self-regulation of our thoughts, independently of external stimuli; and, finally, in an access of various forms of mental disease. In brief, calamities promote the growth of mental disorderliness and disorganization.*

This does not mean that the entire population exhibits these effects; neither does it signify that the disorganization of thought proceeds linearly, increasing in proportion to the intensification of the calamity, regardless of its magnitude or character. The proposition means simply that the disorganization of mental life will be accentuated by any serious catastrophe. But this increase does not preclude the possibility of opposite effects in a certain section of the population. The minds of a select few may be affected positively rather than negatively. It means, further, that if the calamity is slight and short-lived, the consequences will be correspondingly slight and short-lived. We shall presently undertake to demonstrate that while these effects are correlated with the growing intensity of the disaster, the increase need not be linear. It may be, and in fact often is, somewhat undulatory in character, the general trend toward the impairment of mental functioning being interrupted by intermittent flashes of enlightenment, penetrating and inspirational thought. However, these are but short intermissions in the general trend toward mental disorganization. The mind of the select few can escape, to a considerable extent, these effects.

The general reasons for such effects are rather evident. Adequate and fruitful thought demands a considerable degree of detachment from the disturbing influences of external forces; otherwise one cannot concentrate on a problem and think it through. Calamities create a situation in which powerful external stimuli constantly intrude upon the field of consciousness—both mental and emotional— and deprive the mind of the requisite autonomy.

By weakening the body and nervous system through prolonged starvation or sickness, through exposure to the dangers and hardships of war or revolution, calamities impair the successful functioning of our thought. As a rule, one suffering from acute starvation or illness, or exposed to the dangers of the battle field or a revolutionary struggle, is incapable of thinking coherently, intensely, and creatively, except, perhaps, with reference to the limited topic of his calamity. His nervous system and his mind are either directly weakened by prolonged starvation or sickness or are subjected to the bombardment of incessant shocks which disorganize them and deprive them of steady and effective functioning. Many a nervous system cannot withstand the shocks, and succumbs to a form of mental disorder. Others simply lose their ability to function as well as they do under normal conditions.

Finally, calamities destroy many facilities and instruments essential for mental work—universities and other schools, libraries, laboratories, museums, etc.—and impose many other grave hardships and deprivations.

Even prolonged starvation, however, may not prove disastrous to the mind of the select few. Long fasts on the part of many a great religious leader—such as Christ, Mohammed, Gautama Buddha, Mahavira, or Ignatius Loyola—have fructified their mental life instead of disorganizing it. But for the rank and file of ordinary people the disintegrating effects of involuntary starvation are hardly avoidable.

Intense starvation frequently leads to a weakening of the unity and integrity of the "self," which tends to become amorphous and split into two or more "selves," often at war with one another. Mrs. Marsh, in her introspective observation of the effects of starvation, notes this fact: in her mathematical exercises she seemed to possess two selves, one of which tried to make the computations while the other ironically jeered at it, bidding it leave the work to this other self.[15] Hamsun, in his *Hunger*, gives us remarkable pictures of this dualism and disintegration of the unity of the self. His hero, starving and homeless, decided to go to jail. In his cell, when the light was extinguished,

"I sat, a prey to the most singular fantasies, listening to myself crooning lullabies, sweating with the exertion of striving to lull myself to rest. . . . [After many strange manipulations and ideas] suddenly I snap my fingers and laugh: 'This is the very deuce! Ha-ha!' I imagine I have discovered a new word—'Kuboa'! 'By the benign God, man, you have discovered a word—"Kuboa"— a word of profound import. . . .' I enter into the joyous frenzy of hunger. . . . In all calmness I revolve things in my mind. . . . I seek to explain the meaning of my new word. There was no occasion for it to mean either God or the Tivoli; and who said that it was to signify cattle show? I clench my hands fiercely, and repeat once again, 'Who said that it was to signify cattle show.' No, on second thought it was not absolutely necessary that it should mean padlock or sunrise. . . . [After several attempts he finally decides that "Kuboa" must mean something psychical.] *Then it seems to me that someone is interposing, interrupting my argument.* I answer angrily: 'Beg pardon! Your match in imbecility is not to be found; no, sir! Knitting cotton? Ah, go to hell!' Well, I had to laugh. Might I ask why I should be forced to let it signify knitting cotton? . . . I had discovered the word myself; so. . . . I was perfectly within my rights in letting it signify whatsoever I pleased. As far as I was aware, I had not yet expressed an opinion as to. . . . But my brain got more and more confused. . . ."

This split personality, with its fantastic and chaotic association of ideas. continues. The images of policemen, sea, ship, monsters, clouds, and so on follow in disorderly fashion. Finally he says to himself:

" 'Now you will die!' and I lay for a while and reflected that I was about to die. Then I started up in bed and asked severely, 'If I found the word, am I not absolutely within my rights in deciding myself what it is to signify?' . . . *I could hear myself that I was raving; I could hear it now whilst I was talking.* . . . All at once the thought darted through my brain that I was insane."[16]

This illustrates well the disintegration of the unity of self into two or more selves quarreling and fighting, arguing and helping one another, in the chaotic fashion typical of disorganized mental processes.

As death approaches, hallucinations and chaotic delirium —now violent, now quiescent—monopolize the field of consciousness, marked by the most bizarre, fanciful, and haphazard images and ideas.

"The association of ideas becomes devoid of any control, the inhibiting influence of consciousness weakens, ideas flow rapidly and in disorderly fashion. There appear hallucinations of sight and hearing which intrude upon the field of consciousness and induce a multitude of absurd ideas, partly delusions of persecution and partly delusions of grandeur. But these ideas, like the hallucinations, are highly evanescent. The weakened victim is excited, mumbles incoherent words, and gesticulates."[17]

In spite of many an effort, the hero of *Hunger* (a remarkable life document, not a mere literary product) adds:

"But write I could not. After a few lines, nothing seemed to occur to me; my thoughts ran in all directions and I could not pull myself together for special exertion. Everything influenced and distracted me." [18]

Once in a while a brief interlude of clear and inspirational thought ensued, ceasing entirely, however, as the ravages of starvation grew more acute. Try as he would, he found himself unable to compute the cost of 3 5/16 pounds of cheese multiplied by 16.

After even a relatively short period of slight starvation, introspectionists have detected a sense of distraction, a kind of emptiness, a disinclination to act or to think, and so on. [19]

During the famine years 1918-1922 in Russia most of the professors and intellectual workers complained of a decline in their intellectual energy and capacity. Similarly, concentration and accuracy fell off in many occupations, such as those of printers, bookkeepers, and clerks. [20] During these years teachers and professors invariably testified to a deterioration in the mental achievement of the pupils in Soviet schools.

"On the intellectual side, there is a notable decrease of attention and decline of mental work among the children, paralleled by a much swifter onset of fatigue." [21]

It is probable that the highest forms of creative mental work suffer earliest and most severely from physiological starvation. Experimental studies of the suppression of the conditioned reflexes of starving dogs indicate that the latest and most complex "artificial conditioned reflexes" are the first to disappear; next the "natural conditioned reflexes;" and finally the unconditioned reflexes. "The order of the disappearance of reflexes before death by starvation is the reverse of the order of their emergence in the life of the dogs."[22]

Finally, the disorganization of mental activity is attested by the increase in the number of mental diseases reported for major famines, where the problem was the subject of scientific investigation. "In 1918-1920 the mental disease of the population of Petrograd increased notably, and it still continues to increase." One of its main factors, according to the investigators, was starvation.[23]

The Soviet newspapers almost daily reported, during these years, a mass increase of mental disease and derangement.

"In the village of Olkhovka the cases of mental disease caused by famine notably increased."[24]

"In the village of Molchanovka, owing to the famine, three cases of serious mental derangement are registered."[25]

"Many become deranged. . . . There are numerous villages where hardly a single normal human being can be found. All proved to be crazy owing to the famine."[26]

Such data can be multiplied *ad libitum* from Russian reports covering merely the years 1918-1922, to say nothing of the famines in India, China, and other countries.

With certain modifications, the foregoing conclusions may be applied to pestilence, war, and revolution. However different may be the destructive effects of various pestilences, they all lead to a disorganization of the mental activities of their victims—at least for the duration of the sickness—and of a considerable part of the nonsick population as well. The same is true of war and revolution. This is shown first of all by the fact of an increase of mental derangement among the combatants and among a part of the civil population. Besides "coloring" of psychoneuroses, quoted above,

"war acts in a more profound, though still indirect, fashion by provoking temporary spells of excitation and depression, melancholy and neurasthenia through fatigue, mental and physical overexertion, and a sharp change of hygiene, habits, environment, and preoccupations. . . . In other cases war directly affects the nervous system through the horror of certain battle scenes, as well as through the emotions by the shock of bombardment. . . . In these cases we observe spells of mental confusion (with or without hallucinations and delirium) and hysterical attacks of muteness, paralysis, deafness, blindness, anaesthesia of general sensibility, etc."[27]

"The life of the soldier, especially in the front lines, is characterized by the exclusion of individuality in a mass experience which alternates between [a sense of] the danger of death and the desire to escape [on the one hand] and [on the other] complete devotion to a task which entirely consumes the will. Change of occupation, separation from family, and a submission to a new form of discipline (with its petty restrictions) form the initial stresses of the soldier. . . . Boring monotony of prolonged noncombatant service in the rear leads to passivity, indifference, and depression. . . . There is general dulling of the intellectual life. . . . The main sources of mental stress for the front-line soldier are the danger of death, [the sense of] guilt over killing, increased responsibility, separation from the family, and sexual deprivation. . . . Most soldiers on approaching the front line displayed uneasiness and apprehension by restlessness, irritability, artificial jocularity, or silence and withdrawal, or by unusual perspiration, diarrhoea, and frequency of micturition, lasting for a few weeks. . . . In activity under harassing fire is said to affect the mental health of the soldier more than active warfare, while the prolonged uncertainty and fear of a land mine is regarded as the most potent source of mental tension. . . . [Moreover, the conflict between the impulses to kill and to refrain from killing may precipitate a breakdown.]"[28]

The foregoing quotations give an idea of the specific tensions and disorganizing influences of war that induce nervous and mental troubles. Without substantial modification these conditions can be applied also to revolutionary wars and their participants.

In the British Army in the First World War "one third of the unwounded and one seventh of those discharged

42   MAN AND SOCIETY IN CALAMITY

from the British Army were permanently unfit on account of functional neuroses and mental disorders."[29]

"On occasions neuroses made up 40 per cent of the casualties evacuated home [in the British Expeditionary Force]. In 1918, out of a total of 160,000 pensioners, 32,000, or 20 per cent, were receiving pensions for functional nervous and mental disease, while in 1921 this figure had risen to 65,000."

"After exposure to severe shrapnel fire a whole company was noted by Redlich to develop hysterical symptoms—for example, crying fits and vomiting."[30]

These and a considerable body of other data leave no doubt as to the disorganizing effects of war upon the combatants' mental activities.

Even among those combatants who do not develop psychoneuroses the mind does not function normally, especially in battles or other scenes of violent struggle. Normal mental activity becomes stunted and dulled. A few observations of General N. Golovin on a cavalry attack led by him may serve to illustrate this point.

"The decisive moment came. I must confess the moment was fearful, I felt that the eyes of my hussars were focused on me. . . . Having ordered: 'Sabers out' and 'Follow me,' I began to gallop uphill. For a few seconds we were screened from the bullets, but presently we were exposed to fire. . . . The familiar buzzing of bullets became audible. A few shells exploded over our heads. Consciousness was blunted. I remember only that I wanted to cross as quickly as possible the open space between me and the forest. . . . Soon I felt that the enemy's fire was beginning to weaken. . . . With my whole body and soul I sensed this decreasing danger. . . . How I galloped into the forest I do not remember clearly. I remember that an Austrian was rushing toward me with his rifle, and I did not understand why he was not firing at me. When he was quite close to me, he wildly waved his arms—one of my hussars bayoneted him.

"My first clear recollection concerns the moment when I was surrounded by a group of my officers and soldiers. I was struck by the fact that all of them were yelling and gesticulating violently. Recovering, I noticed that I was doing the same— yelling and gesticulating in an attempt to tell them something."[31]

This represents a rather slight modification of mental activities on the part of a general noted for his bravery; yet it constitutes a marked deviation from the normal functioning of the mind. This dulling of consciousness, this half-somnambulistic action, without a clear recollection or understanding of the events experienced,[32] testify to a conspicuous disorganization of the cognitive and other mental processes.

Indeed, the whole pattern of the soldier's life in time of war is conducive to many mental changes, even apart from the activities of the battlefield.

In lesser degree the phenomenon occurs also among the civilian population during a strenuous and prolonged war or revolution. Physical, mental, and emotional strains—due to privation, fatigue, melancholy and depression, anxiety and fear, grief over the loss of dear ones, the revulsion caused by scenes of horror, cruelty, and injustice—all these factors inevitably produce a profound influence upon the mental life of the civilians. It was observed among the population of St. Petersburg and other Russian cities during the First World War;[33] and it has been observed in other countries during the same and other wars.[34]

"In severely bombarded towns [in England, Germany, and Spain] the civilian population suffered from anxiety states lasting for weeks, with disorders of sleep, acoustic hypersensitivity, . . . heart symptoms, polyuria, glycosuria, vomiting, diarrhoea, and amenorrhea. In recent Spanish experience Mira reported a number of cases of a malignant type of anxiety, characterized by lack of concentration, motor inactivity, tachycardia, and panting respiration, in some cases leading to death in three or four days. Typical hysterical fits, especially of screaming, were frequent in Hoche's observation (1916). A psychic epidemic was reported by Wedekind in girls working near the front in a munition factory frequently visited by airplanes. Fits of trembling and prolonged loss of consciousness occurred on the slightest provocation: the sight of over a dozen girls lying on the floor in convulsions was not uncommon."[35]

Here the *law of polarization* is also well attested. Not all, not even the greater part of the combatants (and a still smaller proportion of the civilians), develop these symptoms.

"Aided by community feeling, patriotism, and a religious and philosophic outlook, the vast majority of the soldiers manage to adapt themselves to a situation that appears almost intolerable."[36]

"Most German writers stress the infrequency of psychological disorders in severely bombarded French villages. [In London hospitals the patients did not show any 'marked reactions' to the raids.]"[37]

What has been said of war applies with still greater force to revolutions. The mentality of a considerable proportion of the population is notably disorganized by revolutionary conditions, mental disease, especially in its slighter forms, usually increasing. In the French revolutions of 1830-1831, 1848-1849, and 1870-1871, general paralysis and other mental disorders increased from 9 to 14 per cent in 1830-1831; 27 to 34 per cent in 1848-1849; and by 37 per cent in 1870-1871.[38] Likewise a marked intensification of various psychoneuroses took place in the Russian revolution,[39] as well as in most of the other greater revolutions.[40]

At a later stage, in revolution as well as in a war, "a widespread suggestibility, diminished critical faculty, and increase in wishful thinking" present themselves.[41] A considerable section of the population becomes hysterical; "mob-mindedness" shows a sharp upward trend. The perception of many phenomena becomes one-sided and distorted, concentrating on insignificant data, to the exclusion of the essentials. The logical faculties give place to erratic and chaotic associations. Memory tends to be short-lived. Fallacies and hallucinations abound, including an uncritical acceptance of rumors of plots and "fifth columnists," the confusion of friends and enemies, the delusion of grandeur, and the like. The prevalent mood is one of extreme instability; and an intense and uncontrolled emotionalism is registered in acts of wanton destructiveness and cruelty.[42]

Finally, the weakening and disorganizing rôle of pestilence in relation to mental activities is too well attested to call for demonstration, so far as the direct victims are concerned. Bubonic plague, spotted typhus, cholera, smallpox, and other epidemics incapacitate their victims physically and mentally, and socially, as was pointed out above (see page 21). The mental life of a considerable part of the population is undermined and disorganized to a great extent by fatigue and by fear and other emotional stresses induced by deprivation, horrors and the like. The disorganization assumes somewhat different forms for different epidemics.

Such is the second general effect of calamities, particularly upon the cognitive processes of the direct and the indirect victims. The conclusions reached may be extended to cover all the other types of catastrophe, such as floods, earthquakes, and volcanic eruptions.

3. The Modification of Wishes, Desires, and Volition

In the field of desires and wishes and (in so far as the two can be distinguished) that of will and volition, the principal change brought about by calamities consists in *a reinforcement of the desires and wishes directed toward the mitigation of the calamity and the sufferings imposed by it and in a corresponding weakening or elimination of all contrary desires and wishes.* During a famine the wishes that hinder the satisfaction of hunger tend to be repressed, and those that promote the alleviation of starvation are reinforced. During a pestilence the impulses that thwart safety or recovery are inhibited, while those directed toward avoidance of or deliverance from illness become paramount. In war and revolution the longing for a knock-out blow, for escape from suffering, horror, and danger (for some groups) even the desire for peace at any price, is tremendously accentuated, whereas those desires that either militate against the realization of these objectives or are unrelated to them tend to be suppressed or eliminated altogether.

If we distinguish will and volition from desires and wishes, and if by will me mean a mental effort controlling and often opposing our desires, we note that *this voluntary effort undergoes two opposite changes*, depending upon the persons or groups involved. Volition directed against the satisfaction of hunger, the avoidance of pestilential infection, or escape from mortal peril in wars or revolutions tends to be opposed or neutralized by the impact of contrary forces (consisting of sensations, emotions, and desires).

In the first case, when the volition is antagonistic to other forces it is frequently overborne. In spite of the resolution of famished persons to abstain from stealing food, many fail in their resolve. In battle a soldier may determine not to become a coward and flee from danger. Nevertheless, many do flee because their willpower proves weaker than that of opposing forces.

In other cases we observe the opposite reaction: volition is unshaken or even reinforced by adversity. Thus, political prisoners have repeatedly preferred death by starvation to any concession to their adversaries. The same applies to religious martyrs. Many a combatant has mastered his fear through his willpower, even in the face of death itself. Many a moral hero has deliberately exposed himself to pestilence.

This and the preceding chapter present an outline of the principal uniformities in the transformation of our emotional, affective, volitional, and cognitive processes under the impact of calamities. We are now prepared to inquire how these calamities influence the actual conduct and behavior of the persons involved. The next chapters attempt to answer this question.

PART TWO

THE INFLUENCE OF CALAMITIES
UPON OUR BEHAVIOR AND
VITAL PROCESSES

Chapter Three

How Famine Influences Our Behavior

1. *General Uniformity*

Since calamities notably modify our mental processes, since they transform our organism—its anatomy and its physiological processes—it is only to be expected that they should affect also our overt behavior. These modifications of behavior assume an enormous variety of concrete forms, differing for different calamities and for the persons and groups involved. A mere enumeration of such concrete changes would require hundreds of pages. Such a task is obviously outside the scope of this work. Instead, we shall concentrate on those changes of behavior which are typical and more or less uniformly recurrent. If such central and typical changes are adequately grasped, they easily explain numerous concrete changes of behavior—varying modifications analogous to arithmetical values in a generalized algebraic formula.

The first of these typical changes may be formulated as follows: *Any great calamity tends, on the one hand, to weaken or to eliminate those positive or negative actions —actions of commission and of omission—of our total behavior which hinder or fail to promote the achievement of freedom from a given calamity and its sufferings; on the other, it tends to generate, multiply, and reinforce all those actions that lead, directly or indirectly, to the realization of this objective.*

Let us now elaborate this proposition—first in relation to famine and then with regard to pestilence, war, and revolution.

2. The Change in the Amount of Time Devoted to Food-seeking Activities

Applied to famine, the above proposition means that hunger tends to suppress all activities that either hinder or fail to promote its satisfaction. Until hunger is relieved, it tends to dominate our behavior by means of food-seeking and food-consuming activities. These may be either *pure* food-seeking activities performed exclusively in the interest of satisfying hunger, or *mixed* food-seeking activities, undertaken for the satisfaction of present or future hunger, as well as for that of other needs. Such mixed activities kill two birds with one stone. If a famished artist paints a picture or a poet or composer writes a song in order to obtain money to buy food (like the hero of Hamsun's *Hunger*), by this activity he satisfies both hunger and his creative urge. The activity becomes a *mixed* food-seeking activity.

The first general evidence of the validity of the above proposition is supplied by the facts that *each time when hunger appears or threatens to appear and the obstacles in the way of its satisfaction increase, the amount of time and energy spent in food-seeking activities increases while the time and energy devoted to activities unrelated to hunger decrease.* When food is immediately available, we spend little time and energy in the satisfaction of our hunger. In this case our behavior is similar to that of mice, rats, or dogs whose food is placed under their very nose: they need only eat it, without devoting any time or energy to efforts to obtain it. If, on the other hand there are enormous obstacles in the way of obtaining even a minimum subsistence fare,—if the hungry are placed in a situation similar to that of rats in the experimental labyrinth (with many corridors to be traversed and other obstacles to be overcome before the food is reached),—the proportion of the pure and mixed food-seeking activities in the total behavior of the hungry increases sharply, sometimes reaching 90 or 95 per cent of the total. Correspondingly, the proportion of time and energy devoted to activities unrelated to food declines, sometimes to an insignificant fraction of the total. Under these conditions the activities that hinder the satisfaction of hunger tend to disappear, whereas those aimed at the satisfaction of other than hunger needs remain in so far as they assume the form of the *mixed* food-seeking activities.

The first corroboration of this proposition is offered by the behavior of some of the primitive peoples living in a state of chronic starvation or on its border line. The greater part of their time and energy is spent in pure and mixed food-seeking activities.[1] On the other hand, those primitive peoples inhabiting regions where food is plentiful and easily obtainable are somewhat lazy, devoting less attention to food-seeking activities.[2]

The second series of corroborations is furnished by the behavior of various Arctic explorers (such as Admiral Peary, Mikkelsen, Nansen, and Scott), who were often subjected to acute and prolonged starvation. Reading their diaries, one observes that when they were famished they directed almost all their time and energy toward pure and mixed food-seeking activities—chiefly the former. For days at a time they sought out food caches or engaged in exhausting hunts for birds, bears, and other game, frequently at great personal risk.[3]

The third corroboration is found in the results of the experiment conducted by J. Knowles, who on October 4, 1913, retired to the forests, without any instruments or even clothing, in order to find out whether contemporary man can survive, like primitive man, without the tools and other facilities of civilization.

Studying his behavior we note that, in spite of the most favorable weather, during the first few days of his life in the forest almost all his time and energy were preëmpted by predominantly pure and partly mixed food-seeking activities—fishing for trout in shallow ponds, hunting for blueberries, and so on.

The next evidence is supplied by the mass behavior of people under famine conditions. For instance, in Soviet Russia, during 1918-1922, the time and energy allocated to the pure and mixed food-seeking activities (obtaining ration cards, standing interminably in bread lines, seeking out legal and illegal "food markets," making trips (in the interest of food) to distant villages, planting, cultivating, and guarding vegetable gardens; preparing and cooking food under the most difficult circumstances, etc.) increased to almost 100 per cent of the total, whereas the proportion of the activities unrelated to food (visiting, dancing, attending shows and theaters, walking, doing work that did not promise any food either directly or indirectly, attending church services, etc.) declined enormously. The greater part of the behavior of many consisted exclusively of pure and mixed food-seeking activities. In my study of the budget of time and activities of students of the University of Petrograd (for three months at the end of 1921 and the beginning of 1922)—persons who were situated much more favorably in respect to food than the rank and file of the population—the following data were obtained. In a time budget of one student, out of 1325 hours of waking activities (sleeping hours are excluded) 148 hours, or 11.2 per cent, were spent in *pure* food-seeking activities (the preparation, cooking, and eating of food); in another budget, out of 1341 hours of waking activities 190, or 14.2

per cent, were so spent; still others disclose a total of from 18 to 30 per cent. When to these pure food-seeking activities the mixed food-seeking activities are added, we obtain a grand total of from *70 to 95 per cent.*

With these figures let us compare the time allotted to eating activities by the unemployed white-collar workers of Boston in 1935. To eating activities they devoted, on an average, 1 hour and 29 minutes, or about 11 per cent of their total waking hours.[4] In this connection it must be remembered, also, that the unemployed were the group least favorably situated with respect to food-getting and that their eating-time was not devoted solely to pure food-seeking activities but in part also to mixed food-seeking activities (rest from uninteresting work, chatting with friends, visiting, reading newspapers, etc.).

For the well-to-do classes the proportion of time and energy allotted to pure food-seeking activities is comparatively negligible. Their meals may, indeed, sometimes be greatly protracted, especially in the case of parties and formal dinner; but they invariably represent mixed food-seeking activities, in which the satisfaction of hunger as such often plays an insignificant rôle.

Finally, indirect corroboration of our proposition is supplied by the budget of income and expenses of the poorer and richer classes. The general uniformity observed here is the fact that the poorer the social group the larger the percentage of its total income that is spent for food, and vice versa. Whereas in the budgets of the poor from 40 to 70 per cent is spent for food, in the budgets of the richer classes the percentage is much lower, and in the budgets of the very rich it falls to an insignificant fraction of their total expenses.[5] In the case of persons suffering from starvation, the expenses for food often represent 100 per cent of their income. Nor does this tell the whole story; for in the effort to obtain more food they sell everything they have—clothing, furniture, pianos, pictures, and what not. In Soviet Russia, during 1918-1922, almost everything that the rank and file of the starving city population possessed went to the villages or food dealers in barter for food— from furniture and gramophones to wedding dresses or family heirlooms.

Such are the factual evidences of the proportional increase in the time and energy spent in food-seeking activities under famine conditions, and of the decrease of time and energy devoted to activities that inhibit or fail to promote the satisfaction of hunger.

3. *General Remarks Concerning the Interrelationships of the Various Factors of Behavior*

The preceding proposition is qualified by the term *tends*. Hunger *tends* to bring about an increase of food-seeking activities and a decrease in other activities. If hunger were the *only* force determining our behavior, then all human beings, under the conditions in question, would undergo the aforesaid change of behavior, without any exception whatsoever. However, we well know that man's behavior is controlled by many other forces than food and hunger factors—by the need for self-protection, of group protection, of sex satisfaction, as well as by religious, aesthetic, and other determinants of human behavior. Actual human behavior is the net resultant of all these determinants. The determinant of hunger may stand in either *solidary* relationship to other factors, impelling us toward the same activities as the other factors do; or in *antagonistic* relationship, driving us to perform activities which other factors inhibit; or in *neutral* relationships, where the activities dictated by hunger and those dictated by other factors are neither solidary nor antagonistic.

In our actual behavior we are hardly ever under the sole influence of hunger or of any one of the other determinants. Likewise, it rarely if ever happens that all these factors stand in a perfectly solidary relationship with one another, without any conflict between them and between the activities to which they impel us. In view of the conflict between the several factors—in this case the conflict of hunger with the other factors—a struggle for the control of man's behavior ensues. According to the comparative strength of the various factors three outcomes are possible: first, *the victory of hunger over its opponents*, in which case one's actual behavior is modified in line with our general proposition; second, *the victory of the opposing factors over hunger*, in which case the food-seeking activities do not take place in the way urged by hunger, and one's behavior does not conform to our general proposition; third, *the mutual neutralization of the hunger factor and its opponents*.

All three outcomes are observable in the behavior of persons subjected to famine conditions. In a part of the starving population, hunger obtains the upper hand over all the other determinants of human behavior; in another part the nonhunger factors emerge victorious; in a third part the victor is a factor distinct both from hunger and from its direct opponents.

This illustrates once again the *law of the diversification and polarization of the effects of the same calamity in the behavior of the population concerned.* Leaving its analysis for later chapters, let us next consider the facts that show the victory of the hunger factor over its opponents. This victory is manifested by actions, dictated by hunger, which would otherwise not be committed, and by the nonperformance of actions which in the absence of hunger would have been performed.

4. *The Dominant Role of the Hunger Factor*

A. *The Inhibition, through Hunger, of Self-protection and the Stimulation of Dangerous Activities.* In the totality of our activities there are many which aim to protect us from immediate or indirect dangers to life, health, and well-being. These actions are very diverse, consisting in the prevention or repulsion of attacks by would-be murderers or by predatory animals and poisonous snakes, the avoidance of falling rocks, escape from infection during epidemics, abstention from eating rotten food, protection against unfavorable climatic conditions, etc. Fleeing from an enemy, a dangerous animal, floods, or fire; counterattacks against an enemy; putting on a warm overcoat in cold weather; taking prescribed medicine and staying in bed while sick; avoiding contaminated drinking water; sterilizing food; disinfecting dwelling houses—all these and a thousand other actions are self-protecting in purpose.

Observation shows that animals as well as human beings, when starving, abstain from many such activities and perform many a dangerous action from which they would otherwise tend to refrain. Who does not know of hungry fish, rats, wolves, bears, and other animals being lured to their death by means of baited fishhooks or traps which under other circumstances they would tend to avoid.[6]

"We have visitors occasionally [foxes]. . . . We shoot them every day or so; their relations come along, the rumor having been spread abroad that free meals are to be had close by. . . . The scraps flung outside our door continue to attract new foxes as fast as we can shoot the old ones."[7]

Likewise, who does not know of beleaguered cities and strongholds where the besieged, after a most valiant fight, succumb to the rigors of famine or thirst and capitulate to a merciless enemy? With such facts history is replete.

The recent capitulation of the British at Hong Kong and Singapore to the Japanese was due in part to the lack of food and water. Further examples are furnished by the capitulation of Athens to the Lacedaemonians, of Nicaea to the Turks, of Calais to the English. In many instances such capitulation has meant death to many, if not all, of the victims. Hunger and thirst have here triumphed over many of the instincts and activities of self-protection, military honor, and the like. The strategy of conquest by means of blockade or siege relies primarily upon this factor. To multiply instances, who does not know of cases where famished persons have ravenously devoured obviously dangerous foods which otherwise they would not have touched?[8] Who has not heard of soldiers and criminals who have taken refuge in forests or other hideouts, only to be driven forth by the pangs of hunger in search of food at the risk of being seized, imprisoned, and even killed? The author, when he was being hunted by the Communists in 1918, hid himself in a forest. Twice, however, he and his companion were compelled by starvation to venture forth into the villages for food, in spite of the grave danger of being caught and shot.[9] In Petrograd a number of persons were forced by starvation to steal vegetables and other food from the public kitchen gardens, to falsify documents to obtain food, and the like, in spite of the fact that the death penalty was pitilessly meted out by the Soviets for such actions. Again, the famishing hero of Hamsun's *Hunger* did not notice that two toes of his foot had been crushed by a wagon and hence did not try to bandage them or to take any other remedial measures.

Not infrequently, persons put on a hunger diet by their physician cannot long endure it, and thus depart from the prescribed regimen, to the detriment of their health and even at the risk of their life.

In addition to the direct suppression of self-protecting activities, hunger serves to undermine these activities indirectly through general weakening of the organism and its capacity to resist various injurious influences and through an enfeeblement of the desire to fight for health and life. This is especially true of the later, more acute stages of prolonged starvation. Under these conditions the very "instinct of self-preservation," the will to live, tends to disappear, giving place to apathy and indifference. Hence depleted organisms succumb much more frequently and readily under the impact of adverse conditions, such as unfavorable weather and infection. The extreme form of this indirect weakening of the forces of self-protection is presented by the facts of suicide observed during mass famines.

In Soviet Russia, in the famine years 1918-1922, such facts were observed on a large scale. "In Saratov province the medical statistics indicate an enormous increase of suicide on the part of children and grown-ups due to hunger." Entire families hanged themselves, threw themselves into rivers or ponds, or asphyxiated themselves by means of inhaling poisonous gas in their homes.[10]

B. *The Inhibition or Prostitution of Sex Activities by Hunger*. Sex activities, beginning with falling in love and courtship and culminating in sexual union, occupy a considerable place in man's behavior. They embrace a wide range of phenomena representing either pure or mixed sex activities, including the composition of poems addressed to the loved one, the performance of glorious deeds on her behalf, manifestations of jealousy, the murder of rivals, betrothal and marriage, and so forth.

These activities are sometimes antagonistic to and irreconcilable with those dictated by hunger. In the ensuing conflict, hunger often emerges victorious, in one or another of three forms. First, under the influence of starvation many sex activities are suppressed; secondly, in the case of women they are performed solely for pecuniary gain; thirdly, they assume perversed forms.

1. The weakening or elimination of sex activities by prolonged and acute starvation is effected through enfeeblement of the sexual appetite, through an increase of apathy toward indirect sex activities, and through the suppression of those activities which happen to be irreconciliable with food-seeking efforts.

While it is true that in its initial stages hunger sometimes serves to stimulate sexual appetite, nevertheless prolonged starvation unquestionably weakens the sexual impulses. This has been observed in many experiments with animals, such as rabbits, dogs, and pigeons. According to the experiment of Ugriumoff, when the starvation of dogs had led to a loss of 26 per cent of their weight they could not perform coitus. In Loisel's experiments with dogs, spermatogenesis ceased after 26 days. In those conducted by S. Morgulis several organs related to sex decreased in volume. Likewise, prolonged starvation of human beings not only decreases sexual appetite but often makes conception physiologically impossible, owing to the cessation of the menses (or amenorrhea). For instance, in Soviet Russia during the famine years 1918-1922, the cases of amenorrhea increased from 0.4 per cent in 1915 to 2.5 per cent in 1918 and 6 per cent in 1919.[11]

Such a change is only to be expected, because under famine conditions the organism is weakened, and the expenditure of its energy in sex activities would merely weaken and endanger it still further. Even in normal conditions there is a kind of competition between sex and hunger.

"The sex passion directs the supply of blood and life energy toward sex organs unrelated to the organs of nutrition. For instance, the salivary glands, so important for nutrition, [as a result of] sexual excitement become, so to speak, unimportant organs, and [their functioning is] temporarily retarded, the more so the greater the sexual passion (hence, the drying up of the throat and lips, hoarseness of the voice due to the abnormal dryness of the vocal cords, etc.)."[12]

Hence the conflict between the organs of nutrition and sex. When one is greatly stimulated, the functioning of the other is temporarily retarded. Sex passion inhibits the food appetite, and vice versa.

This law was understood long ago, and was used for purposes of social control of man's sex activities. Among both primitive and civilized peoples fasting has been used as one of the most important means to prevent or repress fornication, adultery, pollution, and other undesirable sex activities.[13] The founders of ascetic religions and monastic orders, the Christian Church Fathers, and others have voiced the idea that "a stomach filled with rich food generates lust. Fasting overcomes it and saves from the sin of fornication" (Cassianus). Similar ideas were expressed by the moral and religious leaders of Brahmanism, Buddhism, Jainism, and other somewhat ascetic religions. They prescribed for their hermits and leaders fasting or else abstention from such food as meat, honey, and wine.

On the other hand, among many primitive peoples (Hottentots, Tasmanians, Ashanties, Caledonians, etc.), not to mention more literate ones, an intensified seasonal sex activity, often becoming a kind of orgy indulged in at initiation festivals and the like, occurs at those times in the year when food is most plentiful, during and after abundant eating festivals, for which food is accumulated in advance. Similar phenomena occurred among many civilized peoples in the early stages of their history.[14]

Among civilized nations such facts as a comparatively

higher proportion of sex crimes in the total criminality of
the well-to-do classes than the portion of sex crimes in the
total criminality of the poorer classes,[15] bear further testimony as to the soundness of the proposition in question.

2. Next form of modification of sex activities generated
by hunger is that of prostitution. Starvation or the threat
of starvation forces many a woman to become a prostitute
in order to obtain food. During famines—in China, India,
Soviet Russia, Europe, and other countries—there are always a considerable number of girls and women who sell
their sex services for a pound of bread or even cheaper.
In China this concomitant of starvation used to appear
regularly, and the price was almost negligible. Chroniclers
of famines in medieval Europe repeatedly noted the phenomenon. *Et ecce quod magis est, conjuges divina ordi-
natione una caro existentes sibi invicem deficiunt, et inter
eos victu parvi muneris thori fidelitas violatur.*[16] In Russia,
N. Lesskoff epically describes it in connection with the
famine of 1840 in Orloff province.

"In the villages girls and women sold to the buyers of the cats'
hides their 'girlish beauty,' that is, their hair and often their honor.
Owing to the abundance of the supply, the price became so low
that women and girls (sometimes quite young) offered themselves
without any additional charge over and above the price of cats.
When the cat buyer did not want to buy a poor cat, the seller
would whine, 'Please buy it, uncle, my dear one; in the evening
I would step out to the well for you.' A cat's hide was mer-
chandise, whereas a woman or girl was thrown in as a mere extra.
This kind of evaluation of women did not insult them in those
times: the torture of starvation was too great for that. As a rule,
peasant women sold their honor for any price offered, beginning
with a nickel; but the buyers in the villages were very few.

More enterprising and pretty women went to the cities, to the
town wells. In the villages young women stepped out in the evening to the cross-road wells, especially those at which drivers,
merchants, and cat-buyers stopped to water their horses. There,
in the gray dusk, again and again was repeated what had happened

long ago at the Biblical well of Laban. . . . And all this was done literally in order not to die from starvation. . . .

No one considered this a crime. The older women openly suggested it to the younger ones. . . . When some of the women returned from the city wells, nobody reproached them or jeered at them. They simply said, "So and so returned from the city wells, . . . fat and even." [17]

This increase of prostitution in connection with famines presents still other aspects. In Soviet Russia, between 1918 and 1922, there emerged a large class of "sodkomsh" and "sovbar," that is, women and girls who served as mistresses of the Soviet commissars and other Communists, the only groups which had more than enough food. They lived openly with their "feeders" for the sake of being fed. Likewise, a vast number of women and girls sold their honor casually, to anyone who could offer some food. In 1921–1922 even a half-legalized trade in women appeared. For instance, in the Tschukadytom district of Belebey county an entrepreneur three times bought three parties of women and girls and transported them in a special car to Tashkent, to supply the houses of prostitution. [18] In addition there were many less sensational forms of increase of prostitution.

Even in normal society, according to different investigators, from 27 to 58 per cent of its prostitutes become such under the pressure of poverty and hunger. [20]

3. Finally, under the influence of a chronic shortage of food—either actual or threatened—many forms of sex activities are modified and sometimes distorted, leading to the renunciation or indefinite postponement of marriage and sex life, in order to avoid overpopulation; the use of contraceptives; abnormal forms of sex satisfaction such as homosexualism and polyandry; the rental of wives for temporary use; and so on.

These three forms of the transformation of sexual activities are evidence of the victory of hunger over competing factors.

C. *The Repression of Freedom Activities by Hunger.* I. Pavlov has indicated that in the total behavior of animals there is a group of activities which he called the "reflex of freedom." By this is meant the activities whereby an animal strives to free itself from obstacles that suppress or limit its freedom of action. A dog, cat, or horse, when bound, attempts to free itself from its bonds. A bird imprisoned in a cage strives to get out; a wild animal confined in a limited space tries to do the same. These activities directed toward liberating the animal from obstacles to its freedom of movement play a very important rôle in the life of the organism, for without them the slightest obstacle would endanger the maintenance and preservation of its life. Pavlov's experiments indicate, further, that dogs differ in the strength of the freedom activities: in some dogs they are well developed; in others, relatively undeveloped. One of his dogs (Umnitza) was very servile; the other, very independent, violently resisting any limitation of its freedom of movement.

A similar group of freedom activities is exhibited by the behavior of human beings. Criminals confined to prison attempt to break loose. Persons bound and gagged struggle to extricate themselves. Curtailment of either freedom of movement or of mental liberty (freedom of speech and of the press, etc.) is ordinarily resisted. Like animals, individuals and groups differ, however, in the strength of their freedom activities.

These activities often enter into conflict with, and are defeated by, the food-seeking activities dictated by hunger. For instance, Pavlov's dog with the strongly developed "reflex of freedom" at first refused to take any food when it was confined within the experimental stall. However, after seven days of starvation, its "reflex of freedom" broke down, and it took food even though tied up in the stall. Similarly, many persons sell their freedom for a "mess of pottage," just as Esau sold his birthright. For the sake of food the hungry are willing to subordinate themselves to and to obey a boss whom they would otherwise despise and resist. We all know of hobos and other indigent persons who during the winter months commit a petty crime in order to be sent to jail and thus to obtain food. Freedom of movement is deliberately subordinated to freedom from hunger. Others willingly submit to servitude, and forego many cherished intellectual activities or assume mental attitudes despised by them. In Soviet Russia, in the years 1918-1922, thousands of persons did this very thing simply because the Soviet authorities (whom they hated) possessed a food monopoly.

This suppression of freedom activities by the existence or threat of starvation explains, in part, the origin and development of slavery, serfdom, and other unfree institutions. Such régimes sprang up not only through the direct coercion but also through the pressure of the factor of starvation. Under its influence many willingly sacrificed their freedom (or *status libertatis*) for the sake of avoiding starvation, subjecting themselves to those who were in a position to supply their slaves and other dependents with a modicum of food.

D. *The Rôle of Starvation in Inhibiting Restraints upon Antisocial Activities.* In the total behavior of man the activities concerned with the protection of life, with the integrity and interests of the social groups to which we belong, occupy a very large place. The social and group-protecting activities related to the family, to relatives and friends, to the community and nation, to political parties, to religious, occupational, and class groups, are numerous and exceedingly diverse. Abstention from cannibalism, murder, theft, and other actions injurious to the members of the group; active work for their benefit through the expenditure of money (including taxes), time, and energy; and fighting and, if need be, dying for the group are among the outstanding examples of such social activities. They practically merge with those prescribed by the religious, ethical, and juridical norms of the respective groups.

Under famine conditions these social activities often conflict with the food-seeking activities induced by starvation. In *part* of the population the food-seeking activities defeat many a social activity, giving rise to antisocial conduct. Under the pressure of starvation many persons commit antisocial acts injurious to their fellows. Conversely, they refrain from many beneficial acts which they would otherwise have performed. Finally, many social activities are performed indifferently and inefficiently owing to malnutrition.

1. *Cannibalism Induced by Starvation.*[21] The most striking example of this desocialization and demoralization of a fraction of the starving population is furnished by the fairly frequent emergence of acts of *cannibalism* on the part of persons who would otherwise view such acts with extreme abhorrence, and who resort to cannibalism only when demoralized by long and maddening starvation, sometimes under the stress of mental derangement. Whether we consider abstention from cannibalism as an inherited reflex or as an acquired disposition,[22] it is probably the strongest inhibition possessed by noncannibalistic people, since the mere idea of such a practice fills them with loathing and disgust. Under famine conditions the practice has been noted among some of the South Sea islanders, the Nukuhivans, some Australian tribes, certain

Indian groups, the Eskimos of Hudson Bay, etc.[23] In the Bible we read, "And thou shalt eat the fruit of thine own body, the flesh of thy sons and of thy daughters . . . in the siege and in the straitness."[24] During major famines cannibalism occurred in ancient Egypt, ancient Greece and Rome, Persia, India, China, Japan, and elsewhere. In medieval Europe numerous instances appeared. Chroniclers note it, for example, in connection with the famines of 793, 868-869, 896, 1005, 1032, 1146, 1233, 1241-1242, 1277, 1280-1282, and 1315-1317. The following extracts are typical.

Anno Domini 1317 et 18 et 19 tanta fuit caristia et fames in Polonia et Silesia, uta quod pluribus in locis parentes filios et filii parentes necantes deveraverunt, plures etiam carnes de suspensis cadaveribus comederunt.

Famis vero quae anno (793) priori coepit, in tantum excrevit, ut homines homines, fratres fratres ac matres filios comedere coegit.

[In 868] tanta fames fuit, ut unus homo alium interficeret et bestiarum more dentibus laniaret. Inventi sunt etiam ea tempestate in eodem pago masculi et femine pro nefas! homines alios occidisse et comedisse.[25]

The same tragic story of parents' killing and eating their children and vice versa, of wives' slaying and devouring their husbands and vice versa, of the snatching of corpses from cemeteries or the gallows, of the professional ambushing, killing, eating of passers-by—this is monotonously repeated in connection with numerous major famines. In France, between 1030 and 1032, one man killed and consumed 48 persons; in Germany, in 897, freshly buried corpses were exhumed and eaten; in Burgundy, in 1030-1031, "human flesh was openly sold on the market." In England cannibalism occurred in such famines as those of 1069 and 1315. In Russia it is recorded by contemporary chroniclers for the famines of 1203-1231, 1601-1602, et alia. "Some of the plain people killed and ate human beings; others devoured corpses."[26]

After the seventeenth century Europe gradually emerged from a state of major or chronic famine; therefore cannibalism tended to disappear in modern European history. But when, as in the case of the survivors from the wrecked ships *Medusa* (1816), *Mignonette* (1884), and others, Europeans were subjected to acute and prolonged starvation, some of them resorted to cannibalism.[27]

The severe and protracted famine of 1918-1922 in Russia was marked by cannibalism on a considerable scale, with all its appalling characteristics. In Moscow, in 1920, a man killed and consumed his wife; in Minsk province two children slew a pal and ate his body; in Busuluck county a peasant woman murdered her seven-year-old daughter and cooked her; and so forth. In many places the cemeteries had to be guarded in order to prevent the exhuming of recently buried corpses.[28]

These facts show that starvation occasionally overrides the strongest taboos and inhibitions, impelling some persons to commit the supremely antisocial act of cannibalism. Fortunately, the overwhelming majority prefer death to such utter demoralization, even when suffering from acute starvation.

2. *Murder, and Other Anti-social Actions Perpetrated against the Members of One's Own Group, Induced by Starvation.* If starvation drives some persons to cannibalism, it induces a much larger number to murder their own parents or children, husbands or wives, or other members of their own group, not to mention strangers and outsiders. In times of famine, the old and useless members of the group, as well as infants, are killed off among a number of preliterate peoples. In other groups they are simply abandoned.[29] In ancient Latium the aged people were killed in

order that the other members might obtain a larger share of the food—*ut reliquis cibaria sufficirent*.[30] In China and elsewhere the exposure of children, their abandonment, or their sale as slaves has attended almost all major famines.[31]

Similar facts have been observed in ancient Mexico, ancient Greece, Rome, and other countries, and among the Arabs and several poorest Hindu castes.[32]

The phenomenon was repeated on a considerable scale during the famine years of 1918-1922 in Soviet Russia. In the Samara (Kuybysheff) museum "there are photographs of children suffocated by their mothers, who had become crazed by hunger.[33] Even more notable were the abandonment of children, and the selling of girls "for export."

"In the cities of Samara [Kuybysheff] province parents are bringing their children from the villages and abandoning them in the city markets and streets. On market days the number of deserted children increases from two to three times. The number abandoned at the Institutions for the Protection of Children likewise steadily mounts."[34]

It is only natural that there should be a still sharper accentuation in the case of milder antisocial practices. The altruistic and humanitarian tendencies tend to be replaced by egoistic or animalistic impulses. As one of the medieval chroniclers observes:

"Nec solum ignotos hoc tempore deficit misericordia, sed etiam inter affines sanguineque contiguos omnis clementia omnisque sublevatio denegatur, quum nec parentes filiis, nec filii parentibus in hac necessitate maxima volunt assistere, ipsisque libet habundantes vitae necessaria ministrare."[35]

In similar terms this recrudescence of antisocial behavior is described by a Russian chronicler of famine in the Novgorod province.

"Mutual irritation grew apace: brother was pitted against brother; fathers showed no pity for their sons; mothers lost all sense of mercy toward their daughters; neighbors denied one another a crumb of bread. Charity became dead among us; only sadness, gloom, and hopelessness reigned within and without our dwellings. Crying children were seen begging in vain for bread and falling dead like flies."[36]

Under these circumstances mutual animosity occasionally leads to accusations of sorcery and the murder of witches and other accused persons, as well as to such superstitious practices as making a candle out of human fat with a view to exorcising the evil spirits responsible for the famine.[37]

During the years 1918-1922 in Russia the milder forms of desocialization due to famine manifested themselves in a variety of forms. In the interest of obtaining better rations, children denounced their parents or other members of the family to the Cheka as anticommunists; soldiers shifted their allegiance from the "red" to the "white" or the "green" armies; members of the Cheka and similar groups (who were much better fed than the rest of the population) executed friends, fellow villagers, and so on. In the Soviet children's homes, as well as in many private families, "there was observed a pathological greed for food. Children chronically exhibited violent irritation, anger, and hatred. They would fight to obtain a warmer place near the stove, or a larger ration during the distribution of food; . . . they stole food from one another and from the administration of the children's homes; the stronger snatched food from the weaker; they lied shamelessly for a chance to obtain food."[38]

E. *The Repression of Minor Religious, Moral, Juridical, and Conventional Activities by Hunger.* If starvation can convert a noncannibal into a cannibal; can impel one to slay his closest kin; can suppress innumerable self-protective activities—if it can thus triumph over a multitude of unconditioned reflexes and instincts, still more easily can it defeat purely *acquired* activities concerned with less important values. The social activities considered in the preceding section deal with the basic values of human life and society—the central norms of religion, law, and ethics. Their roots, as we have said, go deep, being grounded partly in the "subterranean" region of unconditioned reflexes and instincts.

Side by side with these semi-instinctive dispositions there are an enormous number of responses that are clearly acquired, resulting from our social milieu, such as reacting to the sight of an ikon by crossing oneself, to that of a military officer by coming to "attention," to that of a friend by raising one's hat or shaking hands, to that of a notice "Private property" by refraining from acts of trespass; or behaving in one way in a courtroom, in another way at church, in a third way in a store, at school, or at a night club. It is obvious that when these purely "conditioned" activities are antagonistic to food-seeking impulses they are more readily inhibited than the semi-instinctive and basic reactions considered above.

Virtually every religion taboos certain kinds of food in general, and for certain periods (such as Lent) more specifically. The faithful ordinarily observe these prescriptions under normal conditions. But under the stress of acute hunger they frequently violate all such taboos.

Some medieval chroniclers complained that during fast periods people ate flesh and many "unclean" forms of food —mice, rats, and the corpses of animals and even human beings.[39] Many a devout person in Soviet Russia in 1918-1922 ate any food he could get, including what was "unclean" and "sinful."

In other cases the ecclesiastical authorities absolved the violators of religious taboos from penalties in time of famine. Thus in Paris, during several medieval famines, "the bishop of Paris permitted anyone to eat meat even on fast days."[40] A similar suspension of the food taboos was explicitly set forth in many religious and legal codes, which subsumed famine under those *emergency* situations in which even crimes are not punishable. Such actions, if not actually justified, were at least regarded as venial.[41] In brief, religious and juridical food taboos are generally violated in times of famine by a large proportion of the population.[42]

Like the food taboos, the Fourth Commandment is usually observed by believers. But in famines, when it interferes with food-seeking activities it is often violated. Although the Church forbids interment without the appropriate religious ceremonies, during periods of famine thousands of persons are buried without any religious rites. In some cases the Church explicitly absolves its adherents from such a duty. The same may be said of many other ecclesiastical prescriptions,[43] such as those relating to the ritual of church services, the ceremony of baptism, monetary contributions, and the like.

Similar violations are observed respecting juridical, moral, and other norms of conduct distinct from those that prohibit murder and other flagrantly antisocial actions. First of all may be noted offenses against the rights of private property, such as larceny, theft, and forgery. An excellent picture of the inner struggle between food-seeking propensities and inculcated convictions respecting private property is given by K. Hamsun, in his *Hunger*. His hero is an honest man, who entertains deep convictions as to business honesty and the sacredness of private property. The first act of this inner drama consists in the temptation to pawn the blanket of his friend so as to still the pangs of hunger. But, for the time being, his scruples gain the upper hand. He is overjoyed with his resistance to temptation.

"The consciousness that I was still honest . . . filled me with a splendid sense of possessing principle and character."[44] However, he eventually attempts to dispose of the blanket, and then takes money given to him by mistake. When he finally satisfies his hunger, his conscience begins to reproach him for his initial dishonest action, and, to assuage it, he gives the rest of the money to a poor person.[45]

With many others the triumph of food-seeking impulses over conflicting moral or juridical norms ensues much sooner and more readily.[46] The situation in Soviet Russia during 1918-1922 is highly significant in this respect, especially as private property was supposed to be abolished, and as the penalty for theft or any other misappropriation of economic values was most drastic. Nevertheless, the violation of public and private property rights assumed catastrophic proportions. If we take 100 as the index of criminality in 1914 in Moscow, for 1918-1919 we have the following increase: theft, 315; armed robbery, 28,500; simple robbery, 800; unlawful appropriation, 170; forgery, 370.[47] In 1920 the theft of luggage on Soviet railroads was 150 times greater than in 1914.[48] In 1922 2,640,000 pouds of foodstuffs (a poud is 36 English pounds) were stolen on the Soviet railway lines, and several millions pouds of other commodities—a total of 11,400,000 pouds, amounting to 50,000,000 gold rubles. In Leningrad at least 22 per cent and in Moscow up to 70 per cent of the population illegally used two or more ration cards.[49]

Theft and other crimes against property committed under such circumstances are either unpunished or only mildly punished among many preliterate peoples, in ancient Peru, in ancient Greece and Rome, in China, in Mohammedan law, in medieval canon and secular law, etc.[50] Under the same conditions, as we have seen, honest women are driven to prostitution; and even more readily do they, like Esau, trade such values as self-respect, pride, human dignity, honor, and conscience for a "mess of pottage." In Soviet Russia thousands traded these values for a pound of inferior bread or a few ounces of sugar; extolled those whom they despised; accepted jobs which they loathed; etc.[51] Under the stress of starvation men are ready to trade even their liberty for food. Thus, in many famines of the past not a few sold themselves into serfdom or slavery, as evidenced by the history of Greece and Rome, China and India, medieval Europe and Russia.[52] In Russia this occurred, for instance, in 1128 and 1446.[53] Indeed, as has been pointed out, the factor of starvation has played a very important part in the emergence of slavery and serfdom as social institutions.

Before the famine years in Russia many members of the upper and middle classes would have preferred death to the scandal of standing for hours in an illegal market, trying to exchange a pair of old trousers or a dress for food. But during the years 1918-1922 they took this as a matter of course. Multitudes of persons, under normal circumstances, would "rather die than beg." But let them face starvation, and they extend their hands for alms—at first reluctantly and with a sense of shame, then habitually, as a matter of routine; and finally artfully, employing all the tricks of the profession. So it was in Russia with thousands of the former intelligentsia and the middle and upper classes; and the phenomenon had already repeatedly been noted by medieval chroniclers.[54]

F. *The Repression of Aesthetic and Recreational Activities by Hunger.* Though *panis et circenses* supposedly go together, nevertheless, when there is no bread, *circenses* and many aesthetic activities and interests opposed or even unrelated to food-seeking activities suffer. When we are well nourished, we crave beauty and recreation, attending the theater and opera, concerts and the movies, museums and exhibitions; reading poetry or novels; developing our own aesthetic talents (painting, playing musical instruments, etc.); admiring natural scenery or artistic masterpieces; discussing beauty and the fine arts; and the like. Ladies lavish the utmost care upon their hands, face, and hair, spending much time and money in beauty parlors; and they bestow the minutest attention upon the "beauty lines" of everything they buy, from toilet accessories to dresses, suits, and motor cars. With the advent of starvation, however, those activities and interests that thwart or are unrelated to food-seeking purposes tend to go into the discard or else assume entirely different forms, and attention comes to be concentrated well-nigh exclusively upon the grim quest for food.

In Soviet Russia, in 1918-1922, virtually all objects of aesthetic value (paintings, sculpture, vases, rings, de-luxe furniture and fabrics, musical instruments, and the like) were bartered in exchange for food. Similarly, most aesthetic activities that did not promote this interest either declined or disappeared. The same phenomenon has repeatedly marked the course of other famines.[55] Only those aesthetic activities which do not interfere or compete with the food-seeking activities have any chance of surviving.

G. *The Repression of Other Activities by Hunger*. What has been said of the self-protecting, group-protecting, sexual, religious, and similar activities applies in general to all the activities not conducive to the realization of food-seeking purposes. Scientists, scholars, poets, artists, priests, and craftsmen tend to relax or completely suspend their customary activities in times of famine. In Soviet Russia (a wonderful laboratory in this respect), in the years 1918-1922, prominent scientists and scholars gladly ac-

cepted positions unrelated to their specialty; famous artists
painted Soviet propaganda posters; eminent musicians became clerks in the Commissariat of Food; and distinguished
singers, musicians, and composers lent their services on behalf of what they thoroughly despised (stigmatized by the
untranslatable word *khaltura*, as opposed to *cultura*).

H. *The Modification of Ideas, Beliefs, Opinions, and
Speech Reactions by Hunger.* Concomitantly with the
change of our overt activities induced by starvation, we
change also our ideas, opinions, convictions, and ideologies,
together with the respective speech reactions (written and
oral) that manifest them. The direction of the change is
toward a reinforcement of the ideas and ideologies justify-
ing food-seeking activities and a weakening or elimination
of the ideologies and convictions that hinder the acqui-
sition of food and the satisfaction of hunger. This modification of ideologies and convictions, as well as the corresponding speech reactions, can be observed explicitly in
the cases where the persons concerned do not conceal their
ideas, either by silence or by insincere and misleading
speech reactions. In the latter case, starvation turns an
honest person into a hypocrite or downright liar, who entertains one sort of ideas and alleges quite different ones.
While such a person inwardly rates the boss upon whom
his food depends in the most negative or disparaging terms,
outwardly for the sake of the *captatio bonae voluntatis*
of his boss, he flatters him in the most complimentary and
eulogistic terms.

Such is the general pattern of the modification of ideas,
beliefs, convictions, ideologies, and speech-reactions effected by hunger. Let us cite several concrete illustrations.
Suppose that we are confronted by a dry loaf of bread of
poor quality, or by a piece of somewhat putrid meat. If we
are not hungry, we respond to these stimuli by speech re-

actions such as: "Nobody, not even a dog, would eat it. It is nauseating!" But after prolonged and acute starvation our reaction is as follows: "Excellent! Delicious! Wonderful!" and we avidly seize the bread or the meat. The half-rotten flesh of horses that had died of starvation was eagerly, even greedily sought by most of the Russian population during the famine, and it was eaten with as much relish as well-nourished people eat the best steak. The same was true of the flesh of dogs, cats, and even mice and rats. Mikkelsen and Iversen, under the stress of starvation, decided to try the liver of a dead dog which even their own dogs would not eat and which they knew was to some extent poisonous. After cooking it, "We taste it critically . . . ; but the first little mouthful is speedily followed by one considerably larger, and two broad grins of delight with inarticulate murmurs of satisfaction, announce that we find it delicious."[56] What is "tasteless" or even nauseating under normal circumstances becomes "delectable" to a famished person. What is called "malnutrition" in normal times is sincerely regarded (and often with good reason) as "overfeeding" or "luxury" in times of a famine.

In a more complicated form a somewhat similar change occurs with more complex convictions and ideologies and their respective speech reactions. A well-nourished person says, "Private property is sacred." But a victim of famine is likely to exclaim, vis à vis the possessions of others, "To hell with your property!" or, "Property is a theft. Long live the expropriation of the exploiters!" or the like. On the one hand, the speech reaction is "Theft is inexcusable"; on the other, "Theft is excusable." "Ah! what a beautiful picture!", in the other: "I'm not interested. Give me *food!*" Again the proposition "It is inadmissible to profane science, art, and duty just for the sake of mammon. Not by bread alone is man nourished" is countered by the retort

"Bosh! One must live! What if I do temporarily sacrifice to mammon high-sounding duties and the values of art and science!"

In Soviet Russia one could observe these changes *ad libitum* in the behavior of millions toward the Soviet authorities upon whom they depended for food. Journalists, authors, scholars, artists, musicians, doctors, engineers, and persons in all walks of life, though they despised and hated the Soviet bosses, nevertheless tried the way of *captatio benevolentiae* of the Soviet food-givers now by silence, masking their real ideas and opinions, and now in the form of flattery and eulogies (written and oral), contrary to their true convictions. Others, having obtained satisfactory rations through their hypocrisy, speedily convinced themselves of the sincerity of their alleged convictions and remained faithful "converts" to the Soviet faith as long as the food privileges continued. This self-deceit, with its high-sounding phrases, is but a screen behind which the food factor pulls the strings. Such "conversions," "transformations," and "transfigurations" are a mass phenomena in times of famine. A few pounds of bread, a cup of sugar, or a steak is enough to turn the trick. This does not mean that everyone undergoes this transformation of ideas, beliefs, opinions, convictions, and speech reactions. A part of the starving population remains unchanged or changes even in the opposite direction. But another—and possibly larger—part undergoes this "adjustment" (as it is called) of convictions and speech reactions. When such an "adaptation" is sincere, its moral value is even less than that of the clever and cynical hypocrisy of the flatterers; for they at least do not fool themselves.

When the transforming rôle of starvation is thoroughly understood, the rise and fall of various ideologies, the increase and decrease of their adherents, the sharp and rapid changes in the dominant system of beliefs, opinions, and evaluations in a given society, become comprehensible. In Chapter Seventeen we shall deal with these phenomena at greater length. For the present let us summarize the preceding analysis.

1. *General Summary*. (1) Starvation tends to modify most of the fundamental activities and reactions of the victims, including their ideas, beliefs, and speech reactions. (2) The general direction of the change is toward the weakening or elimination of the activities, convictions, and speech reactions that hinder the satisfaction of hunger and toward those that promote the realization of their immediate needs.

5. *The Social Diversification and Polarization of the Effects of Starvation*

If I were to conclude the analysis of the effects of starvation with the preceding paragraph, I should be guilty of the common mistake perpetrated by most of the investigators of starvation—a thoroughly one-sided picture of the phenomenon! These effects, especially the most antisocial ones, rarely manifest themselves in the behavior of all or even of a majority of the population. On the contrary, such actions as cannibalism apply to only an infinitesimal proportion of the population—a maximum, perhaps, of 1 per cent. In some famines no cannibalism appears at all. Likewise, only an insignificant number of persons become murderers, robbers or brigands, or perpetrators of other grave antisocial offenses. The overwhelming majority resist such temptations, thus testifying to the existence of forces that cannot be defeated by the impact of starvation. It is perhaps only the secondary values and purely conventional rules that suffer in the conduct of the rank and file, such as those that relate to church attendance, the proper observance of Sunday and fast days, the appropriate burial of the dead, and the rules of social etiquette.

More than that. If starvation provokes antisocial and brutal behavior in one part of the population, it engenders an opposite reaction in another part. The demoralization of the one is counterbalanced by the ennoblement of the other. Side by side with the desocializing processes there appear conspicuous deeds of altruism, heroism, and religious devotion. Instead of becoming cannibals, the majority share their last crumb of bread with their fellows. Who has not heard of religious leaders, ascetics, and political prisoners who have faced *death* by starvation rather than yield a jot or tittle of their cherished convictions to their captors?

These facts sufficiently attest the exaggeration of the rôle played by starvation in human behavior as compared with other factors—social, moral, religious, etc. If we consider only its effects upon the demoralized *minority*, we have to conclude that it is supreme and overwhelming. In relation, however, to the *total* population, its consequences are seen to be much less significant than is ordinarily assumed. If we take, as an index of the comparative power of starvation, the proportion of persons in whose behavior starvation suppresses those activities, ideas, and speech reactions inimical to food-seeking purposes, we obtain approximately the following results.

Activities Induced by Starvation	Percentage of Population Succumbing to Pressure of Starvation	Percentage of Population Resisting Such Pressure
Cannibalism (in non-cannibalistic societies)	Less than one third of 1 per cent	More than 99 per cent
Murder of members of the family and friends	Less than 1 per cent	More than 99 per cent
Murder of other members of one's group	Not more than 1 per cent	Not less than 99 per cent
Murder of strangers who are not enemies	Not more than 2 to 5 per cent	Not less than 95 per cent
Infliction of various bodily and other injuries on members of one's social group	Not more than 5 to 10 per cent	Not less than 90 per cent
Theft, larceny, robbery, forgery, and other crimes against property which have a clear-cut criminal character	Hardly more than 7 to 10 per cent	Hardly less than 90 to 93 per cent
Violation of various rules of strict honesty and fairness in pursuit of food, such as misuse of rationing cards, hoarding, and taking unfair advantage of others	From 20 to 99 per cent depending upon the nature of the violation	From 1 to 80 per cent
Violation of fundamental religious and moral principles	Hardly more than 10 to 20 per cent	From 80 to 90 per cent
Violation of less important religious, moral, juridical, conventional, and similar norms	From 50 to 99 per cent	From 1 to 50 per cent
Surrender or weakening of most of the aesthetic activities irreconcilable with food-seeking activities	From 50 to 99 per cent	From 1 to 50 per cent
Weakening of sex activities especially coitus	From 70 to 90 per cent during prolonged and intense starvation	From 1 to 30 per cent
Prostitution and other highly dishonorable sex activities	Hardly more than 10 per cent	Hardly less than 90 per cent

Although these figures are highly tentative and approximate, they are hardly misleading. They show that the starvation factor exerts supreme power only in regard to the secondary and minor values and activities. The fundamental values—religious, moral, juridical, etc.—successfully resist its attack in the behavior of the overwhelming majority. The texture of the religious, moral, and other social activities proves much tougher and more indestructible than we usually think. If man cannot live without bread, it is equally true that he lives not by bread *alone*. *Those who observe only the negative—the demoralizing and desocializing effects of hunger in the behavior of the minority—grossly exaggerate the power of this factor, overlooking the other—and much more important—aspect of the total situation.*

The above gives a general idea of the law of diversification and polarization as applied to the effects of starvation, and of the relative power of this factor and competing factors as determinants of human conduct. Later on we shall undertake a more systematic elucidation of the law.

Chapter Four

HOW PESTILENCE, WAR, AND REVOLUTION INFLUENCE OUR BEHAVIOR

1. *General Uniformity*

With the appropriate modifications, the main proposition formulated at the beginning of the preceding chapter seems to be applicable to all these calamities, in that each of them tends to eliminate or weaken those activities which hinder escape from the calamity and tends to generate or reinforce those activities which lead to the realization of this objective. However, in order properly to apply this formula we have to distinguish, first, *the active part of the population directly involved (the victims of pestilence, the combatants in war and revolution) and the passive part of the population (those not suffering from pestilence and the noncombatants in war and revolution); second, the technical modes of behavior which appear to each part of the population best calculated to ensure relief from suffering.* Most people prefer peace to war, and orderly change to the violent change brought about by revolution. But some of these believe that only a decisive victory over the enemy can end the war and its sufferings, while others hold that peace at any price is the best way to eliminate war. Likewise, in a revolutionary society some are convinced that only through the triumph of the revolution can the sufferings of society be eliminated, whereas others contend that cessation of all revolutionary activities, and of the counterrevolutionary efforts engendered by them, is the sole remedy. Once these distinctions are made, the formula can be easily applied to the respective groups.

[83]

2. *The Effects of Pestilence*

As regards the behavior of the victims of bubonic plague, spotted typhus, cholera, smallpox, influenza or other epidemics, little need be said concerning the comparatively initial stages of their illness. Until they become feverish or entirely incapacitated, they are intent on getting well, subordinating every other activity and interest to this purpose. When, with the progress of the pestilence, fever sets in or they become entirely incapacitated, they cease to play an active rôle, becoming merely passive objects in the hands of doctors, nurses, priests, members of the family, caretakers, and so on. Their behavior undergoes so radical a change—from that of a rational agent to the almost purely biological reactions of a helpless, suffering, unconscious, or semiconscious organism incapable of decision or rational choice—that a description of their later "behavior" belongs less to the field of sociology and psychology than to that of pure biology or even biochemistry.

The one aspect of the victim's situation which calls for special mention is his *psychosocial isolation*—the loss of his status as a full-fledged member of society and the snapping of the numerous ties which linked him to the activities and interests of his fellows. This results from a variety of factors: his fear lest they be infected by him; government quarantine measures; and the like. The patient suddenly finds himself cut off from the rest of the human universe —half dead socially, though still biologically alive. In various chronic illnesses the shock of such isolation induces mental depression, despondency, and sometimes even suicide (whose main cause, indeed, is general psychosocial isolation).

The behavior of the *healthy* part of the population changes, as a rule, in the direction indicated by our general proposition. The desire to enjoy immunity from sickness becomes the paramount consideration. In this circumstance the activities that appear to promote this purpose tend to be reinforced and multiplied, whereas those that appear to thwart it tend to become weaker or to disappear. Avoidance of contact with the sick; flight from infected cities and villages; changes of diet and manner of living favorable to health; medical, sanitary, magical, and other means held to be efficacious—these and similar activities expand enormously. If they are opposed by other factors,—religious, moral, aesthetic, juridical, etc.,—a portion of the population, as in the case of starvation, tends to repudiate these considerations. As in time of famine, the most antisocial deeds are perpetrated by a part of the population: the murder of alleged sorcerers and witches, foreigners, doctors, and others who are believed to be responsible for the pestilence; the beating or mutilation of innocent persons, including members of one's own family; the abandonment of the sick, and occasionally their interment while they are still alive; the destruction of property; theft, larceny, and robbery; and sometimes sacrilege and blasphemy. Again, many become extreme hedonists and cynicists, guided solely by the motto, "Eat, drink, and be merry, for tomorrow we die!" engaging in a sensual riot unrestrained by any moral considerations or values.

As to the neglect of the secondary and less fundamental norms and values, when these conflict with the dominant objective they are brushed aside by a much larger proportion of the population. The activities that fail to contribute to the realization of this purpose are performed less frequently and diligently or not at all. Many cease to attend church. The time and energy formerly devoted to public meetings, committee work, and similar "neutral" activities, and even to one's principal vocation, greatly decrease, frequently to the vanishing point.

In brief, *pestilence tends to modify the behavior of the*

healthy portion of society in the same manner in which starvation modifies it, the main differences being that the comparative power of the fear of pestilence and the desire to remain healthy may be different from the comparative power of the fear of starvation and the desire to escape it, and that the concrete activities attacked or reinforced by pestilence may differ in part from those attacked or reinforced by starvation.

3. *The Effects of War*

Here again we must distinguish the change of behavior on the part of combatants actively engaged in and directly exposed to the dangers of war from that of the civil population not immediately exposed to such dangers.

As to the behavior of the combatants (and this applies alike to the courageous and the cowardly, the conscientious and the selfish, the clever and the stupid), *the military factor naturally suppresses those activities that hinder or are not connected with the paramount purpose of defeating the enemy or of escaping death and defeat.* For the duration of the battle and the period immediately preceding it, all other activities are subordinated to the chief objective. Soldiers eat and drink, sleep, curse or pray, run or lie down, play this or that game, read, or write only in the interest of achieving military success or of obtaining momentary relief from the strain of fighting. Even these essential activities are performed and the respective needs are satisfied only insofar as the battle situation permits; for military necessity demands frequently abstinence from sleep or rest, eating or drinking, and requires a soldier to march or fight far beyond the normal limits of his physical endurance.

The individual differences in the conduct of the combatants concern chiefly the *technical* ways in which each modifies his behavior in the general direction indicated. The cowardly soldier may lie down, inflict upon himself a slight wound, or flee to a near-by forest and remain there for hours or days, instead of attacking or counterattacking. The courageous soldier will proceed to the attack and stubbornly engage the enemy. While the two techniques differ, the behavior of the two types of combatants undergoes the same change: activities are subordinated to the military situation.

The same conclusion is reached when the question is viewed from the standpoint of the factors of self-preservation and of group protection and loyalty. In some soldiers the factor of self-preservation gains the upper hand over group loyalty and induces them to flee, to become deserters. In others the factor of group loyalty gains the upper hand or else, in coöperation with the factor of self-protection, dictates the defeat of the enemy as the surest way of achieving self-preservation. All such differences are merely technical variations in the change of behavior formulated by our general proposition, which may be regarded as an algebraic formula in which one may supply different arithmetical values corresponding to the individual techniques of the various combatants. (Concrete examples of individual differences in the technique of behavior will be given in the chapters Ten, Eleven and Twelve on the law of diversification and polarization of the effects of calamity.)

As to the change evoked by war in the behavior of the *civil* population, its character and intensity depend upon many considerations. For example, is the war supported by the civilian population? How immediate is the danger of being killed, wounded, bombed, or pillaged? How serious will be the losses in the event of conquest by the enemy? How strong are the loyalty, patriotism, and morale of the masses? These and many other factors influence

markedly the secondary changes in the behavior of the
civil population in time of war. If, for instance, as is true
of the present war in many countries, the civilians have to
reckon with incessant devastating air raids, the transformation of their behavior is very similar to that of the combatants. If, per contra, the hazards of war are relatively
remote and problematical their conduct may be modified
only slightly, deviating in several respects from that of the
soldiers.

It is nevertheless true that so long as a given population
is involved in major war, its reactions exhibit a marked
conformity to the general proposition under discussion.
*War suppresses or undermines many an activity incom-
patible with its prosecution, and introduces or reinforces
many activities either necessary to or compatible with its
prosecution.* First, the government effects such changes
through orders and decrees embracing various fields of
behavior—economic, political, recreational, etc. Secondly,
there are the inevitable restrictions imposed by the scarcity
of commodities, such as automobiles, and by the disruption
of normal life entailed by the absorption of a substantial
proportion of the male population in the fighting forces.
Finally, the patriotic and disciplined elements voluntarily
subject themselves to numerous transformations in their
way of life. For example, they deliberately lower their
standard of living so as to promote the efficiency of the
armed forces.

Although in their broad outlines the changes in question
follow the pattern of our basic proposition, the technical
modes of filling in the details of the pattern naturally vary
according to the general cultural and social conditions.
They vary also for different groups and individuals. Some
indulge in profiteering, while others sacrifice their wealth;
some hoard commodities, whereas others share what little

they possess, and so on. These divergences merely furnish further instances of the familiar law of diversification and polarization.

4. *The Effects of Revolution*

The behavior of the active combatants in revolutionary wars varies in the same way as that of the combatants in international wars. Likewise the conduct of the civil population not actively engaged in the revolutionary struggle is essentially transformed along lines similar to those that characterize the behavior of civilians during international wars. The main direction of the change is toward the weakening of activities that hinder the revolution or counterrevolution (according to the faction) and toward the reinforcing of those that promote success. In their concrete forms these reactions naturally vary from faction to faction and from individual to individual.[1]

Chapter Five

How Calamities Influence the Vital Processes—Death, Birth, and Marriage Rates and Social Selection

This chapter is a bridge leading from the study of the effects of calamities upon the mentality and behavior of individuals to that of their sociocultural effects. Subsequent chapters deal with the typical, or more or less uniform, changes in social structure and sociocultural life brought about by calamities. Here we shall concisely outline the biosocial effects of calamities upon death, birth, and marriage rates and upon social selection.

1. *Loss of Life*

It goes without saying that all calamities and crises impose a death toll upon the population involved. The loss of life in the bubonic plague which ravaged Byzantium in 543 A.D. amounted to many millions of persons; the Black Death of 1348 and subsequent years carried away from one third to one half of the population of Europe—approximately some 42,836,500, according to the statistics collected at the instigation of the contemporary Pope, Clement VI.[1] In the less severe epidemics—typhus, dysentery, smallpox, diphtheria, cholera, sweating sickness, influenza, various fevers, measles, whooping cough, scarlatina, etc.—the death toll has been smaller than in the foregoing cases of bubonic plague; nevertheless, in many of them the number of victims has been very considerable.[2]

The death toll exacted by many a great famine has also been enormous, owing to the fact that most of the major famines have been followed by various epidemics. Up to the last few centuries "the history of epidemics is almost wholly a history of famine sickness."[3] During the famine of 1921-1922 in the Tartar Republic of Soviet Russia the population decreased by 470,000, or 20 per cent; the population of Bashkiria decreased by 33 per cent; that of the Ural region by 25 per cent; that of the Pougatcheff county, in the Province of Samara, by 50 per cent; that of the city of Kherson by 60 per cent; and so on.[4]

The total number of victims of famine and epidemic during the first five years of the Russian Revolution is counted in the millions. From two to three millions perished in the Russian famine of 1933-1934. Beginning with "the seven lean years" in Egypt and ending with the contemporary period in China and other countries, famines have carried away hundreds of millions of human lives.

Revolutions vie with pestilence and famine in the mass murder of human beings, particularly since the major revolutions are followed, as a rule by famine and pestilence. Large-scale revolutions generally result in a mortality of from 3 to 15 per cent of the population. The total number of victims in the Russian Revolution of 1918-1922 ranged from thirteen to seventeen millions, or from 9 to 13 per cent of the total population. For males between the ages of fifteen and sixty years the loss was about 28 per cent.[5] The French Revolution carried away, during the years 1789 to 1801, from 1,400,000 to 2,000,000. Hundreds of thousands of lives were sacrificed during the English revolution of the mid-seventeenth century headed by Oliver Cromwell. About 300,000 perished in the Roman revolutions from the time of the Gracchi to the end of the civil wars of the Second Triumvirate. In vast populations like that of China major revolutions have taken a still heavier toll. It is estimated that, for instance, the civil war in China in the years 755 to 781 reduced the population from fifty-three millions to twenty millions. Even if we reduce this loss to one half or one third, it remains enormous.[6]

Finally, war competes with pestilence, famine, and revolution in this unholy business. Like notable revolutions, large-scale wars are ordinarily followed by famine and epidemics, which add their casualties to those of the battlefield. The present war has already accounted—directly and indirectly—for more than fifteen million lives. The direct casualties of the First World War were approximately twenty millions in killed and wounded. The lethal power of war has been increasing rather than decreasing with the passing centuries. From the twelfth to the seventeenth century the direct casualties of war were from 2.5 to 5.9 per cent of the strength of the army, and armies were then relatively small in proportion to the total population. Between the seventeenth and twentieth centuries the direct casualties increased from 15.9 to 38.9 per cent of the strength of the army, and armies, moreover, have increased relatively to the size of the total population.[7]

Other, more sporadic and more short-lived, calamities, such as earthquakes, tornadoes, floods, and explosions, likewise exact their toll of human life. But their ravages are relatively mild in comparison with those of pestilence, famine, war and revolution.

2. How Calamities Influence Death, Birth, and Marriage Rates

All calamities and crises, as we have seen, increase the death rate of the population involved. Acute and prolonged catastrophes augment it sharply; insignificant ones, only slightly or even imperceptibly. In major plagues or famines the death rate has sometimes reached 200, 500, or 800 for every thousand of the population, as compared with the normal rate of from 10 to 30. The Black Death wiped out in many localities one half, two thirds, or even seven eighths of the population. In the Soviet famine of 1921 the death rate in many regions reached 200, even 600 per thousand. As to war and revolution, with their outbreak the death rate of the population begins to rise, the more sharply the greater the magnitude of the emergency. If neither famine nor pestilence ensues, the increase of the death rate may remain comparatively slight, rarely exceeding 100 or 200 per cent. But if famine and pestilence supervene, then the death rate of the population may increase manyfold.

With the termination of war or revolution, if famine and pestilence do not continue their ravages, the death rate usually drops to the prewar or prerevolutionary level and then continues its previous trend. During the first two years after the end of a war or revolution it frequently falls even below the prewar or prerevolutionary rate. The reasons for the phenomenon are not far to seek. Wars, revolutions, famines, and pestilences, in addition to their direct effects, seriously undermine the health of the population through worry and anxiety, subsidiary physical deprivations, and many other mental and nervous hardships. When the calamity is over and these facts cease to operate, the death rate begins to decline.

The *movement of the birth rate* during calamities also exhibits a fairly uniform pattern, varying in detail according to the nature and magnitude of the catastrophe. Nine months after the outbreak of a large-scale war or revolution, the birth rate begins to drop. Nine months after the termination of the emergency it jumps abruptly, and during the next two years ordinarily reaches a point above the prewar or prerevolutionary level. Then it returns to the normal level.

The reasons for such a uniformity are again fairly evident. With the outbreak of war or revolution (including civil war) many a prospective bridegroom is called to arms. With the resulting decrease of marriages, the birth rate necessarily declines. With the termination of the emergency, many or most of the soldiers or revolutionaries return home; and many a deferred marriage is at once concluded. Nine months after the consummation of these postponed marriages the birth rate rises and presently attains its prewar or prerevolutionary trend.

During severe famines and pestilences the birth rate also decreases. But exactly when and to what extent depend upon many conditions: the magnitude and intensity of the famine, the nature and severity of the pestilence, and so on. Hence the causes of the decrease of the birth rate differ from those that operate in war or revolution. For instance, prolonged and acute physiological starvation not only decreases the sexual appetite, but, as we have seen (cf. page 60), leads to an increase of amenorrhea, which makes conception impossible.

Upon the return of normal conditions, the suppressed sexual life resumes its former course, and the birth rate returns to the prefamine or prepestilence level. It has been observed that in many cases, as in postwar and postrevolutionary periods, the birth rate of the years immediately following the termination of the emergency exceeds the normal rate.

"After the plague, marriages were everywhere so numerous that the priests were scarcely able to cope with the work. At Cologne, after the plague of the year 1451, which carried off 21,000 people, 4,000 marriages were celebrated in the following year. Nearly all these unions were prolific, and the birth of twins and triplets were more frequent than usual."[8]

In other cases "the women who survived [the pestilence or famine] remained for the most part barren during several years."[9]

Finally, as to the *movement of the marriage rate*. In time of war it too presents a fairly uniform pattern. With the beginning of hostilities it begins to fall, because many prospective bridegrooms are called to the colors. (In some cases, just prior to and at the outbreak of war numerous marriages are hastily concluded, and a temporary rise in the marriage rate takes place.) With the further progress of the conflict the marriage rate continues to decline. During the first and the second year after the close of hostilities, many of the postponed marriages are realized, and the marriage rate rises above the prewar level, only to fall to the normal level within two or three years after the return of peace.

In revolutions we do not find this uniformity: in some revolutions the marriage rate is influenced in much the same way as it is by war; in others, like the Soviet Revolution, we do not observe a decrease in the marriage rate during the course of the struggle. If the revolution does not fundamentally disturb the sanctity of marriage and the family, the marriage rate is likely to follow the same pattern as it displays in wartime. Otherwise (as during the Soviet and other revolutions), the marriage contract represents little more than an incidental sex union in a long succession of divorces and remarriages. Under these conditions the statistical marriage rate naturally does not decline; rather, it tends to rise.

Major pestilences and famines are ordinarily marked by a decrease in the marriage rate, which increases and finally returns to the prepestilence or prefamine rate after their termination. However, here again we note exceptions to the general rule, depending upon the nature of the pestilence, its duration and severity, the duration and severity of the famine, and other circumstances. The decline of the marriage rate during serious famines and pestilences is due partly to a weakening of the sexual drive, to a decreased need for marriage, to a heightened sense of everyone for himself, to a curtailment of the advantages of marriage for purposes of survival, to general demoralization and disruption of the family and marriage ties (cf. Chapter Ten), and to similar factors. As regards the influence of war on vital processes, the described uniformities were observed in the Napoleonic Wars, the Crimean War, the American Civil War, the Prusso-Danish War (1864), the Prusso-Austrian War (1866), the Franco-Prussian War (1870-1871), the Russo-Turkish War (1877-1878), the Serbo-Bulgarian War (1885), the Balkan Wars of 1912-1913, the Russo-Japanese War (1904-1905), the First World War, and certain others.

3. Who Survive—the Fit or the Unfit?

What kinds of people perish in greater proportion in the catastrophes under consideration: the best or the worst? Do these calamities carry away the same share of the fit and the unfit, or do they exterminate principally one kind, favoring the survival of another?

A definite answer to these questions is very difficult, first of all because the very terms "best" and "worst," "fit" and "unfit," are subjective and indefinite; second, because in many cases the necessary statistical evidence is lacking. With these reservations, let us consider the problem, as far as existing data permit, with regard to each type of calamity.

As to the selection effected by war and revolution, many investigators viewed the phenomenon negatively: in their opinion the victims are predominantly those who are healthiest biologically, as well as morally and intellectually superior. War and revolution promote the extermination of the best and the survival of the less fit. In this sense they are disgenic factors, leading to the impoverishment of the hereditary stock and to eventual degeneration and decay. The principal arguments of the proponents of this theory are as follows. The chief losses in international and civil war and in revolutions are incurred by the armies and the active leaders. Their casualties are much higher than those of the rank and file of the civil population. Considering that the armies are made up of the most vigorous age groups; that only healthy persons are enrolled, the physically and mentally defective being rejected; dishonest persons, cowards, and selfish and irresponsible egotists either cannot enter the army or else try to elude military service; that within the army itself the percentage of loss of life among the commanding officers is higher than among the privates and that the officers are superior intellectually to the rank and file of the soldiers,—for these and similar reasons the army represents the best blood of the nation, being far superior to the mass of the civil population. Since the principal casualties are sustained by the fighting armies and fighting groups of leaders, the net result of war selection is the elimination of the better elements and the survival and proliferation of the inferior elements.

According to this theory these considerations are still more applicable to revolutions. If in international wars the conquerors strive to exterminate the most courageous, resourceful, and intelligent elements of the enemy, this is even more true in regard to revolution. Here the Roman motto *parcere subjectes et debellare superbos* (Spare the submissive and demolish the proud) is invariably applied.

Revolution is a process that exterminates first of all and in highest degree the leading elements among the revolutionaries as well as the counterrevolutionaries. Revolutionary terror and counterterror are intentionally directed at the superior constituents of both factions. In this sense, revolution as compared with international war is doubly noxious and destructive.

Moreover, war and revolution result in a host of derelicts —the wounded and deformed, persons with shattered physical constitutions (including the victims of syphilis and other venereal diseases) and those suffering from mental and nervous derangement. If a nation is subjected to frequent wars and revolutions, its vital strength is sapped, and sooner or later it decays. This explains, according to certain investigators, the decline and death of great nations like Greece and Rome.

However popular and convincing this theory may appear, it presents serious weaknesses, including many doubtful assumptions.

Its first defect is that it completely disregards the female part of the population. If war and revolution exterminate preponderantly the fit among the males, they apparently exert a *positive* selection among the females. The decimation of the male population results in a relative excess of marriageable women, and the male survivors accordingly tend to choose as their brides those women who are superior physically, mentally, and morally. As only the married become, for the most part, the progenitors of future generations, and as, from the standpoint of heredity, women count as much as men, this positive selection exerted by war and revolution among the women tends to offset their negative effects among the men.

The second defect of the theory is a somewhat doubtful interpretation of the rôle of heredity. Though better-endowed parents tend to beget better-endowed offspring, this is true only when there is a marked difference between the superior and inferior stocks; and even then the rule presents many exceptions. One of these is that the superior stocks (like that of royal families of Europe) produce not only a somewhat higher percentage of persons of genius but also a higher percentage of abnormal or subnormal persons. The hereditary mental and biological difference between officers and common soldiers, between the army and the civil population, between revolutionary leaders and the bulk of the population, is rather inconsiderable. Hence most of the conclusions arrived at by the proponents of the theory of negative selection are dogmatic assumptions unsubstantiated by factual evidence.

The third defect of the theory is that it overgeneralizes the effects of wars and revolutions. In the past, when men fought with bows and arrows, swords, lances, and similar weapons, physical strength, courage, dexterity, cleverness, intelligence, and experience counted for a great deal, possessing a certain survival value. For this reason, wars or revolutions were formerly positive rather than negative selective agencies. In addition, the superior warriors have always enjoyed better opportunities for propagating their kind, owing to the premium upon physical strength and military prestige in winning the esteem of women. If in modern wars strength, courage, skill, competence, intelligence, and similar qualities still count,—as they seem to, to some extent,—then even modern wars and revolutions are not wholly agencies of negative selection. Again, in many a modern war and revolution, poisonous gas, bombs, shells, machine-gun bullets, and other instruments of destruction exterminate indiscriminately the courageous and the cowardly, the intelligent and the stupid, the honest and the dishonest, civilians as well as soldiers.

Furthermore, if wars and revolutions are viewed not only as interindividual but also as intergroup selective agencies, it is evident that victory and survival are likely to be achieved by that group which is more resourceful and intelligent, more unified, and better prepared—in a word, superior to the opposing group. Viewed in this light, war and revolution are once again seen to be not necessarily the exterminators of the best and the perpetuators of the poorest elements.

Add to all this the fact that peace-time selection is not always positive. Peace-time conditions frequently favor the survival of clever profiteers, cynical money-makers, selfish manipulators, and egotistic bullies, who rarely constitute the biologically soundest or most creative elements of the population, to say nothing of ethical superiority. During long periods of peace one often witnesses the decline of virility and courage; the growth of a spirit of complacency and philistinism dominated by considerations of comfort and material prosperity; and even the increase of actual vice.

One must also bear in mind that in most wars and revolutions the casualties caused by battles constitute but a small proportion of the total loss of life, which is due mainly to sickness among the armies as well as among the civilians. In many a modern war only about one fourth of the loss of life has occurred on the field of battle, about three fourths being attributable to epidemics. (As we shall see later on, the selective rôle of epidemics and famines can hardly be regarded as negative.)

Again, the actual investigations of the comparative physical and mental qualities of the generations born in peace-time and during war and revolution or immediately thereafter have not yielded any uniform results. The same is true of the studies of the physical, mental, and moral attributes of the militant as compared with the pacific peoples. The latter can in no way be regarded as uniformly superior to the former.

Finally, if the theory in question were valid, mankind would have degenerated long ago, for wars and revolutions have been *endemic* in human history. On an average, the European nations have devoted from twenty-eight to sixty-seven years of every century to international wars, or one out of every two years, and have suffered from revolutions or other serious internal disturbances at the rate of one for every period of from five to seventeen years.[10]

The totality of the foregoing considerations warrants the following conclusions: first, theories of either uniform negative or uniform positive selection exerted by war and revolution are one-sided and fallacious; second, the actual effects of these agencies are highly complex, possessing positive as well as negative aspects; third, the net result of certain wars and revolutions may be predominantly negative, whereas that of others may be predominantly positive, depending upon a variety of factors.[11]

So far as physical vigor is concerned, the selective rôle of famine and pestilence is, on the whole, somewhat positive. Those who are constitutionally weaker naturally succumb in greater measure than the strong. Moreover, the more intelligent elements are in a position to take greater precautions against infection during epidemics than those who are mentally less highly endowed. Again, the upper and middle classes are, as a rule, economically better situated to resist the ravages of both pestilence and famine. Finally, since the upper, professional, and middle classes exhibit a lower criminal rate than the depressed strata of the population, and since the latter are generally weaker economically, the selective rôle of famine and epidemics tends to militate against the survival of the ethically inferior elements.

These basic tendencies, however, present many exceptions. In some epidemics greater intelligence or higher morality does not provide for any immunity and does not help much even indirectly. Then the difference in virility, creative intelligence, and morality between the upper and the lower classes is by no means always striking, and in periods marked by the decadence of a given aristocracy it is either imperceptible or even reversed.[12] Again, in times of famine unscrupulous persons tend to acquire more food than those who abstain from dishonest means. In epidemics it is precisely those who are most moral and altruistic who tend to help the victims, thus exposing themselves to greater risk of infection than the egotists who, as in Boccaccio's *Decameron*, flee from danger regardless of any ethical considerations. Finally, criminals, who often obtain their freedom in periods of great emergency, fare better than the noncriminal elements, since they have no scruples against stealing food, or other forms of theft.

For these and similar reasons the prevalent tendencies which we have noted are annulled or even reversed. Nevertheless, all in all, the selection of major famines and pestilences seems to be positive rather than negative or neutral. This is perhaps why the net selection in many a war and revolution has not been so disastrous as one might have expected. As most of the graver wars and revolutions are followed by dearth, famine, epidemics, and harsh conditions generally, and as the number of the direct casualties of war and revolution constitutes only a small proportion (frequently about one fourth) of the total (famine and pestilence account for approximately three fourths of the total victims), *the negative selection due to war and revolution is thus amply compensated by the positive selection brought about by the famine and epidemics generated by the same wars and revolutions.* For instance, in the Russian Revolution, out of the thirteen to seventeen million victims for the period 1918-1922, only from two to three millions perished in battle or at the hands of the firing squads of the Communist and anti-Communist forces. The remaining eleven to fourteen millions succumbed to the famine and epidemics that swept the country during these years. Although the net selection arising from the civil war and executions was negative, this effect was amply compensated by the positive selection associated with the famines and pestilences. Both of the last-named factors operated so efficiently and on such an enormous scale that only those who were physically robust and well supplied with "antibodies" enjoyed any appreciable chance of survival. In addition to a strong constitution, a certain degree of intelligence was also essential. Those who, like the author, lived in Russia during those years lived in a veritable realm of starvation and death. The starvation was so acute and protracted and the epidemics so numerous and diverse that the overwhelming majority could not avoid contact with the diseased and dying or with the foci of infection, including the lice which spread spotted typhus, as well as contaminated food and drinking water.

This positive selection exercised by the famines and pestilences explains why the Russian population recovered so rapidly as soon as the general conditions began to improve after the end of the civil war in 1921 and with the introduction of the so-called "New Economic Policy." The mortality rate, which had reached a fantastic height before 1922, began to decline rapidly after 1922, dropping to an even lower level than the prerevolutionary rate in the years 1923-1929; the birth rate, which had declined enormously in 1918-1922, rose above the prerevolutionary level; the health of the population quickly improved, in spite of the persistence of rather harsh material conditions; and there was even a considerable upswing of creativeness in various fields of culture, such as the arts and sciences, technology, and social organization. In brief, the Russian people experienced an unquestionable biological and mental revival, one of whose fundamental causes was the positive selection of famine and pestilence which neutralized the negative selection of the revolution and the World War. While the cost of this process was terrific (more than ten millions of human lives destroyed by famine and epidemic), nevertheless its net effect seems to have been positive.

Such, in brief outline, are the main uniformities and typical tendencies of the influence of calamities upon the vital processes of the population involved, including the selective factors.

PART THREE

THE INFLUENCE OF CALAMITIES UPON SOCIAL MOBILITY AND ORGANIZATION

Chapter Six

Migration, Mobility, and Disruption of Social Institutions

1. Effects of Calamities upon Migration and Mobility

After the preceding study of the typical effects of calamities upon the mind, behavior, and vital processes we pass now to an investigation of the influence of calamities upon social mobility and organization. What, if any, typical changes do calamities introduce into the normal processes of migration and mobility and how do they transform the social, political, and economic structure of a society? In our analysis of these problems we shall concentrate only upon the transformations that are typical, or recurrent, and upon those typical changes that seem to be the most important. The local, temporary, and minor modifications are for the most part ignored.

In practically every normal society some of its members move from place to place horizontally (from one city, village, and habitat to another), and from one social position to another vertically, an office boy becoming the president of a corporation, a plain citizen being elected president of the state, a poor man becoming a millionaire, or another person being demoted from a higher position to a lower one.[1]

Calamities tangibly affect both processes. *In contradistinction to the gradual, orderly, and voluntary character of migration and mobility in normal times, catastrophes render these processes sudden, violent, chaotic, largely involuntary, and essentially tragic.* They enormously accelerate and reinforce them quantitatively, and they influence them qualitatively in many ways, beginning with the direction of the streams of migration and mobility. They disrupt the existing network of social relationships, and make the social structure chaotic, fluid, and "protoplasmic." In this sense they are one of the most powerful factors of socio-cultural change.

When a major famine or pestilence breaks out, a mass exodus of the population sets in from the areas affected to other areas thought to be relatively free from these evils. With the advent of war or revolution, those living in the areas near the war zone or those regions likely to be occupied by the enemy flee voluntarily to sections believed to be safer, or else are forcibly removed by the authorities, some being deported to concentration camps and other places of detention. In most cases the phenomenon presents the following painful picture. Multitudes of human beings are uprooted from their native soil, separated from family and friends, and forced to leave most or all of their property behind. As a rule, they are unprovided with transportation facilities and do not know their destination. Frequently they lack not only adequate shelter but even food and other minimum necessities. Many—especially the children and elderly persons, the weak and the sick—succumb to the rigors of the exodus, with fatal results.

2. *Exodus and Migration in Famines*

The magnitude of the migration caused by famine depends upon the degree of the satisfaction of hunger by such means as the importation of food into the areas affected and the distribution of the available local surpluses. Since, however, such expedients are generally inadequate, virtually all famines have led to a peaceful or violent exodus. In Rome

"The exodus and mass expulsion of foreigners were the favorite measures of alleviating actual or imminent famine."[2]

"[In the middle Ages] the primary effect of every famine was to force the population to leave their native habitat. . . . When . . . the scanty surplus was consumed, there was nothing left for the peasants to do but to abandon their homes. . . . A typical and ever-repeated trait of the famine picture is the hordes of mendicants wandering aimlessly over the country. Charlemagne noted the phenomenon. We read in his *Passio Karoli* that many died of starvation. *Multi propriis derelictis alienas terras expetant; . . . ut multi patriam deserere et ad alias terras demigrare.*"[3]

These wandering hordes often traveled considerable distances in their "mapless migrations"—from France to Germany, from Bohemia to Thuringia, from Cracow to Russia, from Hungary to the river Don. Vast areas were depopulated to such an extent that the few who remained behind were sometimes able to subsist on the existing food stock. In France, during certain eighteenth-century famines, the émigrés numbered as many as one million. Fairly representative are the cases where from 20 to 70 per cent of the total population of a large area fled.

The foregoing observations apply equally to contemporary conditions. In the famine of 1921-1922 in Russia the majority of the population of the famine regions became nomadic. The city population markedly decreased—for instance in Moscow from 1,854,426 in 1917 to 1,023,-000 in 1920; in Leningrad, from 2,420,000 in 1917 to 740,000 in 1920.[4] If we survey the famines of India during the second half of the nineteenth century, the picture is similar. If from India we turn to contemporary Greece or Poland, the picture is repeated—with this difference, that the German military authorities enormously restrict the scope of the migration.[5]

Many waves of emigration and colonization have constituted merely a variety of the exodus due to famine or food restrictions. The colonizing movements of the Greeks and Romans, and mass movements such as the Crusades, were caused—directly or indirectly—by this factor in conjunction with other forces. The migration of the Irish after the devastating famine of 1846-1847 amounted to not fewer than 400,000 persons in two years, and to 2,064,000 from 1847 to 1859.[6]

3. *Exodus and Migration during Pestilence*

What has been said of famines applies with a slight variation to pestilences. Great epidemics depopulate a region not only directly, by killing a part of its population, but also by forcing another part to flee from the infected centers to other places held to be safer. In Chapters Four and Five we have noted the observations of contemporaries as to how cities and villages were abandoned; how parents forsook their children, and children their parents; etc. In the plague of 1665 "London looked like a desert. The King and Queen had gone with the whole court to the West, to uninfected places in the country." So also did the High Council, the High Court of Justice, Parliament, all the rich people, and many others.[7] With local variations, a similar process has uniformly occurred in all severe pestilences, unless the population was deprived of the possibility of flight, as has sometimes been the case in beseiged cities or in places subjected to sanitary quarantine. Unlike the exodus due to famine, however, the exodus caused by pestilence has been directed mainly from the cities and other centers of dense population to the countryside—that is, to areas more isolated and less affected. For this reason the migration has involved shorter distances. Both types of migration have nevertheless produced a sudden and painful disruption of numerous social bonds.

4. *Exodus and Migration in War and Revolution*

In both wars and revolutions a part of the population flees voluntarily from the fighting zones and from those occupied by the enemy. Another part is forcibly removed by the authorities, some being arrested and banished. The total result is a sudden uprooting of large masses. In the First World War the number of voluntary refugees from the French departments occupied by the enemy in 1918 was over 1,820,000; the number of Belgian refugees in England, France, and Holland was 586,306, in addition to 120,655 or more persons deported from Belgium by the German authorities; the number of Italian refugees in Italy was not less than 632,210; in Russia the voluntary refugees from the regions occupied by the enemy amounted to 3,200,512; in Poland more than 2,500,000 were uprooted; in Serbia, no fewer than 400,000; and so on.[8]

In the present cataclysm the war refugees may be computed in tens of millions. In virtually all parts of the world a considerable and ever-increasing proportion of mankind is being suddenly uprooted and tossed hither and thither by the fury of the war hurricane that is sweeping over the earth.

What is true of war may be said of revolutions. Besides those who flee from the fighting zones every revolution swells the ranks of the refugees and émigré by its terrorism, ostracism, deportation, banishment, and in many other ways. In every Greek or Roman revolution there was a sudden exodus of the general population and especially of members of the defeated party from their native places. In addition, some of the citizens were regularly deported and banished. The same has been true of medieval and modern revolutions, whether in Europe, Asia, or the Americas. In the Russian revolution of 1917 and the following years at least 1,046,000 persons sought refuge abroad, being scattered over virtually the entire planet.[9] Many more millions fled or were deported from their permanent place of abode to some other place within Russia. The victims thrown into the Soviet concentration camps and prisons numbered tens of millions. Probably no less than 20 per cent of the total population shifted its habitat during the first five years of the revolution. Within one year Soviet authorities deported about two million kulaks (or rich peasants) from their villages to the concentration camps of Siberia and northern Russia.

In other revolutions the absolute number of the uprooted was probably smaller, but the relative percentage of the population shifted was in some cases doubtless as high as in the Russian revolution. The enormous compulsory shift of population effected by the Nazi revolution is well known. The latest Spanish revolution performed the same function on a smaller scale.

One additional remark. In comparison with that caused by famine, pestilence, and war, the revolutionary shift probably involves a much higher percentage of the intellectuals, scientific, philosophical, artistic, religious, and political and economic leaders. In a sense, the cream of both factions migrates (or is imprisoned, banished, or killed) with the shifting fortunes of the revolution.

5. Vertical Social Mobility in Calamities

By destroying a considerable proportion of the population any large-scale calamity creates many vacancies in the various strata of the society affected and in its institutions. These vacancies occur not only in the lower positions but also in the higher ones, which frequently have to be filled from the lower ranks. In this way calamities intensify enormously the factor of upward mobility.

Calamities strikingly accentuate also the factor of downward mobility—of demotion to a lower position in the social scale. Especially marked is this downward movement during war and revolution.

In addition to the enormous intensification of the vertical

mobility, calamities notably modify the qualitative aspects of this process, as we shall presently see.

Vertical Mobility in Famine and Pestilence. During the famine and pestilence of 829 A.D. in the priory of Christ Church, Canterbury, "All the monks save five died of pestilence. The Archbishop Ceolnoth filled up the vacancies with secular clerks."[10] This offers a typical example of the effects of catastrophe in intensifying vertical mobility and promoting to higher positions persons who would otherwise have enjoyed fewer opportunities for advancement. Again, as a result of the depopulation of England by the Black Death, the wages of farmhands doubled or trebled, and there was a widespread improvement in their general condition.

"The surviving labourers sought work where they could command the best wages, and at the same time could escape from the few degrading bonds of servitude which still clung to the serfs of a manor."[11]

Serfdom sharply declined, and many a serf became free— that is, climbed to a higher rung of the social ladder.

The same plague intensified the vertical mobility in other ways. A high degree of mortality occurred also within the rich and upper classes. Hence "a great part of the capital of the country passed suddenly into new hands. . . . An immense number of persons came into [the possession of] money who could not all have had the inclination, even if they had the skill and aptitude, [to employ] it as capital."[12] The same was true of ecclesiastical positions. Owing to numerous vacancies, they frequently had to be filled by persons who would otherwise have been ineligible or would have had to wait long to climb to these positions. In 1349 "the clergy were dying so fast that they were obliged to admit numbers of youth, that had only [qualified] themselves for clerks by being shaven, to be rectors of parishes."[13] The Minor Friar Johannes of Winterthur and a Westphalian Dominican, Heinrich of Hertford, testify that in the years 1348 and 1349 "prebends, livings, dignities, rectorships, curacies, . . . even abbeys, priories, guardianships, professorships, and readerships, and other posts, are bought by ignorant, young, inexperienced, and stupid people."[14]

On the other hand, owing to the enormous mortality entailed by famine and pestilence, many a child loses his father and thus his assured position, sinking to a lower social stratum and hence accelerating the downward current of the vertical mobility.

In normal times mobility is a gradual process, governed by definite and rigid rules. Promotion and demotion are from one rung to the next,[15] and many rungs remain inaccessible to certain individuals and groups. During times of great emergency, however, not only do the upward and downward streams swell enormously, but the gradualness, orderliness, and rigidly controlled character of the mobility are considerably undermined.

Vertical Mobility in Revolution. The foregoing observations apply with even greater force to wars and revolutions. One of the essential functions of any revolution is the demotion, en masse, of the prerevolutionary aristocracy and often the middle classes, and the promotion of the lower and perhaps the middle classes. To adapt the famous slogan of the Abbé Sieyès, those who were nothing before the revolution now become everything, and vice versa. Monarchs, aristocrats, the upper classes, the rich and priviledged, even the middle classes, are overthrown by major revolutions, and many former slaves and serfs, peasants and laborers, and other poor and oppressed persons now climb to much higher positions, including the very highest ones. In less radical revolutions the amplitude of the transplanta-

tion is less, but the volume and intensity of the transformation remain far above those of normal times.

This revolutionary mobility is sudden and catastrophic,
and is especially intense in the first phase of the revolution.
In its second phase the trend is sometimes entirely reversed;
for if the counterrevolution gets the upper hand, the
climbers of the first period are overthrown and those who
were demoted during the first period climb back.

Even when the counterrevolution remains impotent, a
considerable reverse circulation occurs during the second
period of the struggle. This is due to the wholesale and
indiscriminate mass promotion and mass demotion characteristic of the first period, which are governed almost exclusively by the political affiliations of the persons and groups
concerned, regardless of their competence or ability. As a
result of such an indiscriminate social selection and mass
transplanting into the upper revolutionary strata, many
persons occupy very responsible positions whose duties
they are incapable of adequately discharging. Conversely,
among the depressed upper and middle classes now in the
position of skilled or semiskilled manual workers there are
many persons whose abilities qualify them to perform the
duties of the upper classes. The new revolutionary society
presently begins to suffer from this defective distribution
of its members among its various strata contrary to the
principle: To everyone according to his ability. The exigencies of life necessitate a correction of the dislocation
through the demotion of many a revolutionary and through
the reinstatement of many of the previously demoted members of the upper and middle classes.

In the first phase of the Soviet Revolution a common
sailor from the Baltic fleet—a very ardent Communist, but
a person who was almost illiterate—was appointed dean
of the law faculty of the University of Petrograd. A fresh-

man was made the president, or rector, of that university. The president of the Supreme Economic Council, which controlled the entire economic life of Russia, could scarcely sign his name. Many persons were made "red professors" in the university even though they lacked an elementary knowledge of their specialty. Persons ignorant of military strategy were appointed commanders of armies and divisions. On the other hand, first-class financiers were relegated to the position of paupers; the best scholars and scientists were thrown into prison or concentration camps and required to perform unskilled manual labor; poets by the grace of God were assigned clerical duties; and so forth.

In consequence of this absurd allocation of functions the entire Soviet economy, army, diplomacy, science, arts, and social structure began to suffer. In order to alleviate this chaos, the vertical process had to be reversed. Accordingly, during the second phase of the revolution (after 1922) many an "upstart" was demoted, and many a member of the former middle, upper, and professional classes was restored to his original position.[16]

A similar process occurs in practically all revolutions. During the first phase of the struggle it smashes the delicate mechanism that normally controls vertical mobility. Instead of the rule: To everyone according to his ability, it promotes or demotes groups and persons exclusively on the basis of their loyalty to the dominant political faction. One may be an ardent Communist or anti-Communist, but that has little or no relation to the question of the successful discharge of his vocational duties. The result of such a policy is *chaos*. Economic life becomes more and more disorganized. Armies are defeated instead of being victorious. The other social functions are likewise discharged unsatisfactorily. Hence the ultimatum of history to the revolutionary government: Either perish or redress the

situation. Hence the reverse circulation which character-
izes the second phase of the struggle, as well as the post-
revolutionary period. The upper and lower strata of
society at the end of the revolution represent always a
mésalliance. The aristocracy and upper classes consist of
a fantastic mélange of successful upstarts derived from the
previous lower and middle classes and of members of the
former aristocracy. Similarly, the underdogs represent
partly those of the prerevolutionary period and, in part,
impoverished and disfranchised members of the previous
upper and middle classes.

The actual mobility in times of revolution is even
greater than the foregoing analysis has indicated; for virtually everyone is dislodged from his social position and
incessantly thrown hither and thither, witnessing a kalei-
doscopic series of shifting positions ranging from the very
top to the very bottom of the social scale and vice versa.
Here are some concrete examples from the Russian Revolution. A senator and First Assistant Secretary of the In-
terior of the Czarist government occupied during the first
four years of the revolution the following positions: that
of a starving gardener, of a prisoner in a concentration
camp, a dealer in insecticides, of a clerk in a coöperative
store, of a typist in the Academy of Sciences, of a teacher
in the Agricultural Institute, and of a photographer. Many
who in the morning were occupying a high position in the
bureaucracy of the Communist government by noon were
arrested and imprisoned, some of them being banished or
shot, and others being eventually released and returned to
high office.

In time of revolution one does not know in the morning
what will befall him in the evening. One's whole life becomes a painful series of surprises and fantastic changes,
permeated by constant uncertainty.[17]

Vertical Mobility in War. With certain reservations the above analysis can be applied to war-time mobility. War also is one of the dynamic forces that profoundly influence the vertical mobility of the combatants as well as of the civil population. With its large-scale casualties it creates numerous vacancies to be filled by new incumbents. Through the death of generals, admirals, and other officers (and the percentage of casualties among the officers regularly exceeds that among the common soldiers and sailors) war stimulates the upward mobility within the army and navy. Presenting a crucial test of the ability of the commanding officers, it acutely intensifies this mobility also through the rapid promotion of the capable commanders and the rapid demotion of the incapable ones (some of whom are court-martialed or handed over to a firing squad). Through such a crucial test many famous warriors, such as Alexander the Great, Caesar and Augustus, Diocletian and Constantine, Charlemagne, Genghis Khan and Tamerlane, Napoleon, Suvoroff, and Moltke, up to the Rundstedts, Timoshenkos, and MacArthurs of the present war, have achieved supremacy in the army, and thus have come to wield supreme power over their respective social groups as dictators, monarchs, presidents, or most influential leaders. In the same way, incapable or unlucky monarchs, marshals, generals, and other leaders have been degraded, taken prisoner, deprived (temporarily or permanently) of their exalted station, or even killed.

The foregoing factors, however, do not exhaust the intensifying rôle of war in this field. War plays this rôle not only in relation to the combatants but also in relation to the civil population of the belligerent countries. Victory or defeat in any first-class war drastically changes the position of the respective peoples on the international ladder of social stratification. Defeat in a life-and-death struggle in the past has meant the utter degradation of the entire population to the level of slaves, serfs, or *peregrini dediticii*. The vanquished have been stripped of their property, their rights and privileges, even of their life. The same is more or less true of modern wars, as illustrated by the present world conflict. Conversely, a victorious nation has always climbed to a higher rung on the ladder of social stratification vis à vis other nations and peoples. This elevation means not only a formal change in status but a substantial increase of the various values—wealth, rights and privileges, prestige and honors, and other advantages—enjoyed by the victorious group. It becomes a "great power," controlling the territory, property, lives, and activities of the vanquished. In this way the position and fate of millions are suddenly transformed.

Similarly, war promotes or demotes even the neutral nations—those that remain aloof from the conflict at its beginning. In the effort to win such a nation (*tertius gaudens*) as an ally, the belligerents grant it various privileges hitherto withheld from it. (Examples are furnished, in the present war, by Turkey and India.) In this way many a third party is promoted.

On the other hand, certain neutral countries that displease one or both of the belligerents are punished for their "inimical neutrality" or "inimical alliances" or for some other policy objected to by one or both parties. Not infrequently, one or both of the belligerent nations invade, subjugate, and despoil a neutral country (despite its innocence), with a view to forestalling an attempt of the enemy to invade it, seize its wealth, or otherwise utilize its resources or strategic advantages. Not infrequently the victor, intoxicated by his successes expands his imperialistic greed and lust for power to such proportions that he refuses to tolerate the existence of any adjacent independent nation and demands its submission, notwithstanding the absence of any provocation or guilt on the part of the neutral country. In these and similar ways war leads to a catastrophic upheaval of the social strata. While revolution achieves this mainly within the limits of the revolutionary society, and only indirectly outside it, war operates principally in the international field.

Considering that most calamities go together,—that famine and pestilence are twins; that large-scale wars and revolutions almost invariably generate famine and pestilence; and that war often provokes revolution and vice versa,—it is easy to see why calamities, in contradistinction to the normal factors that operate perennially and universally,[18] should constitute, despite their intermittent character, the most potent of all the factors influencing the vertical mobility of any human society. Most of our contempories still naïvely believe that wars and revolutions need not entail catastrophic forms of vertical mobility, especially for themselves. Such blindness merely invites disaster.

6. Disruption of Social Relationships and Institutions in Calamities

The extraordinary migration and mobility attending major disasters result, as we have seen, in a drastic disruption of social relationships and social institutions. When the members of a family are suddenly separated from one another by war or revolution, by pestilence or famine, the family unity is seriously undermined. When some of its members are killed, its unity is still further disrupted. It is weakened even more fundamentally and organically by the attitude of "everyone for himself," which results in the abandonment of children by their parents, of wives by their husbands, and vice versa. Hence what was before an institution with a definite pattern of social relationships, with a clear-cut distribution of functions, rights, and duties, is now a mere shadow of its former self.

The same applies to other institutions, such as schools, clubs, church organizations, business firms, labor unions, and political parties. Like an explosive bomb, a calamity descends upon them and impairs or destroys their unity by scattering their members and disrupting their functions. Those that survive are profoundly transformed in their membership, constitution, and functions. The whole fabric of social organization suggests a tattered spider's web. In terms of personality, this means that the members of such a disrupted network of social relationships tend to behave like a spider whose web is torn to shreds. Whereas prior to the calamity they knew what were their respective social functions, rights, and duties, now, having been shifted horizontally and transposed to new vertical positions, they tend to become bewildered if not actually stunned. Many are no longer able to discharge their previous functions or assert their former rights; others do not wish to return to their earlier positions. The old loyalties and social ties are either weakened or destroyed, and the new ones are not yet established. Under these conditions one's behavior becomes formless, chaotic, and inconsistent, uncontrolled by any clear-cut norms, increasingly dependent upon casual external circumstances. Hence there ensues widespread desocialization, demoralization, and even brutalization.

On the other hand, this fluid and indeterminate state affords a *favorable ground for the swift transformation of social institutions—for the emergence of radically different social forms.* Society is now in a plastic state, like half-melted wax out of which anything can be molded. In this sense calamities constitute one of the potent and radical

agents of sociocultural change. Although when the emergency is over, many a society rapidly recovers (reëstab-
lishing its equilibrium, its unity, its institutions, its system
of social relationships), nevertheless it is never the same
as the one that existed before the calamity. Such catastrophes as the Black Death, the Peloponnesian Wars or
the First World War, and the French or Russian Revolution have wrought more profound social transformations
than normal agents of change operating over a period of
many decades. For good or ill, calamities are unquestionably the supreme disruptors and transformers of social
organization and institutions.

Chapter Seven

THE INFLUENCE OF CALAMITIES UPON POLITICAL, ECONOMIC, AND SOCIAL ORGANIZATION

1. Calamities and the General Increase of Governmental Control

In addition to the factors of migration, mobility, and disruption of social relationships discussed in the preceding chapter, *the main uniform effect of calamities upon the political and social structure of society is an expansion of governmental regulation, regimentation, and control of social relationships and a decrease in the regulation and management of social relationships by individuals and private groups.* The expansion of governmental control and regulation assumes a variety of forms, embracing socialistic or communistic totalitarianism, fascist totalitarianism, monarchial autocracy, and theocracy. Now it is effected by a revolutionary régime, now by a counterrevolutionary régime; now by a military dictatorship, now by a dictatorship, now by a dictatorial bureaucracy. From both the quantitative and the qualitative point of view, such an expansion of governmental control means a decrease of freedom, a curtailment of the autonomy of individuals and private groups in the regulation and management of their individual behavior and their social relationships, the decline of constitutional and democratic institutions.

If the calamity is slight and short-lived, its political and social repercussions are correspondingly slight and short-lived. If, on the contrary, it is acute and of long duration, the totalitarian, autocratic, or dictatorial trend assumes a more drastic and less ephemeral character.

Such an increase of totalitarianism manifests itself first in those fields of social relationships in which the calamity creates the gravest emergency. In case of famine, governmental regimentation is applied first of all to the field of food relationships, embracing domestic production, distribution, and consumption, exportation and importation, rationing, prices, and so on. In the effort to regulate these factors, it inevitably extends over almost the entire economic life of the nation, and frequently comprises, as well, a number of noneconomic relationships.

In the event of pestilence, governmental control increases first of all in the field of health, prescribing certain sanitary and quarantine measures and prohibiting certain forms of behavior.

If the calamity is complex, and involves famine, pestilence, revolution, and war, then the increase of dictatorship and regimentation becomes fairly encyclopedic, extending to practically all fields of social relationships. The population either strictly obeys orders or else is thrown into prison or concentration camps or consigned to the guillotine, the gallows, or a firing squad.

Totalitarianism masquerades under a variety of slogans and shibboleths, such as government "by the grace of God," "by the people," "by the proletariat," and "by the will of the Revolution," all of which constitute merely a smoke screen designed to conceal the basic despotism and autocracy whereby the liberties and inalienable rights of the citizenry are trampled under foot. This elemental truth seems not to have been generally apprehended, in spite of the fact that it has been repeatedly stressed by social thinkers from Plato, Aristotle, and Saint Augustine up to Le Play and Herbert Spencer.[1] The only essential difference between various totalitarianism is that one is coercively imposed upon the citizens whereas another is willingly accepted by them. Moreover, it is hard to decide which is mainly compulsory and which, for the most part, is voluntarily accepted. One has hardly any solid ground, for instance, for the argument that the totalitarianism of Sparta or ancient Egypt was more compulsory than that of Stalin or Hitler or even of the war cabinets of modern democracies.

Finally, the transformation of the régime in response to major catastrophes depends very little upon the personnel. No matter who is at the helm, and no matter how strongly the leaders may dislike totalitarianism, an expension of governmental regimentation is as inevitable as the rise of temperature in influenza or pneumonia; otherwise the particular incumbents will be ousted from office and replaced by more amenable officials. If the existing government is wise and competent, it will perform the necessary social "operation" like a firstclass surgeon—skillfully and with a minimum of pain and bloodshed. If it is stupid and incompetent, it will perform the operation with the clumsiness of a butcher, imposing unnecessary physical, economic, social, and mental hardships upon the population. Totalitarianism is not created by Pharoahs, monarchs, and dictators; the Lenins, Stalins, Mussolinis, Hitlers, and other *Führer* are merely the instruments of deeper underlying forces that decree an increase of totalitarianism during signal calamities.

When the emergency is over, the *opposite* trend uniformly sets in—a *decrease* of governmental regimentation. If at that time the same Stalins and Hitlers, Diocletians or Hirohitos, are in the saddle, either they themselves effect this change or they are ousted from control of the state. This uniformity is one of the most fundamental among all the uniformities in the field of social and political phenomena.

Let us now undertake a concise inductive verification of these propositions based upon the relevant historical facts.

2. The Specific Increase of Totalitarianism in Response to Sundry Calamities

In response to the impact of war, pestilence, floods, earthquakes, devastating explosions or fires, and similar catastrophes, more rigid governmental control at once takes place in the form of martial, siege, and other emergency laws. Private property (such as motorcars and boats) is requisitioned; curfew and sanitary measures are introdduced; part of the population is evacuated; and penalties for the violation of the prescribed orders become more drastic. The sequel of the terrific Halifax explosion, which occurred during the First World War, presents a concrete example of the general uniformity. Immediately after the disaster the lieutenant governor sent to the chief of police of Halifax the following order:

"You are hereby authorized to commandeer and make use of any vehicle of any kind that you find necessary for the purpose of removing the injured and the dead of this city."

"Military orders to vacate the North End district followed hard upon the explosion. [Almost at once] the military established a cordon around the devastated district, which no one was allowed to pass without an order."

Various authorities busied themselves with the work of relief and rehabilitation. Legislative acts were passed conferring discretionary power to expropriate property; to repair or reconstruct buildings; to amend or repeal provisions of the city charter and the workmen's compensation act; etc.[2]

The above enumeration indicates that the government extended its authority to cover economic interests, including the rights of private property and those of the working classes; freedom of traffic; and many other basic interests and activities which had hitherto enjoyed a large measure of freedom from governmental control.

This expansion of governmental regulation was even more conspicuous in the case of the great Chicago fire or of San Francisco earthquake and of other sudden calamities.

A. The Increase of Governmental Regulation in Pestilence

Upon the outbreak of a grave pestilence the government of the respective city, town, or country has almost invariably issued regulations extending its control to many social relationships hitherto unregimented by it. In some cities it has instituted quarantine measures prohibiting entrance into the areas affected; restricting the burial of the dead to certain places, and hours; isolating all who were in contact with the sick from any contact with others; and forbidding the occupants of the infected regions to move to other districts. These regulations have been implemented by drastic penalties, including the confiscation of property and even capital punishment. In Rouen, during the plague of 1507, the government decreed "that everything is to be eliminated that could arouse the anger of God, such as gambling, cursing, drinking, and all excesses." In Speyer and Tournai an edict ordered the expulsion or marriage of all concubines, the rigorous observance of Sunday, the elimination of dice games and of gambling in general; the expulsion of drunkards, beggars, lepers, and gypsies; etc.[3] These measures frequently extended far beyond the ordinary sanitary, ethical, and religious regulations. In China, in the famines and plagues of 1313-1318, 1324, 1333, etc. the government "abolished the Buddhist priesthood as the cause of all misfortunes," restrained the tax-gatherers in the districts affected, and regimented the distribution of grain.[4]

In England, during the famine and pestilence of 1269, citizens were forbidden to leave London, to buy food in the outside markets, or to debase the coinage. The government fixed the prices of commodities, prohibited extravagant housekeeping, and so on.[5]

In the plague of 1349 a royal proclamation of December 1 ordered the authorities "to stop the passage beyond sea of them that have no mandate." A proclamation of 1350 decreed that all persons under sixty, "not living by a trade or handicraft, not possessing private means, nor having land to cultivate, shall be obliged, when required, to serve any master who is willing to hire him or her at such wages as were usually paid in the locality in the year 1346," and prohibited laborers from leaving their manor.[6]

B. The Increase of Government Control in Famine

In this field the expansion of government interference and the shift of the political régime toward totalitarianism are still more conspicuous than in the case of pestilence. As in other calamities, this shift may take place peacefully, the existing government itself effecting the change, or it may assume a violent form, the existing régime, incapable of carrying out the process, being replaced by a revolutionary régime. *Other conditions being equal, the greater the contrast between the rich and the poor, the sharper the increase of governmental regulation.*

An increase of governmental economic control during periods of famine or impoverishment has been regularly manifest in the following phenomena. First, in an establishment or reinforcement of governmental control of exports and imports, which has often amounted to a monopoly of foreign trade; second, in an establishment of fixed prices for food and other necessities; third, in registration and tabulation of the total volume of necessities in the country owned by its citizens; fourth, in a complete control of the purchase and sale of commodities, including the amounts to be bought; fifth, in the requirement that private citizens send their commodities to market; sixth, in the requisition, to an extraordinary degree, of private necessities; seventh, in the establishment of numerous governmental agencies for the purpose of buying, producing, and distributing necessities among the population; eighth, in the introduction of a ration system; ninth, in an organization of public works on an extraordinarily large scale.

This expansion of governmental control has sometimes amounted to almost complete totalitarianism, in its communistic, socialistic, state-socialist, fascist, or other forms. The following data offer a few typical instances of the phenomenon.

Ancient Egypt.—The Bible gives us one of the oldest records which clearly show the foregoing correlation. As a result of the great famine in the time of Joseph, the money, cattle, and land of the population of ancient Egypt "became Pharaoh's." The people became the slaves of the government. The entire economic life began to be controlled by the government. In modern terminology this means that everything was nationalized.[7] Other Egyptian records show that this was repeated several times in the history of ancient Egypt. Its Pharaohs and officials often stress in their records the fact that "in years of famine they plowed all the fields of the nome, preserving its people alive and furnishing its food."[8] The frequence of war and famine or the danger of famine in ancient Egypt accounts for the high perennial level of governmental control. And in the famine years and in periods of impoverishment this control seems to have become even more rigorous. Thus in Egypt under the Ptolemys the economic disorganization of Egypt was accompanied by an extraordinary growth of governmental control which led to a transformation of society into a universal state-socialist, or totalitarian, organization.[9]

China.—More abundant and conspicuous confirmation of the hypothesis is furnished by the history of China. It is the history of a society with very frequent famines and with permanent danger of starvation. This accounts for an exclusively high level of governmental control in China throughout its history. The organization of Chinese society has been in essence "an economic state socialism," with "many governmental regulations to control consumption, production, and distribution."[10] And in periods of acute famine or impoverishment, governmental control expanded still further. This, according to the records, invariably happened in the time of the Yao, and in the years of famine during the rule of the Yin, the Chow, the Han, the Tang, the Sung, and other dynasties. Moreover, the attempts to introduce a real state-socialist or totalitarian organization, such as those of Wang Mang or Wang an Shih, regularly took place in periods of grave impoverishment.[11]

Ancient Greece.—Aside from the factor of militarism, economic insecurity was responsible for a large degree of governmental control in Sparta, Athens, Lipara, and other Greek states. R. Pöhlmann says: "The products of the Spartan agriculture were not sufficient to satisfy the needs of the population. The entire economic life rested on a very narrow and uncertain basis. Every economic crisis, every delay or interruption in the importation of necessities, was very dangerous. Is it any wonder that the most rigorous governmental control of economic life became inevitable?"[12] In similar straits was Athens.[13] Attica consumed 3,400,000 medimni of bread, while it produced at most only 2,400,000. In case of a poor crop the danger of famine grew serious.

"As soon as the prices of necessities began to go up, state interference took on unprecedented forms. To cope with the coming famine the state organized an extraordinary commissions of Sitons with unlimited control over economic life." Often the private control of economic relations was almost completely superseded by that of the government, in the production and distribution of necessities and in the field of economic life in general.[14]

In the periods of extreme impoverishment governmental control assumed the forms of the Russian Communism of 1918-1920. The government confiscated private lands and wealth, distributed them in such a way as it found necessary, nationalized what it wanted—in brief, pushed its control to the maximum limit. Such were, for example, the periods of impoverishment after the Messina War, and in the times of Agis IV, Cleomenes III, and Nabis in Sparta, and after the Peloponnesian War in Athens (the periods of the Thirty Tyrants and the Ten Tyrants). Either in a legal way or in the form of revolution, under conservative as well as revolutionary dictators, state interference in such periods attained its utmost limit and assumed the form of state socialism or totalitarianism.[15]

Ancient Rome.—A similar parallelism is seen in the history of Rome. Here the years of famine, such as the years 5, 8, 18, and 52 A.D., were usually marked by a corresponding increase of governmental control. Side by side with these small fluctuations we note that the periods of impoverishment of the masses were followed by an expansion of state interference which amounted sometimes to state socialism or totalitarianism. It is well known that the period from the second half of the second century B.C. to the beginning of the first century A.D. was one of striking economic disorganization. The same period is marked by the Corn Laws of the Gracchi (123 B.C.); by the establishment of a special institution for prevention of famine and for control of a public supply (104 B.C.) (in

Caesar's time it became permanent; in the famine of 22 B.C., Augustus became its head (*curator annonae*)); by the introduction of a rationing system and public supply free of charge; by many acts of nationalization, confiscation, and restriction of private economic enterprise; and by a huge increase in the general economic functions of the government.[16] The apparatus for this ever expanding control of economic life grew into a colossal mechanism served by an enormous number of agents who requisitioned, bought, transported, weighed, and stored commodities. Private business in this field was reduced virtually to zero. The number of the proletariat supplied with free rations steadily grew, amounting in the time of Julius Caesar to some 600,000 in Rome alone. Besides bread the rationing system eventually came to include oil, pork, wine, clothing, the admission to theaters, and even special ration cards for prostitutes (*lasciva nomismata*) which entitled the bearer to the services of one of the Roman prostitutes.

Still more conspicuous was the correlation during the period from the third century A.D. to the fall of the Western Roman Empire. This was a time of economic decay. It also witnessed the establishment of a state-socialistic economic organization in the Western Roman Empire. "The Empire was transformed into a big factory where, under the control of the officials, the population was forced to work. . . . Almost all production and distribution of wealth was concentrated in the hands of the government."[17] In brief, it was a full-fledged totalitarian régime. One who has observed the Soviet Communist system in the period from 1917 to 1922 is struck by the essential similarity of the Roman and Soviet régimes.

The Middle Ages.—Here the same correlation is repeated many times. Already Charlemagne introduced fixed prices under famine conditions (those of 792-793). In the famine of 805 a decree was issued that "ne foris imperium nostrum vendatur aliquid alimoniae"; freedom of contract was restricted; free trade was forbidden; fixed prices were reintroduced; agriculture and industry began to be controlled more severely, and so forth.[18] As famine was very frequent in the Middle Ages, this factor, besides the factor of war, seems to have been responsible for a relatively high degree of government control of economic relations. In famine years this rose still higher. In the history of England such years were 1201-1202, 1315-1316, 1321, 1483, 1512, 1521, 1586, and 1648-1649. In the history of France such years were 1391, 1504-1505, 1565, 1567, 1577, 1591, 1635, 1662, 1684, 1693, and 1709. A historian of the food trade in France sums up his exhaustive study as follows: "As soon as famine broke out, governmental control grew stronger; as soon as it declined, this control weakened also."[19]

The correlation is still more conspicuously exhibited in the history of Russian famines. Those of 1279, 1452, 1601-1603, 1674, 1682, 1723, 1734, 1798-1802, 1805-1806, 1812, 1839, 1848, 1854-1855, 1891-1892, 1905-1906, and 1918-1922 were invariably attended by government control of all exports and imports; the establishment of fixed prices for commodities; direct and indirect rationing of food and other commodities; a search for hoarded stocks; the distribution of free food; compulsory collective and communistic agricultural projects; a sort of W.P.A. and C.C.C. civilian army, controlled by the state and used for the execution of state projects; the systematic curtailment of private business; and outright totalitarianism during the major famines reinforced by pestilence, war, and revolution, such as the acute crises of 1601-1603 and 1918-1922.[20]

Finally, a striking confirmation of all the hypothesis is afforded by the expansion of governmental control during and after the First World War. During the war, not only in the belligerent but in the neutral countries as well, the control of economic life by the government increased enormously. In the belligerent countries it was due primarily to the factor of war, and only secondarily to that of the scarcity of food and other necessities. In the neutral countries the expansion was called forth principally by scarcity of food and other necessities. This factor, in conjunction with those of war and revolution, was also instrumental in generating the extreme forms of communist totalitarianism in Russia, Bavaria, and Hungary in 1917-1919, and somewhat milder forms of totalitarianism (socialism, the "popular front," and fascism) in other countries in the postwar years and especially after the onset of the depression of 1929. These decades have been distinguished in virtually all Western countries by a systematic expansion of government control over both economic and non-economic activities. Where only the depression or the famine factor has been operative, the swing toward totalitarianism has been moderate. But where these factors have been reinforced by war and revolution, the trend has assumed catastrophic proportions, leading in Russia, Italy, Germany, Hungary, Greece, and elsewhere to extreme totalitarian régimes of the communistic, socialistic, fascist, or military type. Private property has been either abolished or drastically curtailed, and the same has been true of private business.

Finally, even in the so-called *anti*-totalitarian, or democratic, countries, such as Great Britain and the United States (especially after 1929), the impoverishment due to the great depression has produced an increase of regimentation. In spite of his personal antipathy toward governmental regulation, President Hoover, after the crash of 1929, extended Federal control to many areas of economic life hitherto left to private persons or groups. As the depression deepened during the subsequent years, the process went still farther under the Roosevelt administration and the New Deal. It is to be noted that the forces responsible for the phenomenon have not been the personal predilections of the particular administration, but, rather, the vastly deeper forces released by the depression. The measures adopted were merely a repetition of those taken by the ancient Pharaohs, ancient China, India, Greece, or Rome, or any other country under like circumstances. As a matter of fact, in all the measures of the New Deal there is scarcely one that does not find its prototype in the expedients invented in the remote past for coping with similar emergencies.

C. *The Increase of Government Control in War*

Herbert Spencer showed convincingly that war causes an expansion of government control and a change of the political régime in the direction of the "militant," or (in our terminology) totalitarian, system.[21] His induction is well corroborated by the historical facts. The reasons for such a mutation of the sociopolitical system in time of war are rather evident. In the first place, the organization of any efficient army or navy makes it a clear-cut totalitarian institution. The soldiers live in quarters not of their own choosing; they eat what is set before them; they wear prescribed uniforms; and from reveille until taps all their activities (save when they are on furlough) are severely regimented. Furthermore, the commanding officer is an autocrat, obedience to whose legitimate orders is obligatory. The commander in chief is entitled to send thousands to die. In a word any good army is a totalitarian organization *par excellence*. As such, and because of its paramount importance in time of war, it naturally influences the whole civil population and the government régime in their trend toward totalitarianism. It becomes the most important school for the inculcation of discipline, centralization, bureaucracy, and autocratic control.

Again, as Spencer rightly remarked, in time of war centralized and autocratic control of the civil population is a necessity. Victory is more likely to be achieved by a country which constitutes a centralized machine, with the government regimenting the population, its activities and resources, in much the same way as the military authorities rule a well-disciplined army. A nation whose citizens in time of war should debate the question whether to fight or not to fight, to obey or not to obey the decrees of the government, to sacrifice or not to sacrifice such a nation would certainly suffer defeat at the hands of the enemy. As victory and defeat are often a question of life and death for the societies involved, large-scale wars have always led to a militarization or "totalitarianization" of the belligerent society in its social, economic, and political organization.

War regularly results in a replacement of the normal laws by martial, siege, or emergency laws, which means an increase of the area and rigidity of government control. It likewise leads frequently to a substitution of military rule for the normal civil government—another form of the totalitarian movement. Again, it may lead to the establishment of a dictatorship, in the sense of the old Roman dictatorship or of a government unlimited by any constitutional restraints. This again represents merely a variety of totalitarianism. War often requires the conscription not only of the man power of the country but of all its resources, including private property. The limitation of property rights; the expansion of government in the field of business at the expense of private business; the replacement, by the government, of private individuals and groups in the production, distribution, and consumption of commodities—such measures are concomitants of practically every strenuous war between complex societies. The complete (factual or juridical) elimination of private property is another phenomenon repeatedly associated with major conflicts, constituting a special case of the loss of constitutional and other civil liberties, which in time of war are usually either greatly restricted or else suspended altogether.

The foregoing reasons are sufficient to explain why the sociopolitical constitution of a belligerent society invariably changes in the direction of totalitarianism.

They explain, as well, why nations that have been most frequently involved in strenuous wars exhibit even in normal times a sociopolitical régime much more totalitarian than that of the more peaceful societies. So long as the vast expanses of the Pacific and the Atlantic Ocean rendered the United States relatively safe from invasion, it could afford to be—and was—much less totalitarian than many European or other nations. When these oceans ceased to constitute serious obstacles to invasion, the United States was forced not merely to expand its army but also to change its sociopolitical organization in the direction of the expansion of government control—the regimentation of industry, business, and civil activities in general.

The ideologies and speech reactions that justify such transformations differ: the totalitarian trend is covered now by "communist" ideology; now by a Nazi "philosophy." The alleged motive is now to defend religion, now to carry the banners of civilization and progress to the "infidels" or "barbarians." But in spite of the disparity of the ideologies and slogans, the central phenomenon remains essentially constant; namely, the expansion and tightening of government control—that is, a shift toward totalitarianism.

A careful corroboration of the proposition by the facts of history makes it one of the strongest inductive uniformities. Its validity is well demonstrated by the history of ancient Egypt, Babylonia, Iran, Greece and Rome, as well as by that of India, China and Japan, Byzantium, the Mohammedan world, the Inca empire, medieval and modern Europe, and America. Those countries which were more belligerent were more totalitarian in their social, economic, and political organization than those which were less belligerent, as is notably illustrated, among the states of ancient Greece, by the contrasting régimes of Sparta and Athens.

The enormous upswing of governmental control during the First World War and in the present conflict offers a further illustration of the general rule. With the outbreak of the First World War all the belligerent countries became to a considerable degree totalitarian, whether they were republics or monarchies, autocracies or democracies. The capitalist economy was replaced by *Zwangsekonomie*, or *Zwangswirtschaft*—that is, by a coercive governmental economy. Private business was substantially replaced by business run by the government. Private property and wealth were increasingly limited through conscription, requisition, confiscation, "nationalization," "socialization," and the like. This process set in long before the communist or fascist régimes came upon the scene. In Russia the Rubicon that separated the capitalist and private-property régimes from those of the communist or fascist type had already been crossed by 1915, when the government (on August 17 and 25) issued decrees entitling it to search for food supplies in any private concern, to requisition or confiscate anything necessary, to check and verify the business records of any private concern, to take any enterprise under government management, etc. The totalitarian system was already born. The rest was a mere extension of it through further totalitarian measures on the part of the Czarist government, then the Kerensky government, and finally the Communist government. The last-named, in a modified form and under different slogans, continued the totalitarian trend of the preceding régimes and carried it to its extreme limit. From this standpoint, Communism was not initiated by Lenin, Trotzky, or Stalin. The most they did was to perform a necessary social "operation" in the most incompetent, bloody, cruel, and destructive way, under the guidance of their "Communist ideology."

Such an extreme form of the totalitarian trend was not caused by a single factor, but rather by the concurrence of all four of the major calamities under investigation— namely, famine, pestilence, war, and revolution. Since each of these calamities in itself tends to produce totalitarianism, it is obvious that their unholy alliance was bound to boost governmental control in Communist Russia to its uttermost limit. The life of every individual was completely regimental, the régime prescribing what, when, and where he should eat or drink, what he should wear, where he should live, and what he should read, say, believe. The "citizens" became mere puppets whose strings were pulled by the Communist government.

The subsequent story is likewise instructive. By 1921 the civil war was virtually over. The factor of international war and in large part that of revolution had ceased to operate. The curve of governmental interference accordingly began to decline. The "New Economic Policy" was introduced, which meant a decrease of government control in the economic and other fields, and a corresponding growth of private autonomy. Toward 1929 the clouds of war began to gather once more on the horizon; at the same time, famine again reared its ugly head, assuming in many regions acute intensity. The preparations for the coming war commenced to eat up the greater part of the national wealth and income. Hence a new upsurge of totalitarianism in 1929 and the following years. By 1935 or 1936, however, economic conditions had considerably improved; the revolution as such was dead; the new régime had become firmly rooted; and the preparations for war were deemed to have gone far enough. The result was a decommunization of the Stalin régime, which increasingly assumed the essential characteristics of the old régime. Many values, such as the family, and Russian poetry, literature, music, and fine arts,—with their Pushkins and Dostoevskis, Tchaikovskys and Lomonsoffs,—were now enthroned again, sometimes on an even higher plan that had been the case during the old régime. Abortions were prohibited and divorces limited. Chastity and virginity began to be praised in the editorials of *Isvestia* and *Pravda*. Marxian textbooks of Russian history were destroyed, being replaced by texts that eulogized the great generals, emperors, statesmen and builders, of the old Russia. Religion and similar values ceased to be sharply persecuted. Individual economic interests were recognized and began to be remunerated; and the privilege of individual possession or lease of real property up to ninety-nine years introduced. But with the outbreak of the Second World War and the Russo-Finnish War the pendulum started to swing in the opposite direction once more. Government control flared up again in an extreme form, though the ideologies and slogans that were now employed were very different from those of earlier years, whose place was taken by a nationalistic and patriotic ideology stressing the defense of the "Soviet Fatherland" and the liberties of the people against foreign aggression.

In other belligerent countries also there was a sharp upswing of governmental interference after the declaration of the First World War, and a notable decline after its close. With the onset of the depression at the end of the nineteen twenties, an upward trend again set in. In Germany, Italy, Hungary, and elsewhere, where the economic situation was that of the "have-nots," the increase was much more accentuated, and eventually led to the emergence of Fascist and Nazi totalitarianism, a form not so extreme, to be sure, as the Russian brand, but extreme enough in comparison with the normal régimes of the respective countries. Since the outbreak of the Second World War the curve of government control has risen so sharply that the capitalistic system that prevailed prior to 1914 now appears as a relic of the remote past. Its place has been taken by a "planned," or "war," economy managed principally by the government. Private property and private business are rapidly going into the discard. Constitutional guaranties are being progressively set aside even in the democracies. In spite of the comparatively short period that has elapsed since the entrance of the United States into the war, the greater part of our industry and finance is already managed by Washington. Most factories now produce what they are ordered to produce, and operate under the direct or indirect control of the Federal government. As to consumer goods, the following list of articles either "frozen" or rationed is highly significant.

The following have been placed under rationing, with the date of the application of the ration order:

Jan. 5.—New tires.
Feb. 23.—Recapped tires for trucks.
March 2.—New automobiles.
April 13.—New and used typewriters.
May 4.—Sugar.

The following have been limited in production or delivery: Gasoline and fuel oils; straight and safety razors and razor blades; metal cosmetic tubes; steel desks; paper clips.

Production has been ordered stopped on these household electrical appliances:

April 22.—Radios and phonographs.
April 30.—Refrigerators.
May 31.—Toasters, waffle irons, flatirons, roasters, grills, percolators, cigarette lighters, dry shavers.
March 30.—Crude rubber banned in 20 household products and restricted in 50 others. (Prohibited in manufacture of brewers' hose, wringer rolls, fountain syringes, acoustic aids, hatters' belts and hat-forming bags, switchboard mats and matting, vacuum-cleaner belts, hard-rubber syringes and dental dams. Reclaimed rubber, however, may continue to be used.)
June 30.—Lawn-mower manufacture to be stopped.

These goods have been "frozen"; that is, their sale is stopped:

Dec. 30.—New automobiles and tires. (Later rationed.)
April 2.—Bicycles of adult size.

If this has happened in what is in many ways the most democratic country in the world, one can readily imagine how swift and far-reaching has been the growth of government regulation in less democratic countries!

As long as the war continues, there is no prospect of a return to the anti-totalitarian system in the field of economic, social, and political relationships. On the contrary, the totalitarian trend is bound to progress (quantitatively and qualitatively) still further, no matter who is at the helm—whether democrats, republicans, monarchists, communists, fascists, or Papists. As has been pointed out, the process does not depend upon the predilections of the party in power. If, during the course of the conflict, any government should attempt to inaugurate an anti-totalitarian trend, it would be ousted from office and would be replaced by a more realistic régime. Only when the war and its attendant evils are over will the opposite process set in; and if the faction then in power should seek to stem the tide, it would meet precisely the same fate.

D. *The Increase of Government Control in Revolution*

What has been said about war applies with still greater force to the social, economic, and political effects of revolution. During a major revolution the government is a complete dictatorship, which flouts such values as the inalienable rights of man, constitutional guarantees, the security of human life, the sacredness of private property. In superficial revolutions the expansion of governmental control is slight; in large-scale revolutions it is limitless and leads to an unrestrained extermination of those who do not support the régime, as well as to an explicit elimination of private property and to its replacement by "communistic," "nationalized," "socialized," or, more accurately, "governmentalized" property. Such has been the case in all the outstanding revolutions of the past: the revolution in ancient Egypt of about 2500 B.C.; many Chinese revolutions (such as those at the beginning of the Christian Era and the one headed by Wang Mang); the Corcyrian revolution in Greece; the revolutions of the Ten Tyrants and the Thirty Tyrants in Athens, and those led by Agis IV, Cleomenes III, and Nabis in Sparta; a long series of other revolutions in the Hellenistic world; the Roman civil wars between Marius and Sulla, and those waged by the First and Second Triumvirate; the revolutions of the third and fourth centuries A.D.; many a medieval revolution (such as that of the Taborites in Bohemia); the English revolution or civil war led by Cromwell (in application to the Irish and the Catholics); the French revolutions of 1789-1801 and 1871; the Russian revolutions of 1601-1603, those led by S. Rasin and Pougatcheff, and the Communist revolution of 1918; the recent Hungarian and Bavarian revolutions of 1918-1920; and the Fascist and Nazi revolutions.

The extent and the concrete forms of this revolutionary totalitarianism vary. In some cases private property is not formally and explicitly abolished. Actually, however, in any notable revolution the private property of the opposing faction is subjected to requisition, confiscation, or even destruction. This applies now to the aristocracy or the rich, now to the Irish or Catholics, now to the Huguenots and other "heretics," now to the Jews, now to the loyalists or rebels, and so forth.

Nor does a revolutionary régime show any more respect for the sanctity of human life. (Typical statistics of the number of persons executed in various revolutions are given above, on pages 91, 185-86). It is one of the most blood-thirsty and voracious monsters, devouring first the rich and the privileged, then the middle class, then many of the lower and impoverished classes, and finally revolution-aries themselves (in the purges of one faction by another). Again, it autocratically prescribes not only political ideas, but frequently also religious beliefs, aesthetic tastes, up to forms of love and marriage. Whoever fails to heed its mandates is likely to be handed over to a firing squad or be sent to the gallows or guillotine.

As has been already pointed out, this upsurge of totali-tarian control does not depend much upon the particular leaders of the revolution or counterrevolution; for if any of them attempt to resist the inevitable trend, they are ousted from office and replaced by those who are willing to swim with the tide.[22]

The most popular revolutionary mottoes are "Liberty" and "Freedom"; yet these values are almost invariably suppressed except with reference to the revolutionary gov-ernment itself and its adherents. Only after the emergency is over does the tree of liberty begin to revive and flourish again.

3. *Summary*

Major crises generally represent a fateful concurrence of various calamities in their acutest intensity. If each of the calamities in itself promotes the growth of totalitarianism, in conjunction they push the trend to its maximum limit. Grave crises are uniformly marked by a virtually complete suppression of autonomy on the part of individuals and groups and by unlimited governmental absolutism and despotism, interrupted, perhaps, by the overthrow of the régime by another faction, attended by a brief period of anarchy.

The phenomenon can be observed in any notable crisis, whether it be the Egyptian crises at the end of the Old, the Middle, or the New Kingdom; the severe crisis at the end of the Greco-Roman civilization and the establishment of the Christian society of the Middle Ages; the crisis at the close of the Middle Ages (in the thirteenth, fourteenth, fifteenth, and sixteenth centuries); or the crisis of our own age. The foregoing analysis explains why at the present time totalitarianisms of all kinds are flourishing: why governments are absolutistic (either de facto or de jure); why the tree of civic freedom is withering; why capitalism and private property are disappearing; why true democracies are becoming a mere memory. As long as the crisis lasts, there is no hope for a reversal of the trend. Only when the emergency is over (and its end does not mean merely the termination of the war) will the converse process set in.

Such is the central and fundamental transformation of the social, political, and economic organization of society brought about by the various calamities that are the subject of our investigation.

Chapter Eight

THE INFLUENCE OF CALAMITIES UPON THE ECONOMIC
STANDARD OF LIVING

Aside from the replacement of free private economy by
governmental economy (largely obligatory), the general
effects of calamities upon the economic life of society consist in three principal modifications: first, in the lowering
of the well-being of the bulk of the population (which
does not preclude, of course, the enrichment of a few
profiteers and other parasites); second, in a tendency to
reduce the economic contrast between the poor and the
rich; and, third, in a sharp reallocation of wealth as between persons and groups.

1. *The Lowering of the Standard of Living*

Any calamity—be it famine, pestilence, war, or revolution—entails an increase of economic misery and a decrease of economic well-being, at least for those upon
whom it falls directly.

Famine involves extreme economic misery. Pestilence
also produces certain economic privations and losses,
though not to the same extent as war and revolution. Large-
scale wars and revolutions are devastating forces of enormous magnitude, destroying cities and villages, industries,
manufacturing and agricultural machinery, crops, etc. Indirectly, they waste the national wealth by using it for
nonproductive purposes (ammunition, armaments, etc.);
by diverting labor from productive tasks to nonproductive
military and revolutionary activities; by disorganizing industry, commerce, and finance; and, finally, by destroying
human life. If we agree to estimate the economic value of

an adult individual at 32,000 francs (as some economists estimate it), it is clear that the killing hundreds of thousands of persons entails an enormous economic waste. Famine and pestilence, generated often by an adverse constellation of external forces, come and go, and after their cessation, society may quickly resume its normal functions and rapidly restore its former well-being. Revolution and war, generated mainly by the internal forces of the societies involved, ordinarily last longer (like a chronic illness), and may hinder the recovery of society for an indefinite period.

The increase of **economic** misery manifests itself more concretely in a variety of ways. In practically any striking calamity, *commodity prices go up* without a corresponding increase in the income of the population. The attempt of the government to control the situation by establishing fixed prices usually—indeed, almost without exception—fails. When it does succeed in imposing fixed prices, commodities progressively disappear from the market and cannot be bought at the prescribed prices. Under these conditions people turn to the illegal "black markets," in spite of severe penalties involving even capital punishment. The prices prevailing in the illegal markets are usually many times higher than the fixed prices. Hence the bulk of the population either cannot buy their goods at all or else can purchase only insignificant amounts.

The problem is still further aggravated by an *increasing scarcity of commodities*. Since economic activities tend to become disorganized; since productive efforts in war and revolution are concentrated on the production of armaments, ammunition, and other implements of warfare; and since all calamities (especially war and revolution) destroy a large part of the existing stock of goods, a progressive scarcity of consumers' goods is inevitable.

Again, as has been said, more often than not the government cannot enforce its prices, and inflation ensues. Money loses much of its purchasing power. In Soviet Russia in 1918-1922 and in Germany in 1923, a million rubles or a million Reichmarks, respectively, scarcely sufficed to buy a pound of bread. In Russia, taking the prices of 1913 as equal to 1, the index of prices for the revolutionary years was as follows: 1917, 3.8; 1918, 23.3; 1919, 230.0; 1922, 182,753.0; 1923, 19,775,000.0. The amount of paper money issued was—in billions of rubles—as follows: 1917, 9.2; 1920, 225.0; 1922, 17,539.5; 1923, 171,000,000.0.[1]

When the government resorts to "all-out" regimentation of economic life by abolishing money and replacing it with commodity rations, and by controlling exports and imports, the production and distribution of goods, and so on, the results are still worse. At best it can provide but a scanty dole, since only a small proportion of the former volume of consumers' goods is being produced; and even this pitiful ration entails a terrific expenditure of time and energy on the part of the population. The rank and file are required to slave on public projects, on "nationalized" farms or in "nationalized" workshops, in various government "labor battalions," and the like. Besides there is endless red tape, as well as interminable "bread lines" (for the distribution of bread, milk, and other necessities). In Soviet Russia, in the years 1918-1922, when everything was "communized," one had actually to expend a greater number of calories to procure the government dole than the food itself contained!

This "all-out" economy has been repeatedly resorted to in the history of human society, and almost invariably it has failed either to maintain the normal economic level or to provide even the most rudimentary requirements. At best it has served merely to ensure the comforts of life for a small minority—namely, the ruling class and its satellites

—at the expense of unuterable misery on the part of the huge army of slaves or serfs who have had to minister to the needs of the totalitarian aristocracy. So it was in ancient Egypt. The lot of the Egyptian "W.P.A." laborers employed in building the pyramids or other public works was that of virtual paupers, though the rations of those who built some of the pyramids were vastly better than the rations received by the bulk of the Russian population in 1918-1922. A similar situation confronted the majority of the population—the slaves and semi-free classes—in the Spartan, Liparian, or Athenian societies when these were highly totalitarian in character. Still worse was the fate of the rank and file of the inhabitants of the Roman Empire in the centuries after 300 A.D., when the Roman economy had become almost as thoroughly totalitarian as the Russian Communist economy of 1918-1922. Further examples are furnished by the Chinese experiments in totalitarianism conducted by Wang Mang or Wang-an Shih, and by the lot of the bulk of the population in the Byzantine Empire, whose entire history was marked by a pronounced totalitarian type of economy.

A close parallel is presented by the history of Japan during the period of the Tokugawa Shogunate, with its high level of governmental regulation of economic functions. Here again the rank and file of the population was kept on a marginal or submarginal level. Likewise in ancient Peru or Mexico, where the economic organization was predominantly totalitarian, we note that the primary function of the depressed masses was to cater to the needs of the ruling faction. If from these countries we turn to medieval Europe and consider such communistic experiments as those of the Taborites in Bohemia, of John of Leiden in the New Jerusalem, or of Thomas Müntzer in Mülhausen, we find similar results. The same is true of various Mohammedan revolutions and of the communist Mazdakist revolution in Persia. Finally, we observe that the undiluted totalitarian economy of Soviet Russia in the years 1918-1922 resulted in the starvation of millions and in the depression of the standard of living to the lowest possible minimum, in spite of the onerous labor imposed upon the masses and of the so-called "proletarian" character of the government. The total monthly wages of the laboring class in Russia for the years 1913-1923, including all the rations and other incomes, were as follows:

1913-17	22 rubles
1918	8.99 rubles
1919	6.77 rubles
1920	7.12 rubles
1921	6.95 rubles
1922	8.22 rubles
1923	17.32 rubles

The consequences proved so disastrous that the government was ultimately compelled to abandon this policy and to seek to mitigate its effects by permitting a narrow margin of individual initiative. Only a trifle less futile has been the more moderate totalitarianism of Nazi Germany, of Fascist Italy, and of Greece, Hungary, and other countries. Even in Germany the situation grows steadily worse, notwithstanding the spoliation of the Jews and the wealthier classes and of three fourths of the entire European continent.

This brief survey of the foremost ventures in totalitarian economy leaves no doubt as to the validity of the general conclusion. Although many still believe that the recent economic experiments are something new, as a matter of fact they are in essence very old. The uniform consequence has been either a degree of wretchedness that has required the abandonment of the policy and the dilution of the totalitarian economy with a measure of private autonomy or else the transformation of the masses into slaves or serfs whose sole function has been to serve the governmental aristocracy and its satellites.

The gist of the matter is that no full-fledged totalitarian economy has ever succeeded in abolishing misery, raising the material plane of living of the masses, and creating genuine economic well-being for the bulk of the population. Only a moderate brand of totalitarianism, granting considerable latitude to private initiative, could achieve this end; and the record of human experience offers few instances of such an achievement.[2]

The totalitarian system, indeed, presents a certain fundamental paradox, if not dilemma. On the one hand, disaster dictates the expansion of governmental control of economic relationships in order to cope with the emergency; on the other hand, the excesses ordinarily engendered by such a policy serve to intensify the evil still further. The only effective remedy would consist in pursuing a *middle* course —namely, in adopting such regulations as would directly assist in meeting the problem without the total elimination of private economy. Unfortunately, the régime in power seldom has the wisdom to choose the golden mean!

2. *The Decrease in the Economic Contrasts between the Rich and the Poor*

Aside from the vultures that fatten at the expense of the majority, *war, and especially revolution in its initial and most destructive phase, release powerful forces tending to rectify economic inequalities.* A major war imposes ever-increasing taxes and levies, which fall most heavily upon the wealthier classes. It directly destroys or indirectly undermines many a fortune, through inflation, requisitions, confiscations, and similar measures. It thus tends to truncate the economic pyramid, converting it into a trapezium and considerably reducing the economic contrast between the poor and the rich. This is particularly true in case of military defeat, when the wealth of the possessing classes is liable to confiscation at the hands of the victor. In this event the rich find themselves frequently worse off than the poorer classes, since they may be less well fitted to earn a living under the altered conditions.

The equalizing rôle of revolution is still more conspicuous. Its avowed purpose is often the deliberate equalization of wealth through the "expropriation of the exploiters," the "redistribution of what has been stolen," or the annihilation of private property. The Egyptian revolution described by Ipuwer and many a Greek, Roman, Persian, Hindu, Chinese and European revolution, expropriated the wealth of the rich, of the middle classes, and even of the comparatively well-to-do peasants. They converted the existing acute pyramid into a relatively flat trapezium, making from 90 to 98 per cent of the population more or less equal—in their poverty and starvation! When the lowest possible minimum of subsistence had been reached, in their second and less destructive phase they undertook to raise the level and, with it, to reconstruct the pyramid of economic inequality, whose upper strata now embraced a mixture of the erstwhile richer and poorer elements. But many years were ordinarily required in order to restore the prerevolutionary standards, and this objective was usually attained only when the revolution had spent its force.

No revolution succeeds in creating lasting economic equality. Those who, during the first phase of the struggle, profess such an objective frequently end their career as convinced and vigorous proponents of the "sacredness of private property." This tragi-comedy has been repeatedly enacted on the stage of history.[3]

When, as during the declining years of the Hellenistic civilization, a society acquires the chronic habit of equalizing wealth through the process of revolution,—the victorious faction of today appropriating the resources of its rivals only to be dispossessed tomorrow,—the inevitable sequel is eventual internal collapse or else conquest by an external foe.

3. *Sharp Reallocations of Wealth during Calamities*

We have already discussed the extraordinary vertical mobility of men and economic fortunes in times of calamity, whereby—especially as a result of war or revolution—the rich are frequently impoverished and the poor are as frequently enriched. Even famine and pestilence play a considerable rôle in this shift of wealth from group to group. The Black Death radically transformed the status of both classes. For instance, as we have seen, the high rate of mortality and the consequent shortage of labor led to a marked improvement in the economic condition of farmhands and other manual workers.

The transfer of wealth during the First World War and in connection with the subsequent revolutions furnishes another notable example of the phenomenon. In addition, the European agrarian movement shifted some 125,000,000 acres (with their buildings, implements, and cattle) from one set of landlords to another, either without remuneration or with only nominal compensation to the former owners. Again, inflation ruined many groups, with a corresponding benefit to others. The annulment of state and communal bonds in various countries impoverished all those who had invested in securities of that type. In Germany alone, the payment of debts and mortgages in a depreciated currency meant the loss of approximately fifteen billion gold marks by the respective creditors and mortgage-holders. Further factors were profiteering and stock-market gambling. The Krupp corporation's net annual income rose from 33,900,000 marks in 1913 to 86,000,000 marks in 1914; the Köln-Rottweilsche firm increased its net income from 4,400,000 marks in 1913 to 14,500,000 marks in 1915. The Gasapparat firm, with a capital of only 1,300,000 marks, received in 1915 an income amounting to 3,600,000 marks. New captains of industry and finance appeared on the scene; and new millionaries and multi-millionaires sprang up, many of whom soon dropped out of the race. In the United States of twenty-three persons who in 1914 had reported a deficit in their income-tax returns ten were enjoying in 1916 a net income of from $500,000 to $1,000,000; and of fifty-nine persons who in 1914 had received a net income of less than $10,000 five reported in 1916 one amounting to more than $1,000,000.[4] In present-day America many firms are making profits of from 100 to 500 per cent; and not a few rapacious middlemen are enjoying an income of from $50,000 to $500,000 per annum.

By way of summary, it may be said that whereas social cataclysms uniformly depress the economic condition of the rank and file, and generally that of the wealthier classes as well, the violent currents which they set up permit many profiteers to batten at the expense of the majority, though a large proportion of these *nouveaux riches* fortunately soon relapse into a state of bankruptcy.

PART FOUR

THE INFLUENCE OF CALAMITIES UPON SOCIOCULTURAL LIFE

Chapter Nine

Two General Effects of Calamities upon Sociocultural Life

Having studied the typical effects of calamities upon mind, behavior, vital processes, and social organization, we pass now to an investigation of the influence of calamities upon sociocultural life. In what ways is it modified by calamities? What are their effects upon ethics, law, religion, the fine arts, science, philosophies and ideologies?

Before investigating these problems we must pause for a moment to indicate two general influences of catastrophes upon the *entire* sociocultural life, in all its varied aspects. Since these two effects concern all the fields of a given society and culture, they can be most conveniently outlined at this point so as to avoid undue repetition in connection with an examination of the more specific effects.

The first of these general influences consists, as has been said, in the *domination or impregnation by calamity of the entire sociocultural life, in all its fundamental processes; the second, in the oft-mentioned diversification and polarization of the effects in question.*

1. *Calamity Molds an Entire Culture in Its Own Image*

When famine overtakes a given society, it becomes the focal point of attention in science and art, religion and morals, and other fields. Science shows unprecedented concern with food problems. Laboratories undertake an elaborate investigation of the best available diets, including food substitutes, and a study of the influence of starvation upon the anatomy, physiology, and psychology of the population. Scientific journals print a much larger number of articles dealing with nutrition, and related topics.

Schools and colleges offer new courses dealing with these problems, and popular lectures on the subject increase enormously.

Religious life is likewise profoundly affected. Special prayers, services, ceremonies, and processions are resorted to with a view to curing or alleviating the evil. If the source of the famine is drought or locusts, religious processions are instituted for ending the drought or exterminating the locusts. Pledges are given to make donations to the Church, to undertake pilgrimages, and the like, conditional upon Divine intervention on behalf of the victims. Hundreds of sermons (oral and written) are composed with respect to the emergency.

Much the same is true of juridical and ethical matters. Multitudes of laws are enacted and edicts promulgated regulating various aspects of famine and food relationships. Innumerable problems arise as to what is moral and what is immoral under existing conditions, such as the questions Shall one hoard? Shall one buy in a "black market"? Shall one eat tabooed foods? Many persons pledge themselves to reform their individual lives, to rectify social abuses, and so forth.

A similar situation is presented by the fine arts, fiction, and poetry, the drama, painting, and sculpture tending to preoccupy themselves with themes drawn from the dominant emergency.

This is even more true with regard to the press and public opinion. Newspaper and other periodical publications are largely monopolized by dispatches, editorials, articles, or stories dealing with famine, which becomes the focal point of attention, as well, in legislative deliberations, party platforms, and private conversation.

The foregoing generalizations are perhaps even more applicable to the effects of pestilence, war and revolution, floods and earthquakes, and like catastrophes. The social repercussions of war are all too evident in the present crisis, manifesting themselves in such varied fields as science and philosophy, education, ethics and religion, the fine arts, politics and economics, business advertising, and recreation. It is the paramount topic of radio offerings—of news items and interpretations, discussions of strategy, patriotic addresses, plays, music, etc. The theme is even exploited for sordid commercial gain—for boosting the sale of such commodities as cereals, laxatives, hair tonics, lotions, tooth paste, cigarettes, and wine through a far-fetched (and frequently nauseating) appeal based on their alleged contribution to military "defense" and "victory"! War has become virtually the sole front-page topic of our newspapers, and it occupies more space than any other item in our periodical publications in general. It dominates the creative activities of our poets, novelists, dramatists, scenario writers, artists, and composers. Our foremost symphony orchestras now open the program, as a rule, with the national anthem. Finally, it is practically the exclusive concern of the Federal government.

As for revolution, there is no need to demonstrate its central rôle in the individual and social consciousness, as revealed by the newspapers, magazines, books, and other publications, the arts and sciences, the religion and ethics, and the economic life of the revolutionary society. The same may be said of pestilence or any other supreme disasters. And when it is over, the reverse process sets in, the calamity progressively fading into the background of social consciousness.

2. The Diversification and Polarization of the Effects of Calamity upon Society

Now let us turn to the second general effect of disasters, namely, the diversification and polarization of the effects of a given calamity in various parts of the respective society and its culture.

Since individuals differ from one another biologically, psychologically, and socioculturally, and since individuals and groups are not equally exposed to danger, the same calamity affects different persons and groups in divers, even opposite, ways so far as the concrete changes in their mentality and behavior are concerned. A given disaster tends to modify the behavior of all members in the direction of the proposition developed in Chapters Three and Four; but as it encounters differences in the biological and psychosocial equipment of individuals and in their exposure to the forces of the calamity, its actual or concrete effects vary widely. Some become brutalized, others intensely socialized. Some disintegrate—morally, mentally, and biologically; others are steeled into an unbreakable unity. In adversity some lose their sense of honor; others are ethically and spiritually reënforced. In certain respects calamity is destructive in all fields of culture; in other respects it proves a stimulating and constructive force, making for a cultural Renaissance.

This diversification and polarization of effects upon the mentality and conduct of various units of the population, as well as upon sundry fields of culture, manifests itself in practically any calamity. "Reactions" produced by it in one part of society are always counterbalanced to a certain extent by the "counterreactions" in its other parts. Its destructiveness is paralleled by its creative stimulation. This generation of diverse and opposite reactions permits a given society and culture to undergo a calamity without being utterly destroyed, to preserve in part their integrity and balance, and to revive quickly after the calamity is ended. It is even a fundamental condition for the termination of the emergency, especially in case of war and revolution.

Otherwise,—if the concrete effects of the disaster were all identical, and tended to be entirely negative, many a society would have been irretrievably destroyed by a single major catastrophe. As we have seen, calamities tend to demoralize, brutalize, and disorganize a society mentally, morally, and biologically. The greater the disintegration in these respects, the less able the society becomes to cope with the disaster, especially during wars and revolutions. Hence the calamity tends to increase, and the society tends to be caught in a vicious circle from which there is no escape.

Fortunately, hardly any notable civilization has ever perished through a single calamity, no matter how great. Almost all societies and cultures have passed through many catastrophes without being permanently and irretrievably ruined. As a matter of fact, most of them have restored their integrity rather quickly after the termination of the calamity. Only a few have been utterly disintegrated—and this only after being subjected to a series of calamities. Such societies and cultures were precisely those in which the diversity and polarity of effects did not occur to any appreciable extent. In most of the others it sooner or later became the main factor underlying the restoration of the disturbed "social equilibrium" and of a creative cultural life.[1] The counterreaction to the initial reactions permits a society to preserve a minimum degree of integrity and, what is still more important, to generate eventually the forces of creative reintegration.

In order to observe this phenomenon more clearly—to understand its *modus operandi* and its consequences—we shall consider first the ethical and religious field. What is demonstrated in this field in regard to polarization will be found to be applicable to virtually all the other spheres of culture under similar conditions.

Chapter Ten

How Calamities Affect the Religious and Ethical Life of Society

1. *The Diversity and Polarity of the Effects of Calamity*

The first general effect of a calamity in this field consists in the aforesaid molding of religious and moral conduct in its own image. The disaster invades the religious and moral consciousness of the society, becoming one of its focal points. This is reflected by a variety of manifestations, embracing prayers and religious services, moral injunctions, legal enactments, juridical procedure, and the like.

The second general effect is the diversification and polarization of religious and ethical phenomena. *Calamities generate two opposite movements in different sections of the population: one is a trend toward unreligiousness and demoralization; the other is a trend toward extreme religious, spiritual, and moral exaltation.*

Calamities split up the bulk of the population—which in normal times is neither very sinful nor very saintly—into three different groups: first, the moral heroes and intensely religious persons; second, the morally debased and irreligious; third, the remnants of the previous more or less balanced majority, who remain at about the same ethico-religious level as before.

Within each of these three groups there are many subtypes. The first movement ranges from the sublimest moral heroism (conforming to the strictest norms of the Sermon on the Mount) and the most intense religious exaltation to a barely perceptible improvement of ethical and religious standards and conduct. Its agents range all the way from martyrs, inspired prophets, mystics, zealous apostles, ascetics, reformers and other altruists, stoics, and so forth, to penitent sinners, converted libertines, and the like.

Similarly, the movement of despiritualization, desocialization, and demoralization comprises in its subtypes militant atheism (denouncing God, ethical commandments, and all transcendental values as "the opiate of the people," or superstition, or a conventional device of the clever minority to exploit the stupid majority); utter moral depravity, nihilism, and cynicism; gross sensuality (whose motto is "Eat, drink, and be merry; for tomorrow we die"); unrestrained exploitation; crass hypocrisy; and selfishness, egoism, and the milder forms of moral deficiency. The human agents of this stream range all the way from open and avowed enemies of God and the moral law, ruthless criminals, extreme sensualists, callous profiteers and exploiters, and shameless hypocrites to ordinary sinners and egoists.

Finally, the "balance" group consists of those who render unto God that which is God's and unto Caesar that which is Caesar's (though as a rule they give to Caesar much more than to God).

Even in normal times two extreme currents exist in the average society. But under the impact of catastrophe they are greatly intensified, and the membership of the "left" and "right" wings grows enormously. Persons hitherto only slightly inclined to be religious or irreligious now manifest an exaggerated trend in one or the other direction. Similarly, an erstwhile moderately sinful person becomes an unbridled profligate.

This diversification and polarization of the effects of calamity upon ethico-religious conduct is not confined to the described phenomena. It exhibits many satellites and subsidiary processes. One of these is *the simultaneous ap-*

pearance of a transcendental Messianic movement within the ethico-religious section of the population, and of an earthly utilitarian movement, aimed at the establishment of a utopia of material comfort, among the libertines and disbelievers. Each of these movements assumes, in turn, many diverse forms according to the concrete conditions of the society. The Messianic movement may range from that of several primitive American Indian tribes to that of Buddha, Mahavira, the great Jewish prophets, the Christian Apostles, and the Church Fathers. Earthly utopianism may range from efforts to improve the material conditions of its partisans, social reforms, and complicated theories of orderly social progress to revolutionary movements seeking by fraud and bribery, violence and bloodshed (including the destruction of its enemies) to establish a materialistic utopia.

This social dichotomy does not mean that the opposing factions—the "saints" and the "sinners"—are equal in magnitude and power or that their magnitude is constant in all calamities. In some cases one movement prevails; in other cases the other movement gains the upper hand. Which one becomes dominant and under what conditions, as well as which members of society become adherents of the respective movements and why, will be discussed later on. If the calamity is fundamental and enduring the polarization assumes a conspicuous and permanent character. In the foremost crises, consisting of great and long famines, pestilences, wars, revolutions, and the like, the polarization is so pronounced that it marks the end of one era and the beginning of another in the life history of the society and culture in question.

After these preliminary remarks let us turn to an inductive verification of the law based on an examination of the relevant facts of history. As such a verification throws a penetrating light upon many important, though obscure, historical processes, we shall devote considerable space to this task. As in any inductive study, we shall start with the more concrete and familiar facts and then, step by step, pass to ever broader series of fundamental sociocultural processes culminating in those crises that mark the end of one epoch and the beginning of another.

2. Corroborating Testimony from the Life History of Individuals

The first corroboration of our theory is afforded by a study of the ethico-religious effects of calamity upon various individuals. During the lifetime of almost every person who has reached maturity, he has experienced one or more disasters. Are the effects of a given calamity upon the ethico-religious conduct of all such persons identical? Do they all grow more irreligious and demoralized or the reverse? Or what?

Observation of the relevant facts in the behavior and mentality of historical as well as ordinary persons shows that the effects are different, often opposite, in different individuals. Some individuals become more religious and moral, others less so; while still others emerge without any marked change in their ethico-religious conduct or beliefs. Let us consider a few typical examples.

The death penalty is certainly one of the worst possible calamities that can befall a person—especially a young person. What reactions, if any, do such persons exhibit during the hours immediately before their execution? The answer is given by the following recent facts.

"J. D. Tuggle, 23, died in the McAlester penitentiary electric chair today for the murder of his aunt and uncle. The blue-eyed farm youth walked into the execution [chamber] . . . calmly puffing on a cigar. Asked by Warden Fred Hunt whether he had any statement to make, he replied: 'No, Mr. Hunt, take care of yourself.' "[1]

"George Cvek, who [had] sneered about the fifteen house-wives he [had] murdered, raped, or robbed, . . . when he came into court for sentencing . . . sneered and spat at Judge James M. Barrett. He told Judge Barrett not to say, 'and may God have mercy on your soul.' . . . A cynical smile played about his lips while attendants adjusted head and leg electrodes and buckled him [for electrocution in the death house]. Only at the last minute before the electric switch was thrown on did his smile fade and his lips move."[2]

"Bernard Sawiski, 19, who died in the Cook County electric chair, was a youth greatly changed from the sneering braggard who [had] told the judge who sentenced him, 'To hell with you; I can take it.' [He had also boasted of his killing of a policeman.] Last September he sat in jail devouring food and candy, happy over winning a bet of a pack of cigarettes that he would get the chair. Last night he took only four mouthfuls of a steak dinner, pushed the food aside, knelt with a priest, and sobbed as he prayed. . . Last night he wrote the policeman's widow, addressing her as 'Dear Mother Speaker,' and saying 'I know I am no good and I hope you forgive me for what I have done to your husband. If I knew then what I know now, this tragedy never would have happened.' Sawiski, who found solace in religion while awaiting execution, left Mrs. Speaker his rosary and asked that she pray for him."[3]

The contrasting effects of the identical calamity upon these youths is clear. Such contrasts are witnessed almost daily in death chambers or before firing squads. Some turn to God and die repentant, others die unchanged; still others die cursing God and all moral values.

Similar contrasts are observed in the ethico-religious behavior of many persons gravely sick or on their death-bed. We are told that at the end even Voltaire called for a priest and made confession. Here are two similar examples. One concerns Codrus Urseus, the tutor of a prince of Forli, and professor at the University of Bologna. Like many other Renaissance humanists, he was antireligious and a libertine. When, for instance, his manuscripts were burned in an accidental fire in his room, he addressed the figure of the Madonna as follows:

"If I ever call upon you in the hour of my death, you need not hear me, . . . for I will go and spend eternity with the devil."

"But when he came to die, he commended in his will his soul or his spirit to Almighty God, exhorted his weeping pupils to fear the Lord, and especially to believe in immortality and future retribution, and received the Sacrament with much fervor."[4]

Such cases during the Renaissance period were not infrequent.

"In the hour of death many [of the Renaissance Epicureans] doubtless called for the Sacrament; but multitudes during their whole lives, and especially during their most vigorous years, lived and acted on the negative supposition" (concerning either the immortality of the soul or belief in God).[5]

The case of Perpaolo Boscoli is still more notable.[6] A similar conversion occurred with many other historical individuals, and numerous cases of this kind are observed today.

On the other hand,—especially in the sensate, or "this-worldly," type of culture,—many cases of opposite character occur almost daily. Like the aforementioned Tuggle, many persons die unrepentant, sometimes boasting of their irreligious attitude, nihilism, and rebellion against God and all moral commandments. Others die essentially unchanged in their ethico-religious attitudes.

If now we turn to instances of grave sickness, loss of dear ones, or any other serious misfortune, we note similar results: some react to it by becoming more religious and moral, others grow more profligate and sinful, while still others reveal no substantial change in their attitude or behavior. The first step in the conversion of Saint Augustine was initiated through the death of a dear friend, and the last step was brought about by the death of his beloved mother.[7] Ignatius Loyola was transformed from a courtier and soldier into a great religious reformer during his protracted recuperation from a wound received in battle in 1521. Saint Francis of Assisi likewise owed his conversion into an exalted moral and religious leader after a period of illness. Egbert, an English youth of noble birth, went to Ireland, where he witnessed the plague of 685 A.D. "Egbert's companion died; and he himself vowed to lead a life of austerity . . . and died in the year 729 with a great name for sanctity."[8] During and after a terrifying storm on the ocean "the idea of the 'spirit,' or of 'the definite consciousness of an intimate personal relationship with God through Christ,' became an obsession" in John Wesley.[9]

A similar transformation was experienced by many other historical persons who, after a calamity, became mystics or religious and moral leaders. Other, supposedly nonreligious, natures have also exhibited an intensification of religious faith under like circumstances. Beethoven was gravely ill with abdominal inflammation in the spring of 1825. The third (adagio) movement of his Quartet in A minor (op. 132), composed immediately after his recovery, was thus inscribed by him: "Fervent thanksgiving to the Godhead of one who recovered, in the Lydian mood." The inscription speaks for itself. With the growth of his deafness and other illnesses during the last fifteen years of his life, we meet in Beethoven's letters more and more frequent references to his meditation upon death and to God and his mercies.[10] During an illness he wrote to the Archduke Rudolph:

"My confidence is placed in Providence, who will vouchsafe to hear my prayers . . . for I have served Him faithfully from my childhood, and done good whenever it has been in my power. So my trust is in Him alone, and I feel that the Almighty will not allow me to be utterly crushed by all my manifold trials."[11]

Instead of Beethoven let us take such a libertine as Boccaccio. The famous author of the *Decameron* began to abandon his free-thinking and libertinism after the loss of his beloved mistress Fiammetta. Subsequent misfortunes, and finally the illness of 1374, altered his mentality and conduct radically, and he ultimately became highly religious and ethical. Cases of this kind could be multiplied *ad libitum*. Adversity acts upon such persons like fire upon iron: instead of disorganizing them, it turns them into ethico-religious steel.

The foregoing facts prove that calamities affect differently the ethico-religious conduct of the persons concerned. Therefore, when calamity falls upon a large population, it is only to be expected that its effects should be diversified and polarized into the three main trends described above.

3. Corroborating Testimony Based on the Study of Specific, Well-Authenticated Calamities

The ethico-religious effects of some recent specific and thoroughly investigated disasters afford further corroboration of the theory. A typical example is furnished by the holocaust at Halifax, Nova Scotia, on December 6, 1917, in which a terrific explosion of ammunition destroyed a considerable part of the city, killing and wounding thousands. The calamity fell upon the city quite unexpectedly. What were its effects upon the ethico-religious mentality and conduct of the population? A few quotations from a systematic study of the social consequences of the catastrophe will suffice to answer the question. The study shows that this calamity caused an almost instantaneous emergence, on the one hand, of moral heroism and intense, almost apocalyptic, religiosity, and, on the other, of demoralization and ethico-religious cynicism.

THE RELIGIOUS AND ETHICAL LIFE OF SOCIETY 169

"The stimulus of the catastrophe results in two different types of responses—that of greed and altruistic emotion."[12]

"Many fell to their knees in prayer. One woman was found in the open yard by her broken home repeating the general confession of the Church. Few would have been surprised if out of the smoky, cloud-ridden skies there should have appeared the archangels, announcing the consummation of mundane affairs. Indeed there were instances, not a few, of those who 'saw' in the death-cloud the clear outlines of a face." Two different denominations now erected a joint church and thereafter worshiped together—a fact attesting the unifying rôle of catastrophes vis à vis religion.[13]

Among many who sustained physical injuries,

"there was no bitterness, no complaint, only a great desire to help some one less fortunate. Another observer said: 'I have never seen such kindly feeling and such tender sympathy.' Men who have lost wives and children, women whose sons and husbands were dead, boys and girls whose homes have been destroyed, are working to relieve the distress."[14]

"A private, with one of his eyes knocked out, continued working the entire day of the disaster. A chauffeur with a broken rib conveyed the wounded trip after trip to the hospital, only relinquishing the work when he collapsed. An unknown man was discovered at work amidst the ruins although his own face was half blown off."

Some of the telephone staff girls worked incessantly for ninety-two hours. Many who were suffering refused relief in order that others might be relieved. "A telegraph operator at the cost of his life stuck to his key and stopped an incoming train in the nick of time."[15]

"The group heroism was no less remarkable." At the risk of their lives a whole battery volunteered to board a ship laden with explosives.

"Catastrophe becomes also the excitant for an unparalleled opening of the springs of generosity." "Cafés served lunches without charge. Drugstores gave out freely of their supplies. Firms released their clerks to swell the army of relief." The Grocers' Guild acted along similar lines.

Financial contributions flooded the city. Halifax gained the appellation of "the City of Comrades."[16]

In a word, there emerged many a moral and social hero whose heroism had been latent in normal times.

Unfortunately, this is only one side of the picture. The other side is represented by depravity, demoralization, greed, gross egotism, and similar unethical and antisocial activities and attitudes, which assumed much larger proportions than before the catastrophe. Disaster divests many of their sociocultural, religious, and moral habiliments and ranges them among "the worst of the beasts," to use Plato's and Aristotle's expression.[17]

["Before the catastrophe] few people thought that Halifax harbored any would-be ghouls or vultures. The disaster showed how many. Men clambered over the bodies of the dead to get beer in the shattered breweries. Men . . . went into houses and shops, and took whatever their thieving fingers could lay hold of. Then there were the nightly prowlers among the ruins, who rifled the pockets of the dead and dying, and snatched rings from icy fingers. A woman lying unconscious on the street had her fur coat snatched from her back. . . . Then there was the profiteering phase. Landlords raised rents upon people in no position to bear it. Plumbers refused to hold their union rules in abeyance and to work one minute beyond the regular eight hours unless they received their extra rates for overtime. And bricklayers assumed a dog-in-the-manger attitude and refused to allow the plasterers to help in the repair of the chimneys. . . . Many squeezed the uttermost farthing out of the anguish . . . of the homeless men, women, and children. Truckmen charged exorbitant prices for the transferring of goods and baggage. Merchants boosted prices. A small shopkeeper asked a little starving child thirty cents for a loaf of bread."[18]

Again, there was a rush for public relief money on the part of many who were not entitled to it and who merely squandered it for "victrolas, silk shirts, furbelows," and other objects of luxury and even for the satisfaction of their lust.[19]

Similar effects have been observed in other carefully

recorded catastrophes, such as the Johnstown flood, the Omaha tornado, the Chicago fire, and the San Francisco earthquake.

Analogous contrasts have already been noted in the present war—in bombed city like London, and, in general, in the invaded countries. During blackouts and air raids certain individuals and groups have exhibited highly criminal tendencies, knifing, robbing, or raping women, and so forth. A portion of the youth under fourteen years of age have manifested a criminal record 41 per cent in excess of their pre-war record, and part of those between fourteen and seventeen years of age a rate of excess amounting to 22 per cent.[20] On the other hand, the same air raids have produced a host of moral heroes bent on helping their fellows at the risk of their own lives, to say nothing of the innumerable persons who have willingly sacrificed their property and other advantages on behalf of those in need.

In the belligerent countries one witnesses the emergence of pleasure-seekers actuated by a purely hedonistic philosophy, and at the same time striking evidences of religious and ethical zeal. For example, A. Boisen's study of contemporary England discloses a "marked increase in the number of the communicants of evangelical religious creeds without comparable loss of membership by the congregations of the more conservative creeds. The rising level of insecurity has driven these people through realization of their personal helplessness into activities calculated to provide merit in the other world." In other words, there is a growing "belief in a benevolent God and a social order founded on divine justice."[21]

Similarly, in Germany

"the Spiritual Church movement launched by the imprisoned Reverend Martin Niemoeller, calling for the unification of the Catholic and Protestant churches throughout Germany 'for their mutual protection' is gathering momentum and adherents 'to a gratifying degree.'

"Reports in synodic circles in Geneva state that the principal supporters of the Spiritual Church movement have been recruited from the intellectuals of Berlin, Munich, Wuerzburg and Koenigsberg, who are proselytizing under difficulties for its realization. Intervention in the plans and meetings of the leaders of the Spiritual Church movement has been frequent and drastic, it is added, with numerous arrests almost daily." [22]

In the United States "The Protestant Episcopal Church reported today that more people were attending services since the United States declared war. A nation-wide survey covering the period from December 7 through the Christmas holidays showed increased attendance almost everywhere, Episcopal National Headquarters announced." [23]

In Boston, "Churches were thronged" as never before on the eve of the New Year. [24] "Crime in Hawaii wanes under war." As a consequence "the policeman's life is dull." [25] "The state prisons [in Massachusetts] are holding the lowest number of inmates since the early twenties. A year ago there were only two spare cells at Charlestown [prison]. Today there are nearly 100. There will be a continuing sharp drop. That was the story in the last war, and apparently it is repeating [itself]." [26]

On the other hand, concerning the same celebration of the New Year in Boston we read the following:

"Young New Year 1942 occupied Boston last night in the gayest, noisiest and wettest welcoming celebration Boston ever witnessed. . . . He [that is, the New Year] literally floated on a tide of liquid refreshments that made history in Boston. Hotels, restaurants, night spots, dance halls, taverns—all were jammed to the doors, the management turning away hundreds who had no reservations. The streets were packed with a celebration that resembled a combination of Christmas shopping, a Legion parade, and a Crimson football victory over Eli. Entertainment reached a new height. At the closing hour of 4 A.M., parking space under the tables was at a premium, a memento of the tendency to overestimate the capacity for invigorating beverages." [24]

And all this on the night of the tragedy in the Philippines, with thousands dying, cities being bombed, etc.

Daily we observe that in spite of the catastrophe of the world war, the night clubs are still thronged; business firms are still concerned principally with profits (adding at the end of their radio advertising a few words about "buying defense bonds"); workers are still striking for better hours or wages or expanded union control; and new "sharks" and profiteers are springing up, intent on preying upon the misfortunes of mankind. The greatest tragedy in history is being shamelessly exploited for selfish commercial purposes. Night clubs, dancing, drinking, chewing gum, laxatives, hair tonics, lotions, cosmetics, tooth pastes, and worse things are advertised in the name of defense, patriotism and victory.[27]

However innocent in normal times, such phenomena in times of momentous crisis are symptoms of acute moral and social obtuseness.

Let us now turn to a detailed study of polarization in the history of each of the four major types of calamity with which we are concerned.

4. Polarization in Famine, Pestilence, War, and Revolution

A. Famines

The polarization of the effects of famine upon ethico-religious behavior has been demonstrated in Chapter Four. We have seen that cannibalism, murder, and other anti-social activities ordinarily emerge during major famines in the behavior of a portion of the population, and that another section exhibits the loftiest moral and religious ideals. The same chapter gives the approximate percentages.

B. *Pestilence*

A study of the actual behavior of the population reveals likewise the diversified and polarized effects of serious epidemics. Let us take first the trend toward unreligiousness and demoralization.

Thucydides' description of the plague in Athens in 430 B. C. admirably serves this purpose. He himself contracted the disease which he reports as an unusually accurate observer of human affairs and a trained historian.

"As the disaster passed all bounds, men, not knowing what was to become of them, became utterly careless of everything, whether sacred or profane. All the burial rites before in use were entirely upset, and they buried the bodies as best they could. . . . Nor was this the only form of lawless extravagance which owed its origin to the plague. Men now coolly ventured on what they had formerly done in a corner. . . . They resolved to spend quickly and enjoy themselves, regarding their lives and riches as alike things of the day. Perseverance in what men called honour was popular with none, it was so uncertain whether they would be spared to attain the object; but it was settled that present enjoyment, and all that contributed to it, was both honourable and useful. Fear of gods or law of man there was none to restrain them. As for the first, they judged it to be just the same whether they worshipped them or not, as they saw all alike perishing; and for the last, no one expected to live to be brought to trial for his offences."[28]

Here are a few citations from the writings of contemporaries of the Black Death of 1348 and the following years—testimonials typical of every major pestilence.

According to Guy de Chauliac, the eminent surgeon, and the personal physician of Pope Clement VI, writing in 1348 of the plague in Italy, "The father did not visit his son, nor the son the father. Charity was dead and hope crushed. [People] were buried without priests."[29]

A contemporary chronicler, John of Reading, "complains bitterly [in the plague year 1349] of the Mammon of unrighteousness which has taken possession of the regulars, especially the mendicants, who, having become unduly rich through confessions and legacies, were seeking after earthly and carnal things."[30]

Still more bitter is the denunciation of worldliness voiced by the Archbishop of Canterbury in his mandates of 1350, 1362, and 1378. He states in 1350 that the priests who survived the pestilence "display insatiable avarice, charging excessive fees and neglecting the care of souls. The second and the third [mandates] make the same charge and add that priests now desire voluptuous pleasures to such an extent that souls are neglected and churches and chapels are empty, to the horror and scandal of churchmen."[31]

Felix Fabri similarly states that during and immediately after the Black Death, even among the monks and clergy, "those who survived were not in monasteries but in the cities, and, becoming accustomed to worldly ways of living, fell from bad to worse; and that there occurred a great decline of all religions in this pestilence."[32]

"A striking [general] feature about the last half of the fourteenth century is the greater amount of lawlessness then prevalent, and the number of outbreaks, both popular and intellectual, against authority . . . and a general demoralization of both the regular and the secular [clergy]."[33]

The descriptions of the Black Death given by Petrarch and Boccaccio stress the demoralization of the Florentines. According to Boccaccio's remarkably accurate observations,

"[some isolated themselves in the country] and lived as separatists. . . . And there they used delicate viands and excellent wines, avoiding luxury [that is, voluptuousness] and refusing speech to one another, not looking forth at the windowes, to hear no cries of dying people, . . . but, having musical instruments, lived there in all possible pleasure. Others avouched that [the best way is] to drinke hard, be merry among themselves, singing continually and satisfying their appetites with whatever they desired, laughing and mocking at every mournful accident. . . . Yet in all this their beastly behavior, they were wise enough to shun the weake and sickly. In the misery and affliction of our City, the venerable authority of the Lawes, as well divine as humane, was even destroyed . . . . whereby it was lawfull for everyone to do as he listed. . . . Between these two rehearsed extremeties of life, there were others of a more moderate temper. . . . Very many, both men and women, forsooke the City, their Parents, Kindred, Friends, . . . One Brother forsooke another, the Unkle the Nephew, the Sister the Brother, and the Wife the Husband: nay, a matter much greater, and almost incredible; Fathers and Mothers fled away from their owne Children."[34]

Again he notes that many religious ceremonies, including religious burials, were suspended and many a church became empty, and he records other signs of the weakening of the religious sense.

Elsewhere he remarks the emergence of theft, robbery, and larceny, prostitution and immodesty, godlessness, the loss of a sense of compassion, idleness, and other tokens of demoralization and irreligiousness.[34]

"In this extreme calamity . . . a custome came among them, never heard of before [that women and girls who fell sick had to be attended by a man], were hee young or otherwise, respect of shame or modesty no way prevailing, but all parts of her body must be discovered to him, which before was not to be seen by any but women: whereon ensued afterward, that upon the parties healing and recovering, it was the occasion of further dishonesty, which many, being modestly curious of, refused such disgraceful attending, chusing rather to die than by such helpe to bee healed."

"In Vienna many of the plague workers who had been serving as nurses had to be arrested as they had rendered more than three hundred women pregnant. . . . The violation of female corpses was the order of the day."[35]

"Although one might think that the proximity of death would act as a deterrent from sin [writes the contemporary of the plague in Dantzig on October 22, 1709], yet desperate minds seem to be encouraged by the scourge of death to still greater misdeeds. For great wickedness is committed by godless men who turn to robbing and stealing and secretly slip into the houses. . . . If only one or two persons are alive in the house, they ill-treat them or even murder them, and take possession of what they desire."[36]

A contemporary, Chrisopolitanus, tells us that in the house of quarantined persons in Parma, during the epidemic of 1468, "there was much indecency and immorality. Terrible and inhuman cruelty and assassination flourished much more than love and friendship."[37]

In the plagues of the Renaissance period many "displayed their atheism in the frankness of their cynical crimes. Atheistic sentiments were by no means rare."[38]

Hundreds of pages would be required in order to set forth all the similar ethico-religious convulsions associated with outstanding epidemics.[39] There is no doubt that every serious pestilence generates powerful currents of demoralization and irreligiousness.

However, this is only one side of the picture. As in other calamities, there is a brighter side—namely, an intensification of the moral and religious sense manifested by the reaction of another section of the population. Though the foregoing accounts by Thucydides and Boccaccio lead one to conclude that plagues produce only adverse effects as a matter of fact these authors—perhaps inadvertently—reveal, as well, an opposite trend. For instance, Thucydides declares that in spite of the enormous risk of infection, many continued to tend the sick and to perform heroically their various missions of charity.

"This was especially the case with such as made any pretensions to goodness: honour made them unsparing of themselves in their attendance in their friends' houses, where even the members of the family were at last worn out by the moans of the dying, and succumbed to the force of the disaster. Yet it was with those who had recovered from the disease that the sick and the dying found most compassion."[40]

The phenomenon is still more clearly exemplified in other notable pestilences. It manifests itself not only in deeds of heroism and self-sacrifice in the ethical sphere, but also in the emergence of an apocalyptic mentality, in mysticism, in religious revivals, in the diffusion of a spirit of penitence and asceticism, and in a disposition to burn or give away one's worldly possessions.

During a famine and pestilence in Wales in the years 1245-1247 "the bishop of Norwich . . . sold all his plate and distributed it to the poor."[41] In the plague of 1347 in Messina "many desired to confess their sins to the priests." "The relics of the saints were brought to their town." "Intercessary processions and pilgrimages were undertaken to Catania to propitiate God." "The people believed that the end of the world was at hand."[42] Boccaccio, during the plague of 1348 in Florence, notes the "incessant prayers and supplications of devout people."[43] In the London epidemic of 1664-1665, according to Daniel Defoe, a man "awoke suddenly as a prophet and announced the Last Judgment."[44] In the plague at Vienna "the people hastened to the churches and with streaming eyes fell at the feet of the confessors."[45] So also in Bavaria and elsewhere.[46] In many places special prayers and magic formulas were resorted to in the hope of stopping the pestilence. "During the Black Death the whole of Europe was persuaded that the end of the world was approaching."[47] Plagues were generally interpreted as Divine retribution for the prevalence of sin, injustice, wantonness, and the like.[48] As in ancient times, "on the outbreak of epidemics, statues and altars were raised to the gods, [and] churches, and costly pillars were erected in honour of the Holy Trinity, the Divine Virgin Mary, and various saints."[49] Special cults of saints, such as Saint Rochus and the Fourteen Martyrs, appeared. "At Easter 1,200,000 [pilgrims to Rome] were counted, and again at Whitsuntide a million from all parts of Europe, who visited the churches of Rome for prayer and penance, and, chanting psalms, filled the highroads of Italy."[50]

Later on we shall see that in the acute crises where pestilence is one of many calamities, the most notable progress toward the ennoblement, purification, and spiritualization of religion takes place. As a matter of fact, the most important steps in the refinement of all the outstanding world religions have invariably occurred in periods of social catastrophe—rarely, if ever, in periods of prosperity and material well-being.

No less certain are the emergence and growth of moral heroism and altruism in the behavior of a portion of the population. Thus, Boccaccio testifies to the deeds of charity performed by persons who aided the sick at mortal peril to themselves. Another example is the attitude of the Cardinal of Arles who, during a plague, declared, "I will rather hold the assembly of the Church at the risk of my life than save my life at the risk of the assembly."[51] In many cities, as at Rouen in the year 1507, the authorities eliminated gambling, cursing, drinking, and all excesses.[52] Houses of prostitution and concubines were abolished. Charitable fraternities and orders sprang up, such as the Brothers of the Order, the Poor Friars, the Burying Friars, and the Capuchins, whose members fearlessly tended and solaced the sick, carried away the dead, performed religious duties, aided helpless orphans, and so forth. Many contracted the disease themselves and died, and those who recovered performed their duties more energetically than ever.[53] Not a few "sacrificed their whole fortune [including even] their beds, to alleviate the needs of the poor."[54]

Though many abandoned their dear ones and friends, others—probably the majority—did not do so. Like our own newspaper reporters, the chroniclers were prone to note the negative rather than the positive data, and thus to present a one-sided picture, overlooking the deeds of heroism and self-sacrifice. Later on, we shall see that the elevation and sublimation of most of the leading ethical codes has been achieved during periods of acute crisis, whereas eras of comparative prosperity and material well-being have contributed little in this direction.

To sum up. Grave pestilences, like major famines, produce different and even opposite ethico-religious effects in the behavior of different elements of the population concerned: in one case they induce demoralization and irreligiousness; in another they lead to moral and religious exaltation.

C. *War*

Like other catastrophes war produces both cowards and heroes, criminals and altruists, profiteers and self-sacrificing persons, libertines and ascetics, hedonists (of the *Carpe diem* or the "wine, women, and song" type) and stoics, atheists and religious devotees. Which of these two types are produced in greater proportion depends upon the character of the war and of the people concerned and upon various other conditions. But the central fact of the polarization of ethico-religious effects remains constant.

This follows from the very nature of war, which subjects both soldiers and civilians to the influence of two contradictory forces, the one impelling them to seek individual self-preservation, the other making for the protection of, and loyalty to, the community (in its broadest sense, the nation or people concerned). With some the egoistic stimulus prevails; with others the social stimulus. In some cases war releases the most bestial instincts of primitive aggressiveness, vis à vis not only the enemy but also one's own fellows; in others it forges the strongest and most unbreakable social ties, evoking companionship in arms, brotherhood in defense of the community, and similar values. From this standpoint, war is perhaps the most potent altruistic stimulus that exists. As such it demands the highest altruism, self-sacrifice, and other forms of moral heroism, particularly on the part of the combatants. This aspect is usually overlooked by its detractors.

Let us now consider a few evaluations of the effects of war offered by certain technical observers of the phenomenon.

"Individualism declines at the outbreak of war and is superseded by mass reactions. . . . The feeling of sharing a common danger leads to a strengthening of community ties and to a levelling of differences and oppositions in social, economic, religious, and political spheres. In volunteers particularly, the increased community feeling leads to a surrender of privileges and to self-sacrifice in the service of the country. Conversely, in some individuals anxious endeavors to protect the ego lead to a ruthless increase in selfishness. In most people the increase in community feeling results in a disregard of minor physical ailments, although hypochondriacal reactions may be observed in some."[55]

The established fact of the polarization of the ethico-religious effects of war refutes the claims of those who contend that they are wholly negative, as well as the contention that they are entirely positive. Here are a few samples of such theories.

"War, an appeal to brute force, is always a degradation, a descent into animalism that demoralizes the victors as well as the vanquished. . . . It brutalizes a man, strips him of all really human ethics, turns him into a beast, and entirely demoralizes him."[56]

"Neither circumstances nor human beings improve in times of peace; it is to war that we must look for progress. From a biological standpoint, aggressiveness has been a condition necessary for progress." A long peace makes men extremely egoistic—devoid of courage, virility, altruism, and self-sacrifice. Effeminacy, idleness, and corruption are bred by peace.[57]

It is evident that both theories are thoroughly one-sided.

The first neglects the altruistic and socializing aspect of war; the second, its egoistic, desocializing, brutal, and demoralizing aspects. If the first theory were sound, mankind would long ago have sunk to the lowest possible moral level; for during its entire history—with slight intermission—it has been constantly at war. My studies demonstrate that in the history of Greece, Rome, and other European countries wars have occurred on an average, once in every two years. The exact percentages are as follows: for Greece, 57 per cent; for Rome, 41; Austria, 40; Germany, 28; Holland, 44; Spain, 67; Italy, 36; France, 50; England, 56; Russia, 46; Poland and Lithuania, 58.[58] Moreover, if the theory were valid, the more militant nations would have been demoralized to a greater extent than the less militant ones, and a given nation would have sunk to its moral nadir in the most militaristic periods of its history.

As a matter of fact, whether we take Greece during the Persian and Peloponnesian Wars, or Rome during the protracted Punic Wars, or the United States during its war for independence, we find that such periods represent perhaps the high-water mark of moral achievement in the history of the respective countries.

If, per contra, the second theory were true, we should expect that the more belligerent a country is, the higher is its moral level. Here again the facts belie the assumption.

Additional evidence in support of the polarization theory and against both of the last-named theories is furnished by a multitude of data, embracing such factors as criminality, puritanism, and religiousness, in times of war and of peace, among the comparatively belligerent and less belligerent countries. When one compares the war-time and peace-time statistics for criminality in a given country, the results are very inconclusive and show no uniformity: in some wars criminality increases; in others it decreases. For instance, in Germany in the wars of 1866 and 1870-1871, and in France in the wars of 1830 and 1870-1871, criminality notably declined. On the other hand, in certain cases it showed an upward trend. Among the countries participating in the First World War, criminality increased in some and declined in others.[59] The same polarity and diversification applies to other moral effects of war.

As to its repercussions in the religious field, we find similar contrasts. Many a famous monarch (such as the Emperor Asoka in India, several Chinese rulers, and Charles of Spain) has undergone a complete change of heart under the impact of war, abandoning his throne or devoting himself to religious (and charitable) duties. A like conversion has been experienced by thousands of obscure persons. The converse is equally well attested, in the case both of combatants and civilians. However, notwithstanding these evidences of polarization, a study of the crucial crises in which war is one of the primary components indicates—as has already been pointed out—that it is precisely in such periods that the foremost world religions have emerged or have been refined and sublimated. Periods of peace and material well-being, on the other hand, are marked by comparative uncreativeness in this field.

D. *Revolution*

What has been said of international wars may be said, with certain reservations, of revolutionary or civil wars. Revolutions invariably disclose the familiar phenomenon of polarization. A considerable portion of the population which has hitherto lived on an average plane ethically and religiously now splits into two opposing camps. The first group perpetrates every imaginable crime and cruelty. The second group exhibits a Messianic or mystical trend, identifying itself with the transcendental Kingdom of God, or a predilection for asceticism, stoicism, or social altruism.

A systematic analysis based on a substantial body of evidence is given in the author's *Sociology of Revolution* (Philadelphia, 1925). A few typical examples will suffice for our purposes.

Respecting the revolution of *c.* 2500 B. C. in Egypt the contemporary Ipuwer writes:

"The laws of the judgment-hall are cast forth, men walk upon them in the public places, the poor break them open in the midst of the streets. . . . A man smites his brother of the same mother. . . . Behold a man is slain by the side of his brother, while he [the brother] forsakes him to save his own limbs. . . . A man regards his son as his enemy. . . . What men do . . . is iniquity. . . . [Travellers] are beaten and wickedly slain. . . . Indeed, the land turns around [the order of things is overturned] as does a potter's wheel. He who was a robber is lord of wealth; [the rich man] is now plundered. . . . Behold, all the craftsmen, they do not work. Behold, [he who reaped] the harvest knows naught of it; he who has not ploughed [fills his granaries]. . . . Civil war pays no taxes. . . . The man of virtues walks in mourning by reason of what has happened in the land. . . . Mirth has perished, it is no longer made; it is sighing that it is in the land, mingled with lamentations." "Would that there might be an end of men, that there might be no conception, no birth."

But while the erstwhile rich are impoverished, the former poor are now wealthy. Ladies are destitute, their former slaves now wearing their dresses, gold, and jewels.[60]

If from the ancient Egypt we pass to one of the oldest recorded revolutions in Greece, the Corcyraean revolution of 427 B. C., the picture is similar. We have a vivid first-hand description from the pen of an eminent historian, Thucydides.

"Death thus raged in every shape; and, as usually happens at such times, there was no length to which violence did not go; sons were killed by their fathers, and suppliants dragged from the altar or slain upon it; while some were even walled up in the temple of Dionysus and died there. . . . Some were slain for private hatred; others by their debtors, because of the monies owed to them."

Thucydides next sets down the following astute generalizations:

"The sufferings which revolution entailed upon the cities were many and terrible, such as have occurred and always will occur, as long as the nature of mankind remains the same. . . . War [and revolution] take away the easy supply of daily wants, and so prove a rough master."

Continuing his remarkable analysis of the transformation of conduct wrought by revolutions and wars, he observes:

"Words had to change their ordinary meaning and to take [on] that which was now given them. Reckless audacity came to be considered courage . . . prudent hesitation, specious cowardice. Moderation was held to be a cloak for unmanliness; ability to see all sides of a question, inaptness to act on any. Frantic violence became the attribute of manliness; cautious plotting, a justifiable means of self-defence. The advocate of extreme measures was always trustworthy; his opponent a man to be suspected. . . . Oaths of reconciliation [were broken]. . . . Religion was in honour with neither party; but the use of fair phrases to arrive at guilty ends was in high reputation. . . . Thus every form of iniquity took root in the Hellenic countries by reason of the troubles. . . . Human nature . . . gladly showed itself ungoverned in passion, above respect for justice, and the enemy of all superiority; since revenge would not have been set above religion, and again above justice, had it not been for the fatal power of envy."[61]

A few data concerning the French revolution of 1789 and the Russian revolutions of 1905-1907 and 1918-1922 suffice to give an idea of the depths of depravity to which a portion of the population sinks. In pre-Revolutionary France the number of executions was very moderate, hardly exceeding a few hundred annually. Per contra, in three years of the Revolutionary terror "it is probable that between 35,000 and 40,000 persons lost their lives as a consequence of terrorism.''[62]

In Russia, whereas the number of executions during the peaceful years of 1881-1905 fluctuated between 9.6 and 18.6 annually, with the outbreak of the revolution of 1905-1906 the figures rose to 547 in 1906, 1139 in 1907, and 1340 in 1908; then, with the liquidation of the revolution, they fell to 717 in 1909, 129 in 1910, and 73 in 1911. In the incomparably greater revolution of 1918 and the following years the number of persons executed by the Communist government during the period 1918-1922 was no less than 600,000, or about 150,000 per annum. And this does not include the other victims of the Red Terror, to say nothing of the victims of the White terror (in the areas under the domination of the anti-Communist, or White, government).[63]

A similar record of violence is disclosed by the revolutions and civil wars in ancient Greece and Rome, in Persia, India, and China, as well as by such conflicts as the Hussite revolutions, the Dutch revolution of 1566, and the Cromwellian revolution in England, to cite but a few comparatively recent examples.

In addition to the murder of one's fellow countrymen, many other acts of cruelty and bestiality are perpetrated by a part of the revolutionary society, including physical injury or torture, mental torture, various forms of sadism, rape, arbitrary arrest, imprisonment, and confiscation of property, theft, larceny, robbery, and brigandage, and the like. Whereas under normal conditions only an insignificant portion (less than one per cent) of the population suffers imprisonment, during a revolution this percentage may be multiplied anywhere from ten to a hundred times. In Russia, between 1918 and 1922 probably no less than one fourth of the adult and semi-adult population was imprisoned at least once.

THE RELIGIOUS AND ETHICAL LIFE OF SOCIETY

Equally striking is the factor of irreligiousness bred by revolution, attested by such early writers as Ipuwer and Thucydides. In some cases it assumes the form of a militant atheism which seeks to exterminate the existing religion as an "opiate of the popular mind." The government or members of the atheistic groups confiscate or destroy churches and other church property, violate religious sanctuaries, deprive church officials of many privileges, etc. In other cases the phenomenon assumes milder forms, such as the growth of a spirit of skepticism and cynicism, the cessation of the performance of religious duties, and an upsurge of sacrilege, heresy, and blasphemy.[64]

No less evident, however, than these negative manifestations is the contrary trend—namely, the emergence, during revolutions, of a heightened religious, moral, and social sense. The reason for this seeming paradox is to be found in the opposing stimuli exerted by revolutionary upheavals. On the one hand, they tend to remove the inhibitions upon man's elemental impulses—his egoism, his lusts and greed, his cruelty and sadism. On the other hand, every revolution is a social movement generated by the sufferings of a part of the population and looking toward the material, moral, social, and cultural improvement of their lot. Idealistic aspirations are hence as inseparable from it as are the demoralizing and desocializing effects, the ennobling and spiritualizing forces tending to counteract the opposing forces. Some, as we have already seen, become "God-intoxicated" prophets, apostles, or religious leaders. Various mystical, ascetic, or stoic movements and activities arise. Others, witnessing the universal suffering of their fellows, become social leaders and benefactors, devoting all their energies to the mitigation of the existing evils, regardless of the party or class affiliations of their beneficiaries. Even more frequent are the acts of heroism or altruism performed on behalf of relatives or friends in danger of arrest, execution, or banishment or suffering from various privations—activities involving the unselfish sacrifice of personal possessions and even life itself. Occasionally some members of the former privileged classes, perceiving the injustice of the prerevolutionary régime, undergo a change of heart in the direction of higher ethical and religious ideals. Next chapter will give many facts of that kind.

Let us now consider a few *mixed* calamities, consisting of revolution, war, famine, and pestilence, and note whether such composite disasters induce demoralization and unreligiousness.

5. *Demoralization and Unreligiousness in Complex and Prolonged Calamities*

In protracted or chronic sociocultural crises all the four types of calamity are usually intermingled. Such periods are marked by famine and other privations and hardships, lack of security, deterioration of health, and the like. They are characterized by internal disorders and external wars, which, in turn, are generally accompanied by pestilence. If each of the four types of disaster alone produces demoralization and irreligiousness, cynicism and nihilism, materialism and sensualism—in ideology as well as in actual conduct—then the mixed crises should produce the same effects. Is such an expectation supported inductively? Very definitely! Let us take a few typical examples, which will serve not only to demonstrate the validity of the induction but also to reveal several characteristics hitherto unstressed.

The severe and protracted crisis in Egypt which set in soon after 2500 B. C.,[65] at the end of the Old Kingdom, lasted, according to different authorities, from 181 to 344 years.[66] Its utter demoralization and irreligiousness have already been mentioned. (See pages 184-85). It was a period of skepticism, materialism, Epicureanism, and hedonism. Here we are concerned only with ideologies of hedonism and of sensualism of the *Carpe diem* type. Several contemporary documents reveal these unmistakably. One is entitled *The Song Which Is in the House of King Intef*. Its dominant motif is the *Vanitas vanitatum*, with the conclusion "Eat, drink, and be merry; for tomorrow we die." It declares that the gods, as well as the most illustrious demigods (such as Imhotep and Hardenef), have passed away.

"Behold their places thereof; their walls are dismantled, their places are no more, as if they had never been. None cometh from thence [from the nether world of death]. . . . Until we depart to the place whither they have gone, encourage thy heart to forget it, making it pleasant for thee to follow thy desire, while thou livest. Put myrrh upon thy head. . . . Increase yet more thy delights, and let not thy heart languish. Follow thy desire . . . till the day of lamentation cometh to thee. . . . Celebrate the glad day; be not weary therein. Lo, no man taketh his goods with him. Yea, none returneth again that is gone thither."[67]

"Here is bared a skepticism which doubts all means, material and otherwise, for attaining felicity or even survival beyond the grave. To such doubts there is no answer [except by means of] a sensual gratification, which drowns such doubts in forgetfulness. 'Eat, drink, and be merry, for tomorrow we die.' "[68]

The same purely hedonistic mentality is reflected in a variant of this song, and in a document entitled *The Dialogue of a Misanthrope with His Soul*.[69]

The latter stresses also the prevalent demoralization.

"To whom do I speak today? Brothers are evil. . . . Hearts are thievish. Every man seizes his neighbour's goods. The gentle man perishes. . . . There are no righteous. The land is left to those who do iniquity."

Still more clearly is it brought out in the *Musings of Khekheperre-soneb*, by a priest of Heliopolis.

"Righteousness is cast out; iniquity is in the midst of the council-hall. The plans of god are violated, their dispositions are disregarded. The land is in distress, mourning is in every place, towns and districts are in lamentation. All men alike are under wrong."[70]

If we turn to the Greek and Hellenistic world of the third and following centuries B. C., and then to the Roman world of the period from the first century B. C. to the fourth century A. D., we witness another long period of social crisis characterized by irreligiousness and skepticism, cynical nihilism, materialism, hedonism and vulgar epicureanism.[71]

"A miserable time in her not very happy history, such was the situation in Greece in the third and early second century B.C. It is not surprising that, downtrodden and humiliated, robbed and pillaged, having lost faith in gods and men, the country was more than ever distracted by political and social unrest. In the atmosphere of war, of organized brigandage and common rapine, life in Greece was utterly disorganized. Demoralization seized upon both the upper and the lower classes, and social unrest, disturbances, and revolutions were of ordinary occurrence. . . . Family life was broken up. Dissipated club life flourished and produced a general lowering of moral tone."[72] "Sacrilege became . . . a matter of common occurrence."[73]

A similar convulsion occurred in the leading centers of the Hellenistic world outside Greece proper.[74] For instance, in Hellenized Egypt the belief in God and immortality notably declined. The hedonistic attitude was sharply accentuated. Sexual perversions assumed extreme forms. The sex mores underwent drastic changes, including a marked increase in the most

"shameless sexual promiscuity. They . . . seduced members of the same family. Relations between father and daughter, son and mother, . . . remained not unknown to Egypt. The [contemporary] authors especially note the cases where a man lived sexually with two sisters or with his mother and her daughter. . . . [Adultery, rape, and prostitution greatly increased.] In the Alexandrian epoch homosexual love entered the mores of the population. . . . Our authors seem sometimes to be sadistically enjoying the enumeration of a variety of turpitudes and sexual perversions, for which they lay the responsibility upon the poetic evening star. They describe all the abberrations of morbid eroticism with the impudent serenity of the casuists: rape, unnatural sexual relations, flagellation, and sodomy."[75]

"The dominant rationalism of the period considered as childish fables all the beliefs of the ancients in an otherworldly life of human souls. . . ."[76]

These types of mentality and conduct are observable also, in an extreme form, among the Romans of the period from the first century B. C. to the fourth century A. D. In the upper and middle classes they often assumed artificially refined forms, followed by almost bestial cruelty. Among the lower classes irreligiousness, vulgar hedonism, and materialism, and similar traits made their appearance. On the tombstone of many an obscure person one reads such epitaphs as the following:

"Horror does not seize me when I think of the putrefaction of my body; nothing further touches us." "I was; I am not; I do not care." "I paid my debt to nature and have departed." "What remains of man, my bones, rests sweetly here. I no longer have the fear of starvation; I am exempt from attacks of gout; my body is no longer pledged for my rent; and I enjoy free and perpetual hospitality."[77]

"Often a grosser Epicureanism recommends that we take advantage of our earthly passage, since the fatal term [death] deprives us forever of the pleasures which are the sovereign good. *Es, bibe, ludi, veni* (Eat, drink, play, come hither) is advice which is several times repeated [on the tombstones. Others are:] 'Indulge in voluptuousness, for only this pleasure wilt thou carry away with thee'; or . . . 'Let us eat and drink, for tomorrow we die. . . . What I have eaten and what I have drunk; that is all that belongs to me. . . . Baths and wine and love impair our bodies; but baths, wine, and love make life. . . . While I lived, I drank willingly; drink, ye who live. . . . The supreme end is pleasure.' "[78]

Evidently, such disillusionment, skepticism, cynicism, hedonism, and materialism must have been very profound and wide-spread to have found expression on the tombstones of ordinary persons.

If we turn now to the prolonged crisis of the Italian Renaissance, stretching from the end of the fourteenth to the sixteenth century, we witness the same phenomena— the effect of irreligiousness, materialism, sensuality, and general demoralization of mind and conduct.[79] The corruption of Renaissance Italy is thus summed up by Machiavelli.[80] "We Italians are irreligious and corrupt above others." In ethics, sensual hedonism and utilitarianism, absent in the ethical theories of the Middle Ages, emerge during the period 1440-1460, reaching unprecedented heights. The leading motif is the familiar "Eat, drink, and be merry; for tomorrow is uncertain" (Lorenzo the Magnificent's "Di doman non c'é certezza").[81] In the upper strata of society, including the Humanists and other leaders of Renaissance art and thought, we find "malicious self-conceit, abominable profligacy, and irreligion."[82] In other classes, "chiefly in consequence of the national disasters,"[83] gambling and bloody vengeance (sometimes assuming fantastic and inhuman forms) were rife; "marriage and its rights were more often and more deliberately trampled under foot than anywhere else";[84] husbands frequently poisoned their wives, and vice versa; brigandage and hired assassination were rampant.

The condottieri and some of the intellectuals openly boasted of their atheism and nihilism, their repudiation of all religious, moral, and other ideal norms. "The enemy of God, of pity and of mercy" was the device adopted by Werner von Urslingen.[85] Such impious outbursts as the following were not unknown: "O thou thoroughly wicked God, if I could but lay hands on thee! Truly I would tear thee to pieces. I deny thee . . . . He is a fool who puts his confidence in thee."[86] Among those at the top (the Visconti and Sforzas, the Borgias, and such condottieri as Braccio di Montone, Tiberto Brandolino, and Malatesta) "the disinterested love of evil, the thirst for blood for its own sake, the devilish delight in destruction,"[87] reigned supreme. The same was true of many of the intellectuals and of a part of the lower classes. "Literature characterized by the *Facetiae*, by Lorenzo Valla's *Voluptas*, and Beccadelli's *Hermaphroditus* could not but shock respectable feelings."[88]

In conclusion, it may be said that a systematic verification of the law under discussion leaves no serious doubt that any grave disaster (such as a famine, pestilence, war, revolution, or earthquake) produces the aforesaid positive and negative ethico-religious polarization in different parts of the population involved. The same is true of mixed calamities and prolonged sociocultural crises. This is especially clear with regard to the negative phase—irreligiousness and demoralization, and their respective philosophies of atheism, skepticism, nihilism, materialism, hedonism, sensualism, etc. Somewhat less attention has been paid in the preceding chapters to the positive reaction —religious, ethical, and social revitalization, purification, and ennoblement, and its attendant ideologies of idealism, the absolutism of moral principles, asceticism, and the like. Hence an additional corroboration of the induction is advisable. In this connection we shall encounter a number of highly important problems as to how, why, and under what conditions religious and moral progress takes place. Let us, accordingly, explore still further the question whether calamities in general—and, especially, severe and prolonged mixed crises—serve to elevate and ennoble the ethico-religious mentality and conduct of a portion of the population involved.

Chapter Eleven

CALAMITIES AND ETHICO-RELIGIOUS PROGRESS

1. Three Special Cases: the Renaissance, Methodism, the Russian Soviet Revolution

Since a minimum of evidence for the positive ethico-religious reaction to separate calamities of famine, pestilence war, revolution, etc. has been given, we shall next deal with a few more specific ethico-religious revivals and then undertake a systematic study of the ethico-religious regeneration associated with prolonged sociocultural crises in several notable cultures.

Among the specific and comparatively well-known cases of ethico-religious revival we shall take those of the Italian Renaissance, of Methodism, and of the Russian Soviet Revolution. They differ from one another in practically all respects except one—a decisive one for our theory—namely, the fact that all three ethico-religious reactions took place under conditions of profound crisis, with its attendant demoralization and irreligiousness. This means that, according to the inductive method of residues, the revival was due to the calamity itself and its negative repercussions.

The Renaissance. We have seen that the Renaissance produced notable demoralization and irreligiousness. Did it generate an opposite reaction? The answer is in the affirmative.

Investigators of the religious revivals of the Middle Ages and the Renaissance stress the following facts:

"They were due to general public calamities or to the dread of such. . . . The Crusades and the Flagellant revival are instances. . . .

[In Italy] the first great companies of Flagellants appeared immediately after the fall of Ezzelino and his house, in the neighborhood of the same Perugia which became the headquarters of the revivalist preachers. Then followed the Flagellants of 1310 and 1334 [years of further calamity], and then the great pilgrimage without scourging in the year 1399. . . . Terrible crises had still at a much later time the power to reawaken the glow of medieval penitence; and the conscience-stricken people, often still further appalled by signs and wonders, sought to move the pity of Heaven by wailings and scourgings, by fasts, processions, and moral enactments. So it was in Bologna when the plague came in 1457; so in 1496 at a time of internal discord at Siena, to mention only two out of countless instances. No more moving scene can be imagined than we read of at Milan in 1529, when famine, plague, and war conspired with Spanish extortion to reduce the city to the lowest depths of despair."[1]

So it was in Ferrara in 1496, frequently in Rome, and in numerous other places in Italy visited by calamity. Such revivals resulted not only in religious processions, scourging, or prayers, but in acts of genuine penitence and moral purification, such as the burning of objects of luxury and worldliness, the decrease of "blasphemy, prohibited games, sodomy, concubinage, the letting of houses to prostitutes or panderers, the opening of shops on feast days,"[2] not to mention the general improvement of conduct and social relationships in line with the Ten Commandments.

A general reaction against sensuality and materialism "was both natural and justifiable. Giovanni Dominici had introduced it at the beginning of the century, and Fra Antonino of San Marco had supported it, while Archbishop of Florence, with the authority of his blameless life, devoted himself to the service of his fellow men. . . . At the head of that movement stood Fra Girolamo Savonarola."[3]

Then came the ascetic Protestantism and the Reformation, soon followed by the Catholic Counter-Reformation (with its mysticism) and the Society of Jesus, which strove to purge the Catholic Church of its worldliness and sensuality and to bring about a revival of religion and morals.

When examined more closely, this process appears to be much more conspicuous in its regeneration and spiritualization than when observed in its general outlines. The dramatic scenes of penitence in the mass religious revivals of Renaissance Italy, as well as in the conduct of many an eminent man of the period (such as Michelangelo), well emphasize its power. The exhortations of an army of itinerant preachers, the spectacle of thousands of persons weeping and burning objects of luxury and worldliness, public confessions, the liberation of debtors from their debts and even from prison, the reconciliation of enemies and the cancelling of their vows of vengeance, the improvement of the condition of the poor, the recall of exiles to their native city, and a general reformation of the mores —these and similar phenomena were typical of the trend in question.

"Violent natures often resolved to enter a convent. . . . The tide of penitence flooded the city and the air resounded with the cry of the whole people: 'Misericordia!' . . . Then followed those solemn embracings and treaties of peace which even the previous bloodshed could not hinder. . . . The spirit of prophecy was unusually active. . . . Nor did [the preachers] scruple to attack princes, governments, the clergy [and the monks]."[4]

The secular and regular clergy, the rich and aristocratic, and many other persons devoted themselves to the reformation of monasteries and other institutions or their own respective groups.[5] Asceticism, mysticism, and intense religiosity manifested themselves in hundreds of other forms —in the fine arts and literature; in philosophy and religion; in social, economic, and political relationships; and in individual thought, feeling, and conduct.

The foregoing may be applied to many other religious

and moral revivals of the Middle Ages, and especially to those of the fourteenth and fifteenth centuries, when "calamities and indigence were especially grievous" and there was "chronic insecurity."[6]

Hence the conflicting characteristics of this era so far as religion and morality are concerned. Intense religiousness and spirituality, asceticism and withdrawal from the world, are found side by side with unreligiousness (including even the profanation of religious symbols for sexual purposes), violent brutality (in the revolutions of the period), sensualism, hedonism, and the *Carpe diem* attitude in the mentality, conduct, literature, arts, and general culture of the epoch. A strong sense of justice and honor coexisted with cynicism, cupidity, and greed.

"It is noteworthy that pious exhortations to think of death and the profane exhortations to make the most of youth almost meet."[7]

The domination of literature and the arts by the idea of death served two opposite purposes: with some it was a sign of turning to God; with others, a reminder of the transitoriness of life and therefore of the advisability of extracting from it all the pleasures it can yield.

To sum up. If all the known religious and moral revivals of this period are taken one by one, most of them are found to have occurred during or immediately after some severe crisis, or in consequence of the danger of such a crisis, and to have emerged and developed concurrently with a corresponding emergence and growth of irreligiosity, demoralization, and sensualism.

Methodism. If from the prolonged crisis of the Renaissance we pass to the somewhat less striking instance of religious and moral revivalism exemplified by *Methodism*, we observe that such a revival likewise occurs under the conditions of a chronic, though less acute, crisis, represented by perennial insecurity and misery, with its attendant lawlessness, crime, and vice. These were precisely the conditions under which Methodism originated and was successfully diffused.

Under what circumstances did John Wesley's movement arise in England, and in what social groups did it experience its initial success and failure? The answer is, in the England of the Industrial Revolution, which was marked by profligacy in the upper classes and by dire misery in the lower (laboring) classes.[8]

Wesley's first and principal successes were achieved among the colliers of Kingswood and the workers of Bristol. The reason is suggested by the following quotation.

"In the early eighteenth century [in England] the middle classes cultivated a very individualistic form of Protestantism, which they found quite compatible with the best sort of worldliness. Above them floated a sceptical aristocracy; and below lay a neglected heathendom. . . . In every town, besides the prosperous masters, journeymen and apprentices, lived a mass of beings, physically and morally corrupt, for whose bodies no one, and for whose souls only the Methodist had a thought to spare. . . . The conditions of existence among the neglected poor provided an environment wherein the transforming spiritual power of the Gospel was amazingly manifest [side by side with vice, brutality, and animalism]. The upper classes remained hostile to Methodism.

"[As a result of the evangelizing of the Methodists] vast areas of English life were saved from aridity or brutality. Religious passion supplanted licentiousness, and revels [though far from all revels] became revivals."[9]

John Wesley himself speaks of the colliers as "a people famous for neither fearing God nor regarding man; so ignorant of the things of God that they seem but one remove from the beasts."[10] On the other hand, he notes, "I fear, wherever riches have increased, the essence of religion has decreased in the same proportion."

Thus the revivalist movement achieved success among "the population of textile towns and [other] manufacturing areas exposed to a prolonged physical and moral calamity."[11]

Perhaps even more convincing is a study of Methodism in the frontier and pioneer settlements of America in 1800 and the following years.

"The scattered homesteads and generally unregulated conditions of pioneer life . . . brought about a loosening of social and religious controls. . . . The almost inevitable lawlessness was rendered still more certain by the fact that a number of rogues and scalawags had migrated along with the more reputable settlers. [Logan County, in Kentucky, became a veritable "rogues' harbor" for "murderers, horse thieves, highway thieves and counterfeiters."]

"[Add to this the] latent fear which was a part of the mental make-up of the pioneer. It was reinforced by actual and ever-present danger. . . . At any moment a man might suddenly meet his end by means of wild beasts or Indians. . . . The Kentucky settlers lived in a state of nerve-wracking guerrilla warfare."[12]

But "when [in Logan County] vice and lawlessness had attained their zenith there the clarion call to repentance evoked the most dramatic response."[13]

From 10,000 to 20,000 persons, from distances up to one hundred miles, came to the revival meetings (such as the Cane Ridge meeting). Bewailing their sins, singing, falling on the ground in ecstasy, groaning, and exhibiting all the external signs of a revivalist frenzy, these hosts of enthusiasts presented a distinct challenge to the lawlessness and lewdness of the unconverted element of the population.[14]

Later on, when these specific conditions had passed, such revivals declined. Eventually Methodism became conservative and respectable—well suited to the circumstances of the securely entrenched social groups. Its original characteristics have been retained, if anywhere, in the isolated mountain communities of Kentucky and Tennessee, where something akin to early American pioneer conditions still prevail.[15]

The Russian Soviet Revolution. Finally, let us turn to Soviet Russia in the years 1918-1922, the most destructive phase of the Russian Revolution—an era immediately preceded by the First World War and replete with such calamities as civil war, terrorism, famines, and devastating epidemics. In addition to the prevailing atheism and demoralization, one is struck by the opposite tendency—the mental, moral, and religious exaltation displayed by a certain element among the population, which produced a conspicuous number of moral heroes, as well as of religious martyrs, prophets, mystics, gnostics, and other devout adherents of the Christian faith. Many a professor who never before preached in the church, now began to do so. Former eminent Marxians and professors of political economy, like Sergius Bulgakoff, not only were converted to Christianity but became priests, monks, or ascetics. If the churches were less crowded than before the revolution, those who attended them were true believers, prepared to suffer martyrdom for their faith (as, indeed, many of them did).

2. *Ethico-Religious Regeneration in Times of Profound Crises*

We are now prepared to undertake an examination of the foremost crises in world history and to inquire whether they serve to support our hypothesis. The answer is again in the affirmative. Nay, more. This inquiry explains why *virtually all the great world religions (Christianity, Judaism, Buddhism, Hinduism, Confucianism, Taoism, Jainism, and the more spiritualized cults of ancient Egypt) arose and flourished under precisely the conditions afforded by such social crises.* Similarly, it throws light upon the origin of outstanding ethical and idealistic movements such as those of the Greek Cynics and Greco-Roman Stoics and the various forms of mysticism and other-worldliness, asceticism, anti-hedonism, and anti-utilitarianism, which were generated under crisis conditions—not in times of security and material well-being.

We shall begin our investigation with the phenomena of ethico-religious progress in ancient Egypt.

Ancient Egypt. For our purposes the first significant fact in Egyptian history is the emergence, at the very end of the predynastic or the beginning of the dynastic period (*ca.* 3300 or 3500 B. C., according to Breasted), of possibly the finest religious and moral doctrine that Egypt ever evolved—namely, the inscription "In the House of His Father Ptah-South-of-His-Wall."[16] The document presents a monotheistic and highly spiritual conception of God (Ptah) closely akin to the contemporary conception of Deity as the moral arbiter. The inscription declares that "mind or thought is the source of everything," that "life is given to the peaceful and death is given to the guilty," the peaceful being "he who does what is loved" and the guilty, "he who does what is hated." With this earliest written document "we are abruptly, and without any gradual transition stages, shifted out of the world of the nature gods into a ripe and developed civilization in which the organizers of religion and government are producing mature abstract thinking."[17]

If the dating of the document is correct, and if the end of the predynastic period was indeed marked by serious war crises and other catastrophes,[18] then its emergence is, according to our theory, quite comprehensible. In the ordeal of mixed calamities the Egyptian population underwent a catharsis and emerged (at least in part) more spiritual, religious, and moral than before—a truly remarkable step in the religious and moral progress of mankind!

The vigorous yet stabilized life of the Old Kingdom reveals, as the *Maxims of Ptahotep and Imhotep*[19] and other
documents show, a well-balanced and prudent moral conduct—a kind of Rotarian ethical sense avoiding both
marked spirituality and sensuality.[20] With the advent of
the profound crisis which marked the end of the Old
Kingdom (*ca.* 2500 B. C.), we note, side by side with intensified irreligiousness, demoralization, and sensualism,
the opposite trend—namely, a heightened religious, spiritual, and ethical sense. Some historians designate this transformation "the collapse of materialism."[21]

The "*Instruction* [of a certain Pharoah, Khety III] *to*
[his son] *Merikere*"[22] carries the moral maxims of the
balanced Ptahotep of the stable period much further. For
example, "More acceptable is the virtue of the upright man
than the ox of him who doeth iniquity"; "Be not harsh";
"Establish thy monument in the love of thee"; "Do
righteousness"; "Comfort the mourner, afflict not the
widow, deprive not a man of the possessions of his father
. . . . Slay not a man whose worth thou knowest." There
are repeated references to the righteous monotheistic God
and to retribution after death.[23]

"Put not thy trust in length of years: the judges [in the other
world] regard a lifetime as an hour. A man remaineth over after
death, and his deeds are placed beside him in heaps. It is for
eternity that one is there, and he is a fool that maketh light of
Them" (the judges of the dead).[24]

"One generation passeth on to another among men, and God,
who knoweth character, hath hidden himself. . . . He is one who
confoundeth by what is seen by the eyes. Let God be served in
his fashion, whether made of precious stones, or fashioned of
copper, like water replaced by water. . . . Well bestead are men,
the flocks of God; for he made heaven and earth. . . . God knows
of the one who does any service to him."[25]

Respecting the general effect of the crisis Breasted remarks:

"The tremendous impression produced by the final break-up of the Second Union [the Old Kingdom], after it had endured for a thousand years, . . . wrought powerfully upon the minds of the men who saw it. Thinking men were thrown back from the consideration of outward splendours to the contemplation of inner values."[26]

"The futility of reliance on material agencies became more and more evident after the end of the Second Union. . . . The sixty-mile pyramid cemetery lay in silent desolation, deeply encumbered with sand half hiding the ruins of massive architecture, of fallen architraves and prostrate colonnades, a solitary waste where only the slinking figure of the jackal . . . suggested the futile protection of the old mortuary gods of the desert."[27]

The reaction was, on the one hand, disillusionment, skepticism, sensualism, and hedonism; on the other, the intensification and spiritualizing of religion and the purification of moral conduct. This comes out in several documents, such as the pessimistic *Dispute with His Soul of One Who Is Tired of Life*.[28] If the *Dispute* is an expression of hopeless pessimism and disillusionment in its earlier parts, in its fourth part it is correctly described as "the earliest Book of Job."[29] The human soul finds salvation, justice, and the Kingdom of God in the world beyond death,—in the transcendental City of God, one might say, —to which the *Dispute* alludes as "yonder."

"He who is yonder shall seize the culprit, inflicting punishment of wickedness on the doer of it. He who is yonder shall stand in the celestial barque. . . . He who is yonder shall be a wise man who has not been repelled, praying to Re when he speaks."[30]

Here, then, we have possibly the first specimen of theological philosophy—the concept that the empirical city of man is full of vice and injustice; that it is fragile; that even death is better than such an empirical life; that the wise man is but a mere pilgrim in it; and that he finds his permanent abode only in the City of God ("yonder"), where he shares the "lot of the blessed dead," as companions of the Sun God.[31]

In *The Lamentation of Khekhepere-soneb*[32] the religious and moral indignation at the iniquities of his time is still more intense, and the call for moral and social justice is still more insistent. Then come messianic prophets who plead for religious and ethical purification in even clearer and more eloquent terms. They castigate the prevalent social injustice toward the lower and peasant classes (as in *The Eloquent Peasant*[33]) with the demand:

"Destroy injustice; bring about justice. Bring about every good thing; destroy every evil thing. . . . For justice is for eternity. It descendeth with him that doeth it into the grave. . . . Such is the uprightness of the word of God. . . . Speak the truth, do the truth. For it is great, it is mighty, it is enduring."[34]

They rebuke the king and the ruling class to their very faces, as in the *Admonitions of an Egyptian Sage* (Ipuwer) and the *Prophecy of Neferrohu*.[35] These documents breathe a moral and religious spirit resembling that of the Hebrew prophets, concluding with an announcement of the imminence of a Saviour and the establishment of his kingdom of righteousness.

"He brings cooling to the flame. It is said he is the shepherd of all men. There is no evil in his heart. . . . Righteousness shall return to its place; unrighteousness shall be cast out."[36]

Various other contemporary documents corroborate our hypothesis.[37]

"It is quite clear that conscience has become something more than an influence on the conduct of the individual. It had become . . . a powerful social force . . . and a policy of social justice had become part of the very framework of government."[38]

One of the feudal lords declares, in his tomb inscription:

"There was no citizen's daughter whom I misused, there was no widow whom I afflicted, there was no peasant whom I evicted, there was no herdsman I expelled. . . . There was none wretched in my community, there was none hungry in my time."[39]

When the Middle Kingdom was consolidated, and order, prosperity, and internal peace returned, religious and moral aspirations notably waned, giving place to a set of prudent, balanced, wholly utilitarian, utterly mundane, and somewhat arrogant traditional beliefs and rules of conduct, illustrated by the *Instruction of Duaf to his son*.[40] Here is no spirit of messianic prophecy, scant appeal to justice, and no denunciation of iniquity. Our bureaucrat-scribe is perfectly satisfied with himself and with his mundane advantages. "A man descants on the supreme advantages of learning, chiefly as a means of escaping from hard work." To him "learning had no charm in itself; it was to be pursued solely because of the advantages and rewards [—because] it enabled its possessor to be an unproductive parasite." "Briefly [in the view of the scribe], God made Egypt for the scribe to exploit."[42] In other literary documents of the consolidated kingdom we encounter amusing stories, tales of adventure and mystery (such as the *Story of the Shipwrecked Sailor*, the *Story of Sinuhe*, the *Tales of King Khufu and the Magicians*),[43] or hymns to the splendor and might of the Pharoahs (for instance, the *Hymn to Senusert*). They all reflect a somewhat hedonistic and utilitarian society bent on amusement.

The picture changes with the close of the Middle Kingdom and the advent of the second intermediate period—another era of profound crisis, preceding the New Empire. While this epoch affords a scanty basis for historical reconstruction, owing to the invasion of Egypt by the Hyksos kings, the few surviving documents preserved from the pre-Hyksos period testify to the piety of the usurping Pharaohs, Neferhotep and Khenzer, who restored the cult of Osiris and cleansed the temple at Abydos, and suggest the prevalence of an acute religious sense, despite its conservatism and traditionalism. This attitude is indicated also by the Egyptian explanation of the Hyksos invasion as an "act of God,"[44] and by the restoration of the cult of Amen-Ra, with its temples and priesthood, by the first Pharaohs (the Aahmes) of the victorious Eighteenth Dynasty immediately after the overthrow of the Hyksos kings and the termination of the crisis.

"Here we have the beginning of that process which resulted at last in Amen and his priesthood becoming the supreme power in the land, with greater resources and authority than even Pharaoh possessed."[45]

When the New Empire became firmly established, rich, and powerful, and successfully expanded into a world empire, religiosity and spirituality once again underwent a decline. Indeed, the zenith of the New Empire—the period of the "Golden Emperor," Amenhotep III—reveals the resplendent epicurean atmosphere of "the lust of the flesh, the lust of the eye, and the pride of life."[46]

Immediately after Amenhotep III the decline of the first stage of the New Empire set in—a crisis which induced, in turn, a religious and moral revolution led by the revolutionary king Akhenaten.[47] Akhenaten's new system (though it miscarried because of the violence of the measures adopted) represented a revitalization and spiritualization of the existing religion and morality, with its ritualism, magic, and barren traditionalism. Although "the criminal Akhenaten" was overthrown by the priesthood of Amon, "the ideas and the tendencies which had given birth to the revolution . . . did not wholly disappear"; and the restored religion of Amon assumed a more spiritual, mystical, and ethical character. "An age of personal piety and inner aspiration to God now dawned among the masses,"[48] as attested by various documents of this critical period.[49]

"After the fall of the Egyptian Empire in the twelfth century B.C. the forces of life both within and without were exhausted and had lost their power to stimulate the moral thinking of Egypt to any further vital development. Stagnation and deadly inertia fell like a stupor upon the once vigorous life of the nation."[50]

However, throughout its long centuries of decline and trying conditions—even after the restoration of *ca.* 700 B. C.—Egypt preserved its existence in the form of a sacerdotal, theocratic state buttressed by the religion and ethics of the Old Kingdom. In other words, when every other expedient failed, the nation preserved its precarious existence by virtue of a social form dominated and permeated by religion.

Thus all the profound crises of Egyptian history serve to corroborate our thesis that social cataclysms generate two opposing trends—that of sensualization on the one hand, and of spiritualization on the other.

China. The thesis is equally well corroborated by the history of Chinese culture. *Confucianism and Taoism* in China emerged and grew during a period of marked crisis and anarchy. The year 518 B. C. and the following years were attended by violent revolutions in Confucius' native state of Lu, and the greater part of China was in disorder.[51] The same conditions attended the rise of Taoism.

As regards the turbulent fourth century B.C.,

"The state of China had waxed worse and worse during the interval that elapsed between Confucius and Mencius [372-289 B.C.]. The elements of disorganization which were rife in the time of the earlier sage had gone on to produce their natural results." Feudalization, incessant internecine wars and other internal disorders, irreligiousness and demoralization were typical of this epoch.[52]

On the one hand we observe extreme sensualism and hedonism, including the ethico-religious nihilism represented by the ideology of Yang-chu; on the other, a pronounced revival of Taoism headed by Chuang-tsze, the formulation of a moral philosophy of universal love by Moh-tih, and, finally, a sublimation of Confucianism under the leadership of Mencius.[53]

In the subsequent history of China we encounter, fairly regularly, further examples of the basic uniformity of diversification and polarization. The periods of acute crisis are almost invariably characterized by the coexistence of positive and negative ethico-religious movements—in the former case either a revitalization of Taoism (less frequently of Confucianism) or the introduction and diffusion of transcendental religions derived from other countries, such as Buddhism and (in lesser degree) Parsiism, Gnosticism, Manichaeanism, and Christianity. Per contra, the eras of comparative stability and material well-being produced an attenuation of Taoism and Buddhism, and, in particular, a ritualistic and positivistic Neo-Confucianism and the dissemination of various forms of positivism, agnosticism, and utilitarian morality.

The phenomena of polarization are well illustrated by the crises associated with dynastic changes. These interregnum periods invariably entailed feudalization, internal anarchy, foreign wars, famine, and pestilence and were not infrequently followed by the conquest of China by foreign invaders, such as the Mongols and Manchus.[54]

With the fall of the Chin dynasty and the accession of the Han dynasty in 206 B. C.[55] the familiar ethico-religious reaction of both types once more set in. The positive religious and moral movement was enriched also by the introduction and rather rapid diffusion of Buddhism (Chinese sources record the presence of Buddhist missionaries already in 217 B. C.).

The next anarchic period (with external wars) dawned at the beginning of the first century of our era, signalized especially by the protracted civil war of the years 9 to 23 A.D.

The first half of the century witnessed the ascendancy of mystico-transcendental Buddhism, which in 61 or 65 A.D. was declared to be the third state religion of China.

Another era of anarchy and social calamity was inaugurated at the close of the Han dynasty, lasting roughly from 184 to 280, and embracing a crucial peasant revolution, the civil wars of three pretenders to the throne, feudalization, and the concomitant factors of famine and pestilence. It is characterized at once by a revitalization of Taoism and Buddhism (and also, to some extent, of Confucianism) and by the contrary currents of unreligiousness and demoralization.[56] The revitalization of religion went so far that even certain of the emperors undertook to preach the doctrines of Taoism or Buddhism. Edicts such as that of the Emperor Ming-ti (227-239), issued after the eclipse of the sun in 233, demonstrate this "apocalyptic" mentality explicitly.

"We have heard, says the Emperor, that if a sovereign is remiss in government, God terrifies him by calamities and portents. These are divine reprimands sent to recall him to a sense of duty. . . . [Declaring that he had failed in a proper discharge of his duties, he continues that it] therefore behoves Us to issue commands for personal reformation, in order to avert the impending calamity. [The implied relationship between God and man suggests that of a father chastising his son.] Do ye governors of districts, and other high officers of the State, seek, rather, to rectify your own hearts; and if anyone can devise means to make up for Our shortcoming, let him submit his proposals to the throne."[57]

The fourth, fifth, and sixth centuries and the beginning of the seventh constituted the *Chinese Middle Ages* (as Grousset and other historians call them), with a high tide of anarchy and other catastrophes, interrupted only by short intervals of comparative order.[58] Like the European Middle Ages, this period was religious-minded, with Buddhism and Taoism in the ascendant; with Confucianism on the decline; with the introduction of foreign religions,

such as Mazdaism (or Zoroastrianism), Manichaeanism, and
Nestorian Christianity (in the sixth and seventh centuries);
and with an enormous concentration of social thought on
various theological and moral problems, which occupied
the central place in the thought and conduct of the population.[59] Some of the Emperors, such as Wu-ti (502-549),
having abolished capital punishment, actually retired to
monasteries, or relinquished the throne and devoted themselves to Taoism and religious duties. The state itself (with
Nanking as the capital) was transformed into a sort of
Buddhist theocracy organized and ruled in accordance with
the principles of Buddhism. Between 581 and 618 the Sui
dynasty made Buddhism the official religion. "No fewer
than 3792 new temples were built; 106,580 statues of gold,
silver, sandalwood, ivory, and stone were made for the
sanctuaries; thousands of old temples and statues were
restored." Art was primarily religious in character and was
largely in the hands of the monks.[60]

Omitting the revolution of 755-763, let us pass to the
next epoch signalized by major upheavals (revolutions,
wars, and the like), which began in 875, at the close of the
T'ang dynasty, and continued, with brief interruptions,
until the establishment of the Sung dynasty, in 960. It was
distinguished by the familiar positive and negative ethico-
religious movements. The positive reaction manifested
itself—in addition to clashes between Manichaeanism,
Mazdaism, Nestorian Christianity, Taoism, Confucianism,
and other faiths—in new currents of Chinese religious and
philosophical thought; in the decay of Buddhism, and in a
revival of Confucianism. Whereas during earlier centuries
Buddhism had constituted a distinct spiritualizing and
moralizing force, by this time it had become dull, ritualistic, conservative, and parasitical. The eminent scholar and
mathematician Fu Yi had already noted in his memoirs
in 624:

"Its doctrines are full of absurdities and extravagances. Its disciples now spend their lives in laziness. . . . If their habits are different from ours, the reason . . . is their desire to be free from taxes and other duties. By their reveries and trances they stimulate the simpletons to hunt for a chimerical felicity, to the neglect of their duties and the laws of the country. This sect has now more than 100,000 bonzes and as many female nuns unmarried. It is in the interest of the State to force them to marry. Owing to their unproductive laziness they are the burden of the society."

Similarly, the celebrated philosopher and exponent of Neo-Confucianism, Han Yu (768-824), known also as Han Wen-kung, stressed the fact that "Buddhism does not understand the value of the social ties binding together the father and the son" (and, through this filial piety, all the members of society).[61]

Similar polar movements characterize the subsequent transition period marked by the end of the Sung dynasty and by the Mongolian conquest, and the transition period signalized by the fall of the Ming dynasty and by the Manchu conquest, which inaugurated the Ching dynasty—a line of rulers that lasted until the revolution of 1911.

If we now turn to the periods of relative stability, order, and material well-being, we find the situation no less instructive. In all such epochs we note the *revival and re-establishment of Confucianism* (frequently an erotic perversion of Taoism or else a comfortable philosophy of *dolce far niente* and of drifting with the tide), *together with various positivistic, empirical, and agnostic currents of philosophical thought which, in the latter stages of each period of stability, tend to become more and more positivist and agnostic, and, in the field of moral conduct, increasingly relativistic, hedonistic, and utilitarian, finally reaching the nadir of downright religious and moral cynicism and nihilism.* As was the case in Egypt, ethico-religious mentality and conduct grow more "balanced," more "sensible," "more respectable," and more mundane.

Religion and ethics become better organized, but at the expense of lowered intensity, zeal, and aspiration. The contrasting juxtaposition of prophets and messiahs, saints and martyrs, on the one hand, and libertines and profligates on the other, is replaced by a "balanced," "decent," "practical" Babbitry or Rotarianism, whose adherents grudgingly yield unto both God and Caesar his due. At a later stage this "sensible" ethico-religious Babbittry begins to disintegrate, and, as the next crisis approaches, finally gives place to downright unreligiousness and moral anarchy.

From this standpoint it is perfectly comprehensible why, in such periods of stability in Chinese history, Confucianism, in its varied Neo-Confucianist forms, has almost invariably revived. Even in its pure form, Confucianism, in contradistinction to Taoism, is primarily a noble system of practical morals and practical religious mentality,[62] rooted predominantly in this world and only partly in "Heaven." As such it contains fewer elements of transcendentalism than Taoism, Buddhism, or most of the other great religions. Its practicality is the reason why in periods of crisis, when religions of "high voltage" were in demand, it declined, and why in periods of stability it invariably revived, in a still more mundane, ritualistic, and utilitarian form of Neo-Confucianism.

One has to bear in mind that each revival of Neo-Confucianism represented a sharp deviation from simon-pure Confucianism. What Hu Shih says of Neo-Confucianism under the Han dynasty may be said of it in all subsequent revivals.

"Confucianism was always a timely system of teaching; it always caught up the fashions [and superstitions] of the age. . . . It is to be expected that the New Confucianism established under the patronage of a ruler of such multifarious and insatiable credulity and under the leadership of such equally credulous scholars—that this New Confucianism should be a great synthetic religion into which were fused all the elements of popular superstition and state worship, rationalized somewhat in order to eliminate a few of the most untenable elements and thinly covered up under the guise of Confucian and pre-Confucian classics in order to make them appear respectable and authoritative. In this sense the New Confucianism of the Han Empire was truly the national religion of China. It was a great conglomeration of popular beliefs and practices of the time through a thin and feeble process of rationalization. . . . One may easily see that the New Confucianism of the Han Empire was quite different from the agnostic humanism of Confucius or the democratic political philosophy of Mencius."[63]

The same author clearly explains the repeated perversion (if not the total elimination) of Taoism in such periods of stability.

"The long years of revolution and war had devastated the country, and the new empire found everything in ruins. . . . What was needed was not positive and meddlesome reforms, but peace, and order to allow the people to live and recuperate. So the early statesmen of Han practiced the policy of peace and *laissez faire*, and scholars and thinkers tended to exalt the philosophy of Taoism, which taught non-action and non-interference with Nature."[64]

In other cases Taoism was perverted into an exotic justification of the most refined, but most antisocial and decadent, forms of erotic aestheticism and sensualism.

Side by side with this repeated emergence of Neo-Confucianism and of a partly perverted Taoism (which reminds us of the similar revivals, in ever-modified forms, which took place in Egypt under the Old Kingdom, during the stable stages of the Middle and New Empires, and particularly during the later stages of Egyptian history), the stable periods of Chinese history generated various positivistic, agnostic, materialistic, and utilitarian currents of thought, followed by many social reform movements, including Chinese brands of socialism, communism, and totalitarianism. The reformistic activities of Wang-An-shi (1068-1085 A.D.) and Ts'ai Ching are typical of these.

Thus, not only the periods of profound crisis but also those of comparative stability and order in the history of China well support our theory of the polarization of ethico-religious mentality and conduct in times of acute stress, as well as the thesis that periods of crisis have regularly generated new and loftier religious and moral standards or have led to their revival in a more exalted form. Purified by the ordeal of suffering, a part of the population, defying all the forces of calamity, rises to higher and nobler levels of religious and ethical thought, feeling, and conduct.

India. Let us continue the verification of our contention in the light of the History of India. The following summary of alternate crises and stable periods in the principal states will suffice for our purposes.

Case No. 1. The first relevant fact for our theory is that the religion and morality of the *Rig Veda* (not of the later *Yajur-Veda*)[65] emerged during and immediately after the profound and protracted crisis of 2000-1000 B.C., which culminated in the great war of *ca.* 1000 B.C., described later on in the *Mahabharata.* This pre-Vedic and early Vedic period was attended by numerous struggles between Hindus and Jains, Brahmanas and Kshatriyas, Kurus and Pandavos, Aryans and non-Aryans, and Vasista and Visvamitra groups, and by various other internal crises. "It was an age of light and darkness, peace and unrest, progress and decline, prosperity and adversity caused by long and terrible famines," evolving religions of rationalism, theism, atheism, and materialism. Prior to 1400 B.C.[66] some of the politics and moral practices were corrupt to the extreme. In brief, the religion and morality of the *Rig Veda* evolved under the familiar conditions of intense and prolonged crisis, with its polarization of ethico-religious consequences.

Case No. 2. The next instance of extraordinary revival

and ennoblement of religious thought and ethical standards is presented by the period from the sixth to the fourth century B.C. This era witnessed the rise of Buddhism (Gautama Buddha's chief activity fell between 532 and 487 B.C.) and of Jainism, represented by Mahavira (whose activity fell between 497 and 467 B.C.). Moreover, the period produced a notable spiritualization of the Vedic religion and morality, which by 600 B.C. had become "a mere bundle of lifeless rites and tenets."[67] This spiritualization manifested itself in the development of the sublime philosophical and ethical thought of the *Upanishads*, the *Bhagavatas*, and the *Saiva* sect, and then in the nucleus of the *Mahabharata* and *Ramayana*—to cite but the most epoch-making steps in the evolution of the Vedic system of religion and morality.

What is still more significant is the fact that these positive trends operated as a counterpoise to the atheism, materialism, and sensualism of the age.

These three religious movements [Buddhism, Jainism, and the currents of thought associated with the Upanishads and Bhagavatas] were not isolated events, but merely the product of the age. The bold Upanishadic speculations were the outcome of a critical spirit which revolted against the mechanical ceremonials of the Brahmana age. But freedom of thought and a spirit of inquiry once aroused are not likely to observe any limit, and it is no wonder that the sixth and fifth centuries B.C. saw a great outburst of intellectual activity which defied all traditions. . . . The result was a wild growth of new views, . . . sects, . . . religions. Some of these . . . proved a victim to unbridled passions and lack of all moral or intellectual discipline. Thus while the tide of free speculation led on the one hand to the rise of important sects like Buddhism, Jainism, Saivism, and Bhagavatism, it culminated on the other in a system like that of Charvaka or immoral practices masquerading in the name of religion."[68]

If, now, we examine the sociocultural conditions that produced such an extraordinary polarization of ethico-religious thought and conduct, we find that they were highly critical and catastrophic. These centuries witnessed repeated invasions of India—by Cyrus and Darius, Alexander the Great and his successors, and other conquerors. There were incessant wars among the Hindu political states, especially the struggles for the supremacy of the Kingdom of Magadha and those of the Nanda kings of Pataliputra. There were also chronic revolts against the supremacy of the Brahman caste, against various rulers, and in the interest of other causes. Finally, devastating hailstorms and swarms of locusts, famines, pestilence, and like disasters abounded.[69]

Miscellaneous Cases. Instead of going systematically into case after case of the subsequent periods of alternate crisis and well-being in India, we may accept as roughly valid the following statement of a historian and then confront it with the ethico-religious behavior and thinking of the population involved.

"Amidst all this ceaseless flux of the political units that constituted India throughout all these ages, there stands out one fact, namely, that whenever great empires were in existence, such as the Maurya or Gupta or even that of Harsha, India enjoyed not only internal tranquility and the blessings of a good administration, but also security on the frontiers. Whenever this imperial unity was wanting, it follows as unmistakeably that the anarchical elements inside [and foreign invasions and wars] asserted themselves."[70]

"Every interval of peace and prosperity under a strong central government was quickly followed by internal dissension which opened the door to the invader, always ready for an opportunity to loot the prosperous cities of the Indian plains."[71]

Here we see the same uniformity which was stressed in connection with the history of China and of Egypt. Let us, on the one hand, take the periods of stability and prosperity of the Indian empires at their virile stage, such as the empires of the Maurya or the Gupta, and observe the contemporary ethico-religious situation; on the other hand, let us take the anarchistic periods of the interregnum between such empires and note the ethico-religious phenomena that prevailed in these calamitous times.

When such a systematic inductive study is undertaken, we find the uniformity very closely akin to that encountered in the history of China. The eras of prosperity, peace, and stability regularly produce a revitalization of Brahmanism or Hinduism (like Neo-Confucianism in China), but a Brahmanism or Hinduism stripped, to a considerable extent, of the intense transcendentalism, lofty ethical tone, and deep philosophical thought of the Upanishads. It is formalized and ritualized, made "practical" and "utilitarian"—"handy" for the authorities and the dominant caste, as well as for the superstitious masses. In a few instances the place of Brahmanism or Hinduism was taken by Buddhism (under Kanishka, for example), "adjusted" along similar lines to the conditions of prosperity.

Side by side with such revivals of the traditional religion and ethics of India, the periods of prosperity are marked by an upsurge of secular philosophical thought and literature—positivism, skepticism, utilitarianism, materialism, and sensualism. They are relatively devoid of the sharp antitheses typical of crisis conditions. In brief, the ethico-religious thought and conduct of these stable periods are "sensible," "balanced," and well organized, but shallow.

Conversely, times of calamity reveal the juxtaposition of extreme libertines and of fervent ascetics and God-intoxicated devotees, with their respective ideologies, and a decline of the "moderate," "sensible," and "practical" beliefs and norms typical of periods of stability.

Such is the uniformity. As applied to conditions of prosperity, we encounter it in the virile stage of the Maurya, Gupta, Harsha, and a few subsequent empires.

Thus the first—the virile—phase of the Maurya Empire

(*ca.* 321-186 B.C.) was prosperous, comparatively stable, and orderly.[72] Since its establishment was brought about by revolts against Alexander the Great's successors, led by Chanakya (a Brahman) and Chandragupta, we are not surprised that Brahmanism and Jainism should have been favored and Buddhism (until the time of Asoka) somewhat discredited. In the daily schedule of Chandragupta's activities there was not much time devoted to religion.[73] The administration was firm and strong, though harsh. "When crime did occur, it was repressed with terrible severity."[74] "The sound doctrine is inculcated that 'all undertaking depends upon finance.' Hence foremost attention shall be paid to the Treasury."[75] "As regards daily life, we find the public side of it sufficiently gay."[76] Gambling and other vices prevail, though in moderation. Family life is somewhat lax. Nothing suggests either a keen religious or moral sense or pronounced depravity. The picture of ethicoreligious life is relatively sober and balanced—devoid of both extremes.

The situation temporarily changes in the second phase of the Maurya Empire, during the reign of the great Asoka (*ca.* 272-232 B.C.). Soon after he ascended the throne (in 256 B.C.) a devastating war broke out, during the course of which more than 100,000 were slain, 150,000 were carried away as prisoners, and still greater numbers of the noncombatant population perished from war, famine, pestilence, and similar calamities.

Overcome with remorse for the horrors of his policy of blood and iron, Asoka now espouses Buddhism, becomes ordained as a member of the Buddhist Sangha, and devotes the rest of his life to religious, charitable, and humanistic activities, building thousands of temples and hospitals, develops stimulating missionary activities, helping the needy, rendering his administration "faultless," and insists upon the "life hereafter" as the main objective of human beings. ("His Majesty thinks nothing of much importance save that which concerns the next world.") There was a tremendous upsurge of ethico-religious activity induced by the misery bred by the recent war.[77]

The years 183-86 B.C. marked the decline of the Maurya Empire. It was succeeded, with short interruptions, by "five hundred years of chronic misery" (up to about 300 A.D.). Revolutions and wars, invasions by Greeks, Bactrians, Parthians, Scythians, incessant dynastic changes, feudalization, swept over the country. In conformity with our hypothesis, we observe the polarized movements of acute religiousness and demoralization. The first manifests itself in an intense revival of purified Brahmanism and Buddhism; in the division of Buddhism into the Mahayana and Hinayana branches (A.D. 78); and in the rise of several other ideational and transcendental religions and philosophies. (It is a highly symptomatic detail that a more moderate, less austere, Mahayana Buddhism flourished chiefly in the more stable areas of India. It was a variety of utilitarian Neo-Buddhism, analogous to Neo-Confucianism.)

Per contra, we note the "rise of a debased element in the religions of the day which is generally referred to as Tantrikism. Though more closely associated with the Sakta sect, some of its characteristics, such as magical beliefs, degraded erotic practices—all leading to gross indecency and lax morality—are common features observed (in many sects of the time). Some Tantra indulge in theories and practices which are revolting and horrible."[79]

With the establishment of the Gupta Empire (*ca.* 320-500 A.D.) order, stability, prosperity, and external well-being returned. This era was the Golden Age of the fine arts, literature, and science. On the other hand, it exhibits a notable lowering of the intensity of ethico-religious life, as well as a decrease of extreme depravity and irreligiousness. None of the Gupta monarchs was preoccupied with any religion. Buddhism underwent a sharp decline. A more practical form of Neo-Brahmanism (akin to Neo-Confucianism) gained the ascendancy. The administration was so firm and strong that no serious crime wave, revolt, or similar disturbance assailed the country. It was an age of "balanced" ethico-religious behavior.[80]

The centuries following the fall of the Gupta Empire—apart from the brief period of the Harsha dynasty (ca. 606-647)—were disturbed by civil and external wars, incessant invasions and conquests (by Huns, Moslems, Turks, and Mongols), pestilences, and famines. (There were several terrible famines, such as those of ca. 700, 919-918,—when the land became "like one great burial ground,"—and 1099.) "Few centuries can rival the Kashmir . . . kings and queens [and those of some other feudalized regions of India], who gloried in shameless lust, fiendish cruelty, and pitiless misrule."[81]

Numerous sects sprang up which worshiped the most repulsive deities, with drunken and erotic orgies and grotesque rites. A considerable proportion of the scholars became skeptics and agnostics. On the other hand, Brahmanism, purified and deepened, revived (under Shankara and other leaders), whereas Buddhism declined.

"The old simple creed of Buddha, with its lofty morality, had become cluttered by forms and ceremonies to such an extent that the true religion was completely lost sight of. . . . Corruption and superstition had insidiously crept into the church, and the luxurious and comfortable lives led by some of the Buddhist monks had shaken the confidence of the people and undermined its prestige."[82]

Such a religion evidently cannot flourish in times of calamity. A number of sects of highly transcendental character appeared. All kinds of gods were worshiped. Hindu society was stirred by such religious reformers as Ramanuja Acharya. Pilgrimages became common.[83] In brief, there was a notable concentration of social thought upon the problems of ethics and religion.

It lies outside the scope of this work to follow systematically the subsequent periods of alternate crisis and comparative stability in connection with the law of polarization. Suffice it to say that the highly complicated history of India in later centuries (with its Moslem rulers, the "Slave Kings," the local dynasties of the Khilji and Tughluq, the period of drastic disintegration followed by the establishment of the Mogul Empire, and so on, up to the English domination) affords abundant corroboration of our theory, provided proper consideration is given to the Mohammedan religion itself during the time of the Moslem domination.

One more remark about these centuries. In spite of the ups and downs of the ethico-religious life of India, its intensity has remained rather high, with a corresponding moral and religious debasement at the opposite pole. India is at once "God-intoxicated" and "devil-intoxicated." Considering that it has been in a chronic state of calamity, interrupted by only brief periods of stability and material well-being, such a high intensity of both trends is quite comprehensible—indeed, inevitable—in the light of our hypothesis.

Judaism. Let us now cite a few additional historical cases of polarization. Since they are much better known, a brief indication will suffice.

The history of Hebrew religion and morality again testifies to the validity of our hypothesis. As W. F. Albright rightly remarks,

"Real spiritual progress can only be achieved through catastrophe and suffering, reaching new levels after the profound catharsis which accompanies major upheavals. . . . Every such period of mental and physical agony . . . yields different social patterns and deeper spiritual insights."[84]

"The question of theodicy always comes to the fore during prolonged times of crisis, when human emotions are winnowed and purified by sustained catharsis. So it was in Egypt between 2200 and 2000 B.C., so it was in Babylonia after 1200 B.C., and so it was among the Jews between 700 and 500 B.C."[85]

Such movements, declares another historian, "appear usually in periods of calamity, of the contradiction between ideals and reality, divine promises and actual slavery."[86]

Let us examine a few of the phenomena in question.

The first case is represented by Moses' religion and moral commandments. They were associated with a period of acute crises in the life history of Israel (including the escape from slavery in Egypt, the exodus, wandering in the desert, wars, and the like). The pre-Mosaic religion and ethics of Israel were very different from the Mosaic code, which constitutes an enormous step in the direction of mono-theism and the spiritualization and purification of the earlier religion and mores.[87] It is hardly necessary to add that this trend was preceded or accompanied by flagrant impiety and sensualism, as illustrated by Sodom and Gomorrah.

The second case concerns the charismatic leaders—the Judges, Samuel, Saul (*ca.* 1020-1000 B.C.), David (*ca.* 1000-960 B.C.), etc. Their emergence, with their exercise of purely moral authority and their message of divine grace, coincided with grave crises in the life of Israel.

The third case is furnished by the time of Solomon, a period characterized by security, prosperity, and material well-being. A refined epicureanism prevails, side by side with ritualistic and formalized religious observances. There is little evidence of religiosity.[88]

The fourth case is presented by the catastrophes of the

ensuing centuries, which began with the division of Solomon's empire into two states in 925 B.C. and continued, with minor vicissitudes, down to the fourth century B.C., resulting in complete loss of independence, the destruction of Jerusalem, the Babylonian and other captivities, and similar disasters of the gravest kind. The era discloses both ethico-religious trends—the positive and the negative—in acute form. The positive reaction is represented by the prophetic movement, which brought the religion and morals of Israel to their culminating point. This line of prophets began, in the ninth century B.C., with Elijah and Elisha, who were followed by Amos, Hosea, and Isaiah in the eighth. Then came Jeremiah; during the captivity, Ezekiel, the author of the book of Job,[89] and the Isaiah of Deuteronomy; and later such prophets and ethico-religious and political leaders as Nehemiah and Ezra. On the other hand, idolatry, sensuality, and even human sacrifice abounded.[90]

The fifth case is taken from the third century B.C., when the conditions in Judea were somewhat less catastrophic. As a result, "this comparatively quiet situation weakened the exclusiveness of the Jews. We hear much less about Messianic expectations and find in Jerusalem a large faction prepared to accept Hellenization."[91] A comparatively mild moral and religious stoicism, as reflected by the teachings of Antigonus of Socho, Ben Sira and Enoch, on the one hand, and on the other, by the idealistic epicureanism of *Ecclesiastes*, marks the end of the third century B.C.[92]

Finally, it is to be noted that here, as in Egypt, the last stage of the independent or semi-independent Jewish state and the last phase of the world mission of Judaism[93] assumed the form of a *theocracy*. This does not mean that theocracy necessarily ushers in the dénouement, but that, when all other forms of sociopolitical organization fail, the theocratic form enables a given society to survive, and—what is much more important—preserves the essence of its culture, to be transmitted to posterity.

Additional cases. To the foregoing cases we may add three more, derived from other religions and cultures.

One is from the Hittite culture of the thirteenth century B.C. An extant document tells of a Hittite king who confessed his unjustifiable attack upon the Egyptian Empire and attributed to his moral obliquity the subsequent outbreak of pestilence as a punishment sent by God—another instance of calamity and remorse followed by purification through the enactment of better laws and the recognition of the sacredness of moral obligations.[94]

Another case is drawn from the history of Babylonia. The period between the reigns of Sargon of Akkad and Hammurabi was replete with civil disorders, wars, and calamities of various kinds. The surviving documents urge the improvement of conduct through greater justice and recommend the quest for immortality (or the nearest thing to it).[95]

After *ca.* 1200 B.C. there ensued another era of grave social stress, which produced a remarkable document, known as "the Babylonian Job," disclosing the prevalence of injustice, sensuality, and general misery. While the conclusion of the work is not so sublime as the Biblical Job's "God hath given and God hath taken, Blessed be the name of Lord," it is nevertheless highly exalted in view of the essentially commercial culture of Babylon. The document voices a profound belief in "the inscrutability of divine justice and the need for the most complete humility and self-abnegation in one's relation to God."[96]

Greco-Roman culture and Christianity. The last final corroboration is afforded by the Greco-Roman culture signalized by the rise of Stoicism and Epicureanism and, in particular, of Christianity. We have already witnessed the development, in the Greco-Roman world, of the positive and negative trends elicited by the cataclysms of the fourth and following centuries B.C. The process culminated, on the one hand, in a further intensification of unreligiousness, moral nihilism, and depravity between the first century B.C. and the fourth century A.D.; on the other, in the rise of various Oriental religions, of Stoicism, Neo-Platonism, and Neo-Pythagorianism, which eventually succumbed to Christianity, with its belief in the Kingdom of God, its indifference toward the values of this world, and its asceticism and monasticism.

Renan aptly summarizes the conditions under which the Apocalyptic mentality of Christianity originated.

"When one reads the Apocalypse without knowing the date and the key to it, the book would appear to be the work of a most capricious and individualistic imagination; but when its strange vision is replaced by the picture of the period between Nero and Vespassian, when the Roman Empire experienced its most acute crisis, the Apocalypse will be found in marvelous accord with the popular mind of the period. . . . Blood was flowing everywhere. Nero's death opened the period of the civil wars. The struggle of the legions in Gallia was horrible. Galilee was the arena of an extraordinary extermination; the war with the Parthians was extraordinary homicidal. The cruelty of the military and civil mores banished all pity from the world. . . . To the massacres was added famine. In the year 68 the supplies of Alexandria were insufficient. In March, 69, the inundation of the Tiber was exceedingly disastrous. . . . A sudden flood from the sea covered mourning Lycia. In 65 a horrible pestilence afflicted Rome; in the fall there were thirty thousands dead. In the same year an enormous conflagration destroyed Lyons; Campania was ravaged by tornadoes whose devastation spread to the gates of Rome. The natural order appeared to be upturned. . . . What, however, created the greatest terror were earthquakes. . . . There was the terrible eruption of Vesuvius in 79. On February 5, 63, Pompeii was almost ruined by the trembling of the earth. . . . Certain areas like Philadelphia experienced almost daily shocks. In the year A.D. 17, fourteen cities were demolished. . . . The years 23, 33, 37, 46, 51, and 53 there were again similar misfortunes in Greece, Italy, and Asia. . . . Beginning with the year 59, almost every year was marked by a great disaster.

"All this created a sort of somber atmosphere in which the imagination of the Christians found the strongest excitation."[97]

Such were the conditions of decadent Greco-Roman paganism, which produced, on the one hand, irreligiousness, skepticism, agnosticism, materialism, and moral depravity, and, on the other, Christianity, with its mystics, prophets, martyrs, and ascetics.[98]

3. Summary

The total evidence presented in this and the preceding chapters leaves no doubt as to the polarization of the ethicoreligious effects of calamities upon the behavior and mentality of the population involved. It demonstrates likewise that *the principal steps in the progress of mankind toward a spiritual religion and a noble code of ethics have been taken primarily under the impact of great catastrophes. The periods of comparative stability, order, and material well-being, and hence of complacency, have scarcely ever given birth to a truly great religion or a truly lofty moral ideal. Herein lies, perhaps, the justification for the signal tragedies of human history.*

Chapter Twelve

Sinners and Saints in Calamity

1. *Two Additional Problems*

Two important problems involved in the law of polarization have been left without adequate analysis in the preceding discussion. First, precisely what members of the population become "sinners" or "saints" or else retain their earlier status under the stress of calamity, and why? Second, what is the relative strength of the opposing trends, and what conditions determine which of the competing forces shall gain the ascendancy?

2. *Who's Who among the Sinners and Saints*

The concrete factors determining why some members of the population are transformed into irreligious and demoralized profligates, whereas others become more religious and ethical, are many and diverse, including the biological constitution, age, and sex, the degree of exposure of individuals to dangers and hardships, and the like. However, these conditions are subsidiary, local, and temporal—not the fundamental selective factors.

Assuming that all these factors are identical for a given group, we find that *those persons (a) whose system of values is well integrated, (b) whose values are not limited to the material and sensory aspects of the empirical world but envisage, as the end values, those of transcendental character (of the "City of God"), and (c) whose system is rooted not only in their ideology and speech reactions but also in their general conduct (and is hence free from the contradiction between words and deeds), furnish the overwhelming majority of the adherents of the intensified ethico-religious movement.*

Conversely, from the ranks of those whose system of values is poorly integrated, constituting a chaotic congeries of either the "high-brow" or the "low-brow" type, and whose end values are confined chiefly or exclusively to the material and sensory aspects of the empirical world, is recruited the majority of the opposing camp.

Finally, those whose system of values is fairly well integrated, but consists predominantly of the nobler type of material and sensory values, tend to retain their erstwhile ethico-religious position.

The foregoing propositions are concerned principally with the integration or nonintegration of values, together with the character of the end values[1] and their embodiment not only in one's ideology and speech reactions but also in one's deeds and general conduct. Moral and religious standards are *not innate*, but are derived from the society and culture in which one is born and reared. Values are inculcated through reaction to the sociocultural milieu. If a given system is well integrated, and deeply rooted in one's mind and behavior, its "Thou shalt" and "Thou shalt not" are so compelling that one resists their injunctions much more successfully than a person possessing merely a congeries of heterogeneous and haphazard standards. The former suggests a boat equipped with a powerful and efficient rudder; the latter, a craft bereft of steering gear. A sudden squall (that is, any momentary temptation, any biological urge) makes of it a mere plaything, incapable of resisting, of maintaining a steady course in life's stormy sea. Still less capable are such persons of resisting the stress of starvation, war, revolution, or any other serious calamity. This surrender of persons with nonintegrated values to the impact of temptations and hardships is greatly facilitated by the extraordinary capacity of the human mind to rationalize and justify the most ignoble actions. They convince themselves that their yielding to the pressure of calamities is justifiable, and rational, as dictated by considerations of "reason," the "summum bonum," "solidarity," "the interests of the proletariat," "national interests," "self-preservation," the "natural preference of pleasure to pain," the "laws of nature," and what not—motives which assume hundreds of primitive or highly sophisticated forms. They easily persuade themselves that they had to kill, steal, perform cowardly acts, rape, and so on for the sake of this or that high-sounding value. They readily believe today that A is B; tomorrow that A is C; and the day after tomorrow that A is non-B. Often they are sincere in this self-deceit. But this "sincerity" is so specious, so amenable to the shifting forces of calamity, that it is worthless. Since their values are not integrated into a unified and consistent system, but represent a mere accidental agglomeration, or congeries, they afford no basis for effective resistance to the pressure of adversity, since this pressure neither wholly contradicts nor wholly complies with them. A conglomerate congeries can be added to or subtracted from, or its items can be rearranged—nothing more.

Since any action, however antisocial, demanded by a calamity fails to contravene the unintegrated values of the type of person in question, the impulse to perform such an act is not resisted as it is in the case of one possessing a consistent and integrated system of values. When, for instance, a catastrophe tempts one who is actuated by the religious and moral standards of Christianity to kill a person in order to obtain food, the impulse conflicts with his fundamental system of values and therefore tends to be inhibited.

The second condition of the proposition is *the nature*

of the basic, or end, values. Among the persons possessing integrated systems, those whose supreme values are purely material and sensory—wealth, health and comfort, food and drink, love, and a miscellany of pleasures of varying degrees of refinement—are more likely to become "sinners," under the stress of adversity than those whose end values are rooted in the transcendental Kingdom of God (or its equivalent under different names). The latter are more inclined in the direction of an intensification and purification of ethico-religious life than in the opposite direction. The reasons are rather evident, provided that in both cases the system of values does not represent mere ideology and speed reactions but actual conduct. Every material, sensory system, whether based upon pleasure, happiness, or utility, or a combination of these, is bound to be (explicitly or implicitly) not only egoistic but also relative or conditional and hence unstable and shifting.[2] If sensory happiness is the end value, then one is concerned first and foremost with *his own* sensory happiness. For its realization one is entitled to pursue *any* course of conduct which is most expedient under the circumstances. If one is hungry, then in order to avoid suffering or starvation he is justified in snatching bread from somebody else—even in killing; for this motive constitutes one of his supreme values.

Those who are devoid of any integrated system of norms succumb to the antisocial, antimoral, and antireligious impact of disaster without reflection, without the elaboration of an intricate ideology of self-justification, much like animals which, when hungry, seize food when and where they find it, often killing other animals in the process of satisfying their needs.[3] In contradistinction to such persons, those endowed with an integrated sensate, "this-worldly" system of values readily contrive theories wherewith to extenuate and rationalize their antisocial conduct. It is precisely this group that produces the militant atheists, the nihilists, the "enemies of God, pity, and mercy," since it is unrestrained by any divine or absolute taboo upon the effort to obtain happiness or pleasure at the expense of others. Dostoevsky rightly declared, "If there is no God and no absolute value, everything is permitted." Such a philosophy, indeed, ultimately leads to the disintegration of these relative, material norms themselves,[4] and thus to utter religious, ethical, and social cynicism.

Very different is the situation of those whose character is rooted primarily in the absolute, transcendental, eternal verities of the Kingdom of God (or its equivalent). Their end values, being immaterial, remain valid when all material values are threatened with destruction. Not regarding pleasure, sensory happiness, or utility as of supreme importance, they are not tempted by such considerations in times of disaster, nor do they shrink from suffering as something essentially evil. Since they are swayed by the categorical imperative of God's commandments, they cannot be easily induced to violate their lifelong principles in response to the exigencies of mundane emergencies. Indeed, in adversity the categoric imperatives unconditionally demand resistance to any temptation whatsoever. When such a system of values is deeply ingrained in their ideology, speech reactions, and general conduct, they can seldom if ever be desocialized, demoralized, or despiritualized by disaster, tending, rather, to become moral heroes and religious zealots.

Finally, the foregoing considerations explain why the behavior of persons with partly transcendental and partly sensory norms tends to remain fairly static under calamity conditions—"decent," devoid of extremes, neither "hot nor cold."

The validity of these propositions is well supported by a factual verification, which demonstrates that the adherents of the negative movement of irreligiousness and demoralization have always been recruited from two types of persons. Its leaders, organizers, ideologists and propagandists have regularly been atheists and disbelievers, materialists, relativists, hedonists and sensualists, or hypocrites and frauds, with an integrated sensate system of values; while their followers have been drawn preponderantly from persons and groups devoid of any integrated system of values.

On the other hand, the intensely religious and ethical character of the opposing trend clearly reflects the transcendental or ideational nature of the system of values possessed by its partisans. Virtually all such movements have been conducted under the banner of God, the Messiah, Brahma, Nirvana, or the like. The very fact that the rise of the leading religious and moral codes, and notable ethico-religious progress in general, is associated primarily with calamity conditions affords obvious and uncontroversial evidence for the fundamentally transcendental or ideational character of the positive polarization.

Lastly, the balanced, "neither hot nor cold" system of values has been represented, as a rule, by the bourgeoisie, or middle classes—the "decent" Rotarians and Elks—of all ages. They fluctuate somewhat in the scale of ethico-religious values, now becoming slightly more demoralized, now slightly more spiritualized; now supporting the faction of profligates, now that of the saints. This relatively balanced position insures them against both extreme demoralization and irreligiousness and extreme moral heroism and religiosity.

3. Is the Magnitude of the Polarized Movements Equal in All Calamities?

Whatever measuring stick of the power or magnitude of the respective movements is adopted,—whether the number of adherents, the number of criminal or heroic actions, or the influence of the competing ideologies,— their relative strength has hardly ever been equal, nor has either one proved invariably stronger than the other. The relation shifts from calamity to calamity, depending upon a variety of conditions. Instead of attempting to compute statistically the comparative magnitude of each movement, it is more fruitful to indicate approximately the typical constellations in which now one, now the other, gains the ascendancy.

The concrete factors are numerous and diverse, especially in connection with minor calamities. In crucial, epoch-making catastrophes there is one which is rather decisive—namely, the fundamental character of the culture that is already in process of decline. If the disaster occurs at the close of a sensate,[5] or "this-worldly," period of culture, during the *initial* stages of the crisis the reaction of demoralization and irreligiousness tends to prevail over the opposing trend; but with the prolongation of the emergency (provided the society in question does not meanwhile succumb) it generally loses ground in favor of its opponent—the movement of religious and ethical regeneration. In the subsequent stages of the catastrophe the latter trend becomes increasingly dominant and self-assertive. It attacks irreligiousness and demoralization as manifested both in thought and in conduct; it revaluates the entire sensate system, eliminating many of its items as superannuated, negative, or pseudo values. This tremendous work of reformation, reorganization, and revaluation operates to elevate transcendental religious and ethical norms to the dignity of end values, and, conversely, to demote the material, sensate values hitherto supreme.

The movement thus progressively bridles the forces of anarchy, demoralization, and desocialization, decreasing revolutions and other internal disturbances, as well as external wars; and it finally ushers in a new era, with its remodeled constitution and its new social institutions, culture, and system of values. When this point is reached, the catastrophic transition is over, and the society enters upon the next epoch in its life career. Shaped by the intense religious and moral forces that have been released, this fresh culture becomes more ideational and idealistic, permeated in all its main compartments (including the sciences and fine arts, philosophy, and the various forms of social organization) by transcendental religious and ethical norms, and oriented toward God and His commandments as the supreme end values.

However, under the stable condition of this epoch, *the intensity of the religious and moral movement generated during the period of catastrophe begins to decline*, and settled forms of organization, credos, and dogmas progressively emerge which are now unchallenged, being sustained by the prestige gained in the earlier fighting stage. For this reason, even an ideational or idealistic culture, in its dominant and settled phase, tends to grow complacent, moderate, and luke-warm in its religious and moral aspects as compared with the movement that produced it under the stress of calamity.

Then there were militant martyrs; now no martyrs are required, being replaced by passive priests or monks, or other servants of the established church or theocracy. During the earlier critical period there arose prophets and founders of new religions; at the settled stage we find, instead, a hierarchy of ecclesiastical dignitaries, with well-defined ranks, privileges, and duties. During the transition phase religious and moral leaders needed divine inspiration and unflinching courage, and their task called for incessant physical and intellectual effort. These attributes and endeavors are now no longer required, being superseded by a routine observance of established rules and creeds, and often by a comfortable way of life devoid of serious hardships or dangers. The place of divine inspiration, of prophetic or mystic revelation, is taken by prescribed rites, administrative efficiency, and bureaucratic functions. For all these reasons it is easy to understand why, even in a predominantly ideational or idealistic culture, permeated by religion and moral values, the intensity of the ethico-religious life declines as compared with its initial heroic phase. The history of ancient Egypt, and that of Confucianism, Taoism, Brahmanism, Buddhism, Mohammedanism, Christianity, and other great ethico-religious movements, demonstrates this clearly, as we have already seen.

At the time of their emergence and growth under crisis conditions, their intensity, their creative vital force, was at its maximum; this was their truly heroic age. After they had become dominant, they tended increasingly to become merely well-organized machines (often marvelously efficient), with ingeniously developed dogmas, theological systems, and rituals—huge religious and moral bureaucracies, with magnificent buildings and vast wealth. The vitality of the Holy Spirit animating the Church and, through it, the entire culture, somehow tended always to decline until, sooner or later, the religious and moral organizations in question became little more than a hollow shell from which the living spirit had escaped.

This process has usually entailed the granting of unwarranted privileges to the agents of the established religion, who have frequently led a parasitical existence at the expense of the masses. Such a situation has ultimately led, as a rule, to an acute crisis resulting in the permanent or temporary decline of the prevailing religion. This crisis, in turn, has brought about its revitalization, spiritualization, and purification, whereupon it has reëmerged in a regenerated form that of a Neo-Ammonism or Atonism (among the Egyptians), a Neo-Judaism, Neo-Confucianism, Neo-Taoism, Neo-Brahmanism, Neo-Buddhism, or Neo-Christianity (represented by the Christian Renaissance periods of the eighth, ninth, twelfth, and thirteenth centuries and of the Reformation and Counter-Reformation).

Such are the comparative life curves exhibited by the positive and negative ethico-religious movements when a profound crisis occurs during the declining stage of a predominantly sensate culture and society. Familiar instances of both trends are afforded by the history of Greco-Roman culture during the early centuries of our era. The dominant form of Greco-Roman culture prior to the second century A.D. was sensate.[6] We know that the trend toward irreligiousness, materialism, and immorality was much stronger during the Hellenistic period than was the opposite ethico-religious movement. We know also that under the stress of crisis the positive movement began to grow until, with the triumph of Christianity, it gained the upper hand and ushered in the medieval ideational form of culture. Finally, we know that the most intense, most heroic, and most sublime era in the history of Christianity was precisely that of its inception and struggle under the catastrophic conditions of the Greco-Roman world of the first four or five centuries A.D. That was the age of the apostles, martyrs, and Church Fathers, of lofty moral heroism, of inspiration and divine grace, when the Holy Spirit permeated and quickened the entire Christian Church. Since the official recognition of Christianity by Constantine the Great the superhuman heights of its initial heroic stage have never again been attained, although it succeeded in imposing its own dominant culture upon the Middle Ages, and though its ethico-religious level has remained, on the whole, very high. The exceptions are the periods of corruption brought about by the unbridled growth of hierarchical organization, wealth, ecclesiastical and secular authority, ritual, and dogma, and culminating in the crises of the pre-Reformation, the Reformation, and the Counter-Reformation.

Somewhat different is the nature of the polarized movements when a drastic crisis occurs at the last stage of a declining *ideational* culture—as, for instance, at the close of the Middle Ages[7] (from the end of the twelfth century to the sixteenth or seventeenth century) or in ancient Greece (at the end of the sixth and throughout the fifth century B.C.).

In such a setting, in the initial phase of the crisis the negative ethico-religious movement is more moderate and conservative, still controlled by the religious and ethical values of the declining ideational culture. The opposite reaction (the positive) is likewise relatively restrained, retaining the prescribed forms of the existing religion and moral code and developing within this framework. There may even be a period when the two reactions go hand in hand, producing a synthesis and reconciliation. With the prolongation of the crisis, the negative reaction gathers momentum, becomes bolder and bolder, creates its own ideologies and dogmas, and openly attacks both the declining religion and ethics and the ethico-religious movement unleashed by the emergency. In most cases it collides with the positive trend and temporarily undermines it or even overwhelms it.

Once having attained supremacy, the negative movement is fatally inclined to become more and more anti-social, nihilistic, and irreligious. As such it aggravates the disaster instead of alleviating it, and thus progressively alienates an ever-increasing proportion of society. In an effort to cope with the evil, this part of the population now turns to the opposite movement as the most efficient instrumentality for realizing its purposes.

The positive movement accordingly exhibits an upward trend. Through its ideology it begins to combat the ideology of the nihilists and atheists; through its vital ethico-religious spirit it successfully inhibits immoral tendencies; through its altruism and devotion, its practical social activities, it compels the negative reaction to retreat from its extreme position, and to become more sensible and balanced, less sensual and egoistic, more creative and constructive.

When this stage is reached, through the combined forces of the positive ethico-religious movement and of the tempered and balanced sensate movement the foundations are laid for a new constructive epoch in the life history of the society—for a predominantly sensate culture freed from most of its destructive tendencies, its militant atheism and its libertinism. These are now replaced by the balanced values of a humanistic mundane philosophy and religion (be it Pantheism, Deism, "the religion of mankind," or simply religion as a necessary means of social control); by a sober (sometimes even puritanical) utilitarianism proclaiming "the maximum of happiness for the maximum number of human beings"; by socialistic experiments and social reforms aimed at alleviating the sufferings of the masses; by a noble system of sensate fine arts; by science and technological inventions; and so on. These sober sensate values are reënforced by the transcendental ethico-religious norms carried over from the earlier period. The new culture thus represents sensate culture at its best, with its creative forces released and its destructive tendencies bridled, supported by the positive ethico-religious movement generated by adversity and now working hand in hand with the reorganized religion and morality of the preceding period.

The most familiar examples of the phenomenon are furnished by the history of Western culture from the end of the twelfth to the seventeenth century. At the end of the twelfth century the dominant ideational culture of the Middle Ages already exhibited signs of decline. The crisis manifested itself in enormous waves of revolutions in the thirteenth, fourteenth, and fifteenth centuries. As a matter of fact, these centuries for the whole of Europe were the most turbulent and disorderly throughout the entire history of Western culture with the exception of the twentieth century.[8] To revolutions were added wars, pestilences (including the terrible Black Death), and famines.

These calamities naturally gave rise to both movements—first to violent depravity and semi-atheism. This tendency spread rapidly and assumed an extreme character in revolutionary groups, as well as in intellectual groups and among the masses of the population. The opposite movement also developed, but it seems to have been weaker than its competitor. However, as time went on, and as the population began to suffer from the excesses of the nihilistic movement, a reaction set in. Various ascetic and mystical sects sprang up; eminent religious leaders like Savonarola appeared; later on their work was supported by ascetic Protestantism, then by the Society of Jesus and the Counter-Reformation. Toward the end of the sixteenth century this movement had already succeeded in curbing the prevalent depravity, cynicism, and atheism. Even such cynics as Machiavelli conceded that human society cannot be successfully controlled by purely empirical means, and that religion is indispensable for this if for no other purpose. "The sagacious politician will always respect religion even if he has no belief in it," he declared. The positive ethico-religious movement thus increasingly checked the atheism, licentiousness, and antisocial trend of the negative movement, sobered it, and made it constructive rather than destructive. The ground was accordingly broken for a working cooperation (within limits) of both the polarized movements in the task of creating a renovated society. This task was accomplished; and from the seventeenth to the twentieth century we have had a sensate culture—first restrained, yet vital and creative, and since the beginning of the present century displaying unmistakable symptoms of disintegration and decline.[9]

Such are the typical life curves exhibited by the two polarized movements when the crisis occurs during the decline of an ideational culture and continues throughout the initial phases of a sensate system.

Chapter Thirteen

THE INFLUENCE OF CALAMITIES UPON SCIENCE AND TECHNOLOGY

1. *The Two Principal Effects*

Two general principles—the imprint of its own image upon scientific and technological activities, and the law of polarization—sum up the main effects of calamity upon science, including the social sciences, the humanities, and technology. The first manifests itself in the concentration of scientific and technological thought upon the calamity problem and the means for its solution. The law of polarization is revealed in the opposite effects induced by social disaster. While the former has already been adequately discussed in Chapter Nine, the phenomenon of polarization calls for restatement and additional comment.

2. *The Law of Polarization in the Field of Science and Technology*

In its application to science and technology the principle of polarization means that severe calamities exert simultaneously a negative and a positive influence over these cultural phenomena. On the one hand, they disorganize the existing scientific and technological institutions and hinder successful work in these fields. On the other hand, they exercise a stimulating, revitalizing, and regenerative effect, especially after the crisis has passed.

Negative effects. War, revolution, famine, and pestilence destroy or put out of commission many scientific institutions, universities, and laboratories, and thus paralyze or disrupt normal scientific study. They cause many scientists and inventors to be shifted to tasks unrelated to their

242 MAN AND SOCIETY IN CALAMITY

customary pursuits, and allocate scientific funds to other purposes. For successful scientific investigation or technological invention a considerable degree of peace of mind and undisturbed concentration of thought are essential. Calamities undermine concentration and independent thinking. They arouse passions and emotions—fear, hatred, depression, compassion, and the like—and hence impair mental objectivity. Fruitful mental functioning is further impaired by sickness and starvation. Again, important studies have to be abandoned because of the general precariousness of life under calamity conditions.

Add to this the intolerance characteristic of times of war and especially of revolution. Major revolutions and, in lesser degree, wars directly destroy many scientists and thinkers, including the most eminent. Socrates, Michael Servetus, Giordano Bruno, and Lavoisier in earlier centuries and the hundreds of scientists and scholars executed in the Russian Soviet revolution are typical examples. A much larger number of scientists, scholars, and thinkers are either banished or else forced to flee. Confucius, Anaxagoras, Plato, Aristotle, Dante, Hobbes, De Maistre, Chateaubriand, Karl Marx, and thousands of Russian and German scientists and scholars illustrate the point. Other thousands perish in prisons and concentration camps during wars and revolutions.[1]

Furthermore, revolutionary and war governments autocratically determine what theories, opinions, and ideologies shall be adopted, and pitilessly proscribe or persecute a scientist or scholar who dissents from these "governmental revelations" (*sic*). Again, such governments grant positions, salaries, research funds, laboratory facilities, and so forth only to those who agree to support and subscribe to their fiat or pseudo science. As a result, independent and creative scientific work, the disinterested search for truth, sharply declines. Pseudo science, fostered by the government or by powerful factions, by its very nature cannot be fruitful: it turns into trite and stale political propaganda, ceasing to constitute science in any proper sense of the term. The so-called scientists, academicians, professors, and researchers appointed by the powers that be become mere bureaucrats, propagandists, ideologists, and "yes men" in the service of those who dictatorially control the mind of the people.

All this is empirically demonstrated by the decrease of technological inventions during the First World War in the foremost belligerent countries. For instance, in Great Britain the number of patents on inventions issued for the years 1910-1911 was 160,386, and for the decade 1911-1921 only 138,909. In the United States the *rate* of increase of patented inventions by five-year periods was (taking the number of inventions in 1841-1845 as equal to 100) 218, 525, and 2170 for 1846-1850, 1851-1855, and 1856-1860; for the five-year period of the Civil War, 1861-1865, it fell to 757. It likewise declined for the years 1916-1920, which exhibit a rate of increase of 2281, as opposed to 2936 for 1911-1915.[2]

Positive effects. If our analysis were to stop at this point, we should be guilty of the error of one-sidedness; for, as has already been pointed out, calamities not only inhibit creative scientific and technological work but also stimulate and foster it. Disaster imperatively urges men to contrive something new wherewith to alleviate it or to prevent its recurrence. Both the government and society in general make an intense effort to facilitate by every means those inventions that may be of service in coping with the crisis. Extensive funds are appropriated; special laboratories are built and equipped; all available scientists are mobilized; and similar measures are adopted. In time of famine these measures are directed toward relieving starvation. In time of war, society appropriates large sums and mobilizes all the available scientific and technological resources in the interest of producing more efficient implements of war—better explosives, armaments, poisonous gases, airplanes, ships, tanks, etc. In time of pestilence, attention is concentrated on public hygiene and medical science. In time of revolution the emphasis is similarly laid upon measures calculated to ensure victory, particularly in the fields of warfare and propaganda.

Calamities promote scientific and technological progress also by creating new situations for observation and experimentation. They offer an opportunity to examine many aspects of social life which in normal times are hidden. Pestilence affords rare opportunities for the study of various biological and medical problems; famine, for the investigation of a host of biological, psychological, and sociological questions. War and revolution furnish exceptional facilities for the exploration of certain mathematical, chemical, physical, biological, and psychosocial phenomena.

Calamities stimulate scientific thought indirectly through unusual situations which disrupt routine modes of thought and observation. They raise a host of new problems urgently demanding an answer even in the minds of ordinary people. Demanding an answer, they stimulate thought, direct it into fresh channels, suggest new modes of study, and thus contribute to the progress of science and technology. In a word, they unfold new vistas, perspectives, and approaches. Finally, they serve as a drastic test of the validity of heretofore unchallenged theories and opinions. Tested in the crucial fires of calamity and found wanting, a given theory is invalidated, and scientific thought is forced to find a more adequate one.

The stimulating rôle of war. As a result of this stimulating rôle of calamities many a discovery and invention has been made in the natural and social sciences. Probably most of the earliest mathematical, physical, chemical, and technological inventions were achieved in connection with war. We know that the inventions and discoveries in these fields by Archimedes, Thales of Miletus, Democritus, and others were directly attributable to the needs of warfare. Many of the achievements of Leonardo and Galileo, Tartaglia, Descartes, Torricelli, Leibnitz, Von Guericke, Papin, Newton, Johann and Daniel Bernoulli, Euler, Maupertius, Gay-Lussac, Chevreul, Graham, Cavalli, Mayevsky, Hooke, Boyle, Mariotte, Lomonosoff, Towneley, Robins, Hutton, Didion, Poisson, Halley, etc. are ascribable directly or indirectly, to the same cause.[3]

In recent wars this connection has become still closer. As P. L. Kapitza rightly says, the Haber process for producing synthetic ammonia not only prolonged Germany's resistance in the First World War but also provided her with fertilizers. The heavy chemical industry arose when Leblanc met an urgent wartime need for soda; the earliest sewing machine was invented and first applied in response to the demand for military uniforms. Likewise the recent development of synthetic rubber, synthetic gasoline, and the coal-tar industry was largely due, directly or indirectly, to military requirements; so also blood transfusion, the control of typhus and other infectious diseases, and the invention or perfection of various other techniques. In the present world struggle virtually every scientist is mobilized for military work and provided with the requisite funds and facilities. Solving the urgent problems of war, they solve, as well, many a general problem of science. The invention of new weapons and armaments; the solution of new engineering problems; the improvement of explosives, airplanes, cannon, tanks, antitank guns, ship construction, and so on—all this is facilitated enormously by war. While it is true that the principal progress is made in the narrow field of science and technology that directly ministers to military requirements, nevertheless some progress is also achieved in connection with those problems that constitute the perennial subjects of scientific investigation.

What has been said of the engineering, mathematical, and physicochemical sciences may be said also of the biological, medical, and psychosocial sciences. War has facilitated the study of human anatomy and physiology, especially of the medical and surgical disciplines. It was a potent factor in *the first efforts of social engineering, in so far as an army was one of the first forms of scientifically built social organizations.* Since the earliest times, military activities and the social phenomena connected with them, have represented one of the most important fields investigated by the social sciences. In the treatises on history, political science, economics, sociology, and social philosophy, from the earliest to the most recent, war has occupied a central place. So has it been in the history of Greek, Roman, Chinese, Hindu, and Euro-American social thought. Most histories of the traditional type have been concerned preeminently with military phenomena. But the study of war has involved indirectly many other social phenomena, and has served incessantly as a crucial test of various ill-advised theories. The First and especially the Second World War have already invalidated more theories in the field of the social sciences than all the critical treatises of earlier decades.

The net effects. The foregoing emphasis upon the positive influences exerted by war does not mean that they are always greater than the negative effects. The net result is hardly uniform for all cases. In some the negative effects prevail; in others, the positive. This explains why, for in-

stance, the statistics of discoveries and inventions fail to
show a decline in all the belligerent periods, such as the
decreases cited for Great Britain and the United States for
the years 1861-1865 and 1916-1920. The only uniformity
is the fact of the twofold influence of war: it is neither
wholly negative nor wholly positive, but plays a double
rôle.

The stimulating rôle of famine and pestilence. What
has been said of war applies to other disasters as well.
Famine and *pestilence* have also facilitated, directly and
especially indirectly, the progress of human knowledge
and technological invention. To be sure, the inventions
and discoveries attributable directly to famine and pestilence have seemingly been of a routine nature rather than
of fundamental importance. Since both of these calamities
tend to incapacitate the population physically and mentally, it can hardly be expected that they should greatly
stimulate creative scientific thought. Most of the "discoveries and inventions" in times of famine have consisted
mainly in the introduction of *Ersatz*, or substitute, foods—
dogs, cats, mice and rats, horses, frogs, snakes, grass and
other herbs, roots, the bark of trees, moss, and, in exceptional cases, even human corpses.[4] Another set of "discoveries and inventions" has consisted in the somewhat
more efficient manufacture of food substitutes, such as
those employed in Germany during the First and the
Second World War and in Russia during the revolutionary
famine years—the utilization of the blood of animals in
bread; the admixture of various ingredients in food to replace protein, albumin, and other components; and the
like. A further device has been the establishment of collective farms or similar enterprises. Needless to say, such
"inventions" have been of negligible importance, suggest-
ing the tactics of an impoverished person who, though

unable to feed his horse, nevertheless whips it unmercifully to make it run faster!

Similarly, the inventions attributable to pestilence have been few in number and of trifling moment, owing to the disorganizing effects of epidemics and the heavy toll which they exact among physicians and among students and observers of the phenomenon.

However, when the disorganizing and paralyzing effects of famine or pestilence finally cease, the desire to prevent their repetition serves as a powerful incentive to discoveries and inventions in the fields in question. If it had not been for famine or its ever-present danger, the primitive tribes would have shown far less initiative in this direction. Those which are favorably situated economically by reason of the lavish gifts of nature are less industrious and exert their minds less arduously than groups placed in an unfavorable position.[5] Again, many a creator of the highest artistic values, such as Mozart or Beethoven, has been actuated— at least in part—by the necessity of earning his daily bread. Per contra, the secure pecuniary position of the posterity of the well-to-do tends to make them lazy and unproductive, aligning them with what Veblen has called the members of the "leisure class."

As has been said, the facts indicate that after a famine is over, new measures and inventions are frequently contrived with a view to preventing or minimizing the danger of its repetition. According to the oldest Chinese chronicle, the *Shû King*, or *Book of History*, edited by Confucius, the Great Yü (*ca.* 2205 B.C.) "sowed grain and showed the multitude how to procure the food of toil" after a famine caused by a disastrous flood.[6] Since that time the connection between famine and agricultural progress has often been demonstrated. After the famines of the eleventh century in Russia we note the introduction of wheat and other cereals, millet gruel, and several new vegetables; the area of cultivated land was expanded; and a number of technical improvements of agriculture were put into practice. After subsequent famines additional efforts were made to increase the fertility of the soil; to introduce potatoes and new vegetables; to expand and improve bee culture and cattle-breeding; and so on. Side by side with such measures the government undertook to establish agricultural schools, special courses in agriculture, research laboratories, agrarian publications, and the like.[7]

With certain reservations, the foregoing applies to other countries as well. The development of agriculture and husbandry has been due, in large measure, either to the direct influence of actual famine exerted during the post-famine periods or to its perennial menace.

The same is true of *pestilence*. Both of these disasters have led not only to specific inventions and discoveries aimed at their alleviation, but also to a further exploration of the field of biological science in general.

"Of the greatest importance for the suppression of the plague was the increase in cleanliness and civilization throughout Europe —[the establishment of quarantines and hospitals, the reconstruction of cities to make them cleaner, the introduction of new methods of treating disease, and so on].

What David Hume says of the rebuilding of London after the fire and plague of 1666 applies also to other cities.

"The town was very rapidly reconstructed, . . . making the streets broader and more regular than before. . . . The plague, which generally broke out with great vehemence twice or thrice a century, and in fact every time appeared first in the most filthy corner of the town, has never been heard of since this misfortune."

"Experience gained during various epidemics contributed essentially to the consideration of hygienic aspects in the construction of towns and dwellings."[8]

It is not too bold a generalization to declare that the successful medical treatment of all major epidemics— bubonic plague, typhus, cholera, dysentery, diphtheria, influenza, smallpox, measles, etc.—has been discovered or refined, for the most part, during or immediately after their ravages.[9]

The stimulating rôle of revolution. Finally, *revolution* has also exerted a positive influence upon the natural sciences and especially the social and humanistic sciences, and for reasons similar to the positive influence of war and other calamities. Typical examples are furnished by the Cromwellian revolt, the French Revolution, and the Russian revolutions. The revolutionary periods of Greece, Rome, and other countries afford further illustrations.

The impact of revolution upon the social and humanitarian sciences has been immense. Since ancient times social thinkers have been impressed and fascinated by the phenomenon. It is one of the central topics of the oldest Confucian texts in China,—*Shû King* and Li-Kî,—as well as of the principal Taoist texts (*The Classic of Purity* and *The Writings of Kwang-tse*), not to mention the works of Mencius and other Chinese social thinkers. It plays a dominant rôle, likewise, in ancient Hindu literature—the *Law Books*, the *Narada, Brihaspati*, the *Code of Manu*, and such political and economic treatises as the *Nitisastras* and *Arthasastras*.[10] It is one of the fundamental themes of Plato's *Republic*, his *Laws*, and some of his *Dialogues;* of Aristotle's *Politics;* of the historical treatises of Herodotus and Thucydides; and of the chief works of Cicero and the Church Fathers. It dominates also the social writings of the medieval thinkers—the proponents and opponents of tyranny from Alcuin to Saint Thomas Aquinas and Suárez. Ibn-Khaldun, Machiavelli, Hobbes, J. Bodin, Vico, Locke, Montesquieu, Rousseau, Karl Marx, Herbert Spencer,

Auguste Comte, Hegel, Nietzsche, J. de Maistre, de Bonald, Haller, etc., allot to it generous space. On the basis of their study of the phenomena of revolution they derive conclusions and generalizations bearing upon the entire fabric of social and cultural life, including its structure and dynamics.

The stimulating rôle of revolutions (particularly after their termination) manifests itself, moreover, in the refutation of sundry hoary theories which cannot stand their acid test, and in the emergence of fresh and more fruitful concepts. In this sense, revolutions, like wars, serve as brooms that sweep away the cobwebs of outmoded theory and bring fresh air into the stale atmosphere of social thought.

These considerations explain why most of the outstanding systems of social science and social philosophy have appeared on the eve of, during, or immediately after periods of catastrophic upheaval. Under such turbulent conditions were evolved the Confucian and Taoist codes in China; the *History* of Thucydides; Plato's and Aristotle's systems of social philosophy; and those of Cicero, Seneca, Saint Cyprian and Saint Augustine, Joachim de Flore, Albertus Magnus and Saint Thomas Aquinas, Dante, Nicolas of Cusa, Marsiglio of Padua, Luther, Calvin, and Melanchthon, Ibn-Khaldun, Machiavelli, Hobbes and Locke, Montesquieu, Rousseau, and the Encyclopedists, Auguste Comte, J. de Maistre, de Bonald, Fichte and Hegel, Le Play and Karl Marx, and Benjamin Franklin, Hamilton, and the Federalists: These and many other social thinkers either lived a part of their life under critical social conditions or were personally involved in various political and social conflicts. A rough estimate indicates that from 70 to 85 per cent of all eminent social thinkers have suffered ostracism, imprisonment, or banishment or have become voluntary exiles, from their homeland.

Thus the influence of calamities upon science and technology provides additional testimony to the polarization of their effects. Some are positive; others are negative. As to which of the two trends prevails in a given crisis, there is probably no uniformity, though major catastrophies tend to produce predominantly negative results.

Chapter Fourteen

INFLUENCE OF CALAMITIES UPON THE FINE ARTS

1. *Temporary Effects*

Major and prolonged calamities affect the fine arts in several ways. First, they temporarily weaken the interest in art phenomena, as well as aesthetic creativeness, by incapacitating those artists who are the direct and indirect victims. We have seen that in famine aesthetic activities decline (see above, pp. 74-75). The same is true of pestilence, war, and revolution. Secondly, calamities invade the field of the fine arts and become one of their central topics. Thirdly, they inject into the fine arts (at least temporarily) a mood of melancholy, pessimism, and even despair, as well as an atmosphere of the *pathétique* and macabre; painting and sculpture, music and literature, the theater and the dance—all are permeated with these moods and this atmosphere. For instance, after the Black Death the *danse macabre* motif swept over the countries affected, fairly saturating the fine arts with pictures of Death in the company of kings and popes, serfs and merchants, young and old, men and women, in the widest range of situations and postures. Corpses, often terrifying in their realism, invaded painting and sculpture and other fields. Even the tomb monuments succumbed to the obsession, representing a veritable apotheosis of Death. Melancholia became a dominant *Leitmotif*. The fine arts grew increasingly *pathétique*, tragic, and terrifying—in a sense, more sadistic. "The art of the fourteenth and the fifteenth centuries bespeaks sensitiveness. . . . *Douleur* is the great inspirer of this age. . . . The Passion is its keynote."[1] Beginning with the second half of the fourteenth century, "the images of corpses,

[253]

death's heads, and skulls multiplied in the churches, in stained-glass windows and in pictures."[2] Similar traits mark the literature, poetry, and music of the period.

"At the close of the Middle Ages a somber melancholy weighs on people's souls. . . .

"The note of despair and profound dejection is predominantly sounded not by ascetic monks, but by court poets and chroniclers —laymen living in aristocratic circles and amidst aristocratic ideas—[Eustache Deschamps, Jean Meschinot, Georges Chastellain, Jean Gerson, and others]."[3]

The same is true of music. For instance, *O Roche beatissime*, composed during the sixteenth-century plague in Italy by Jhan Gero, voices "a cry of terror", perhaps rivaled in this respect only by "the corpses of the three kings in the Campo Santo at Pisa," writes Ambrose.[4]

This note of despair and *douleur*, of the macabre and the *pathétique*, is elicited not only by famine and pestilence but also by war and revolution. One sees it clearly in the art of the critical centuries of Hellenistic Greece, the third and second centuries B.C., exemplified in the field of sculpture by the celebrated Laocoön group. One recalls that the verses of Theognis, an exile of the Megara revolution, are deeply despondent and pessimistic. One observes that the art of the end of the sixteenth and seventeenth centuries, following the turbulent and bloody times of the Renaissance, the Reformation and Counter-Reformation, and the Thirty Years' War, is marked by the same characteristics.[5]

"The religious (and also secular) art of the seventeenth century was supercharged with an almost pathological, in a sense sadistic . . . emotionalism and patheticism, particularly in the pictures of the martyrs, in tortures and sufferings, which are depicted in all their visual horror. The scenes of the cutting out of tongues, of [burying] people alive, of [disemboweling], and so on—these scenes, depicted in their [most minute and gruesome] details . . . [are now rife]."[6]

In the secular field,

"the artists of the seventeenth century ordinarily depicted only the most violent scenes of ancient history: Lucretia stabbing herself, the dying Dido and Cleopatra, Sophonias drinking poison, Seneca opening his veins. . . . The spectacle of these gruesome paintings is almost unbearable."[7]

It is an art replete with cruelties, horrors, and death.

Fourthly, in war and revolution the fine arts become, to a considerable degree, *mere instruments of propaganda, and hence pseudo-arts*. In their subject matter, their objectives, and their external form they are forced to bow to the purposes of the existing emergency. Artists are "mobilized," being charged with the task of stimulating patriotic or revolutionary ardor. Nowadays they are even required to furnish entertainment for the soldiers of revolutionary or national armies. Plays and movies, novels and poetry, music and paintings, are turned out expressly with a view to meeting such demands. The plays of the French Revolution provide typical examples. *Modern Equality, The Tenth of August, Buizot, The King of Calvados, The Republican Widow, The Guillotine of Love, The Last Judgment of the Kings, The Marriage of J. J. Rousseau, The Storming of the Bastille, Friendship and Fraternity,* and so on were its favorites. Their principal slogan was: "Off with the chains," "Down with the tyrants, kings, clergy and aristocrats" or "Long live freedom!"

Similar propaganda plays, novels, poems, music and paintings have appeared in other revolutions and wars.

During the first five years of the Soviet revolution any sort of so-called futurist, modernist, or cubist art was highly favored by the Communist government—indeed, coercively imposed. Later on, this fad was replaced by "classic" or other forms of art. Similar fads have attended the Nazi and Fascist revolutions.[8] These types of pseudo-art are generally short-lived, fading out with the termination of the crisis which produced them.

As regards the negative aspect of the phenomenon, it may be said that in any war, and especially in revolutions, works of art that are contrary to the objectives or tastes of the powers that be are likely to be prohibited. In the Russian Soviet revolution, for instance, Tchaikovsky's *1812 Overture* and *Marche Slave*, some of the operas of Rimsky-Korsakoff and Moussorgsky, and Dostoevsky's *The Possessed* were at one time under the ban of the government. During the French Revolution, *Pamela*, *The Marriage of Figaro*, certain of Molière's dramas, and other literary, musical, and theatrical works were similarly suppressed by the Jacobins. The same was true of the Cromwellian revolt in England. In time of war, art which is unpatriotic—which is created by citizens of the enemy nation—likewise tends to be banned. Thus during the First World War the operas of Wagner and other German composers were regarded as taboo by the Allied powers.

2. *Aesthetic Creativeness in Calamity and Post-calamity Periods*

Existing theories present divergent views as to the influence of war and revolution upon artistic creativeness. Some claim that their effects are wholly negative; others, that they are the "best fertilizer of the plant called Genius."[9] The truth probably lies somewhere between these two extremes. If major disasters tend at first to diminish artistic creativeness, nevertheless, when the initial stage has passed, the fine arts often exhibit a sharp upswing, attended by the production of genuine masterpieces, the emergence of notable aesthetic values, and the introduction of new and significant techniques.

If there had been no wars, we should have been deprived of many of the foremost masterpieces of literature, music, painting, sculpture, and even architecture. The great epics of all nations—such as the *Iliad*, *Odyssey* and *Aeneid*, the *Ramayana* and *Mahabharata*, the *Eddas*, the *Nibelungenlied*, and *Beowulf*—tend to glorify war and its heroes. The same is true of such epics and other literary masterpieces (mostly of later date) as Malory's cycle of Arthurian romances, the *Alexanderlied*, the *Song of Roland*, *Tristan and Iseult*, *Hugues Capet*, Boccaccio's *Teseide*, Boiardo's *Orlando Amoroso*, Ariosto's *Orlando Furioso*, Tasso's *Jerusalem Delivered*, Camoens's *Lusiad*, Ercilla's *Araucana*, Ronsard's *La Franciade*, Montalvo's *Amadis de Gaule*, and Milton's *Paradise Lost*. Many of the tragedies and comedies of Aeschylus, Sophocles, Euripides, and Aristophanes, Shakespeare, Corneille and Racine, Voltaire and Schiller likewise center around war—its heroes and its victims—as do numerous novels (for instance, Tolstoy's *War and Peace*, and recent best sellers like *Gone with the Wind* and Remarque's *All Quiet on the Western Front*). An enormous amount of poetry is also preoccupied with martial themes. The same is true to a considerable extent, of even the *Bible*.

The situation is similar in *music*. Military songs and marches were one of the very earliest forms of music. Military prowess has been one of the main themes and the chief inspiration of a host of musical compositions. A considerable number of operas, such as Wagner's *Ring of the Nibelung*, the *Flying Dutchman* and *Rienzi*, Glinka's *A Life for the Tsar* and *Russlan and Ludmila*, Rimsky-Korsakov's *Kitege Grad*, Moussorgsky's *Boris Godunov* and *Khovantschina*, Rossini's *William Tell*, Grétry's *Dionys le Tyran*, Meyerbeer's *Les Huguenots* and *Le Prophète*, Beethoven's *Fidelio* and *The Ruins of Athens*, Weber's

Oberon, and Verdi's *Aïda,* either are inspired by war and revolution or have a military or revolutionary setting or background. Other examples are Schubert's *Marche militaire;* certain works of Chopin, Mozart and Handel; Beethoven's *Eroica* symphony; Strauss's tone poem *Ein Heldenleben;* and Tchaikovsky's 1812 *Overture* and *Marche Slave.*

In *painting and sculpture* the martial deities (Mars, Jupiter and Athena; Marduk; Thor and Odin; and so forth), famous conquerors and military heroes, the victims of war and revolution, and battle scenes are favorite subjects. In genre pictures the military element constitutes from 3 to 70 per cent of all the topics (according to country and the period).[10]

Finally, in *architecture* a large proportion of the masterpieces commemorate war or revolution and their heroes—for instance, Phidias's Parthenon; Augustus's Ara Pacis; the columns of Trajan and Marcus Aurelius; some of the foremost structures of Egypt, Assyria, Babylonia and Persia; and many a pantheon, triumphal arch, armory, castle and fortress.

This brief list of masterpieces in the various fields of the fine arts suffices to suggest one of the ways in which wars and revolutions have served to heighten aesthetic creativeness.

These forces have played a more subtle rôle in generating an atmosphere which seems to have brought out the latent powers of a number of geniuses in the realm of the fine arts. The phenomenon is similar to what we have noted in the field of natural science, the social sciences, the humanities, philosophy, religion, and ethics. This subtle stimulation is indicated by the fact that periods of internal and external disorder—with their abnormal mobility—have been marked by an extraordinarily high percentage of men of genius. In Greece the golden age of the fine arts was the fifth and fourth centuries B. C.—the age of Pindar, of Aeschylus, Sophocles, Euripides and Aristophanes, of Myron, Phidias, Polygnotus, Praxiteles, Agoracritus, Callimachus. These centuries were at the same time the most belligerent and revolutionary epochs.[11]

The golden age of Roman art, in turn, was the first century B. C. (signalized by Virgil, Horace, Lucretius, Cicero, Varro, etc.). The same century was the most revolutionary and the second most belligerent period in Roman history.[12]

In Italy internal disturbances were rife from the eighth to the seventeenth century, reaching their climax in the thirteenth, fourteenth, and fifteenth centuries, and then rapidly declining, while external wars attained their maximum intensity between the fifteenth and eighteenth centuries.[13] The epoch between the thirteenth and sixteenth centuries constituted the *Blütezeit* of Italian creative genius in the fine arts and related activities. During these turbulent, disorderly, and mobile centuries Italy led all Europe in these fields, producing Dante, Petrach, and Boccaccio, Savonarola, Politian, Lorenzo Valla, Pico della Mirandola, Vittorino, Marsilio Ficino, A. S. Piccolomini, Machiavelli, and Guicciardini; eminent scholastics like Saint Thomas Aquinas and Nicolas of Cusa; the *ars nova* in music, and the musical Renaissance, distinguished by Gabrieli, Gesualdo, Palestrina, Vittoria, Orland di Lasso, and Monteverde; and celebrated painters, sculptors, and architects like Giotto, Perugino, Leonardo da Vinci, Raphael, Michelangelo, Benvenuto Cellini, Donatello, Giorgione, Botticelli, Fra Bartholomeo, Correggio, Titian, Bramante, Brunelleschi and Alberti. Among the illustrious painters of Italy the thirteenth century, according to the computation of Cooley, produced 7; the fourteenth, 7; the fifteenth, 38;

the sixteenth, 23 (most of these being born in the first half
of the century). The subsequent centuries boast only a
few painters, none of whom is of the first magnitude.[14]

In France, according to the detailed study of A. Odin,
the majority of eminent men of letters belong to the
periods 1376-1400, 1591-1605, and 1801-1815 (the fourteenth to the nineteenth century, inclusive). These periods
were at the same time most tempestuous in respect to war
or revolution or both.[15]

In the United States, up to 1851 the highest percentage
of births of prominent literati of the white race for any
given decade occurred in 1791-1800; the next highest, in
1811-1820; the next 1801-1810. The same decades, and the
period of 1791-1820 were (up to the Civil War) possibly
the most turbulent in the entire history of the United
States.

In England the years 1351-1475 were among the most
belligerent; they witnessed, in addition, the Black Death
and rather acute internal disturbances. This period produced *The Vision of Piers Plowman*, Chaucer, and a considerable upswing of English literature generally.

The flowering of literature and music under Queen
Elizabeth came soon after the first half of the sixteenth
century, which was one of the highly belligerent periods
of English history; and even the Elizabethan Age itself was
far from peaceful, either internally or externally.

The next great notable renaissance of English literature
and music, associated with what is loosely styled the period
of Queen Anne, was preceded by the Cromwellian revolt
and the revolution of 1688. The years 1676-1725 were
among the stormiest in the annals of the British Isles.

Reynolds, Romney, Gainsborough, and other eminent
British painters were born in the first third of the eighteenth century—a particularly militaristic epoch.[17]

Finally, the revival of English literature which marked the first part of the nineteenth century occurred during and immediately after the grave wars of the end of the eighteenth and the first quarter of the nineteenth century.

In Russia a notable upswing of literature (Derjavin, Pushkin, Gogol, etc.), music (Glinka, etc.), and other arts took place between 1751 and 1850. The period of 1751–1825 was one of the most belligerent and that of 1751–1755 one of the most revolutionary in Russian annals.

Similarly, the singular vitality displayed by Russian literature and art during the second part of the nineteenth and beginning of the twentieth century was attended or immediately preceded by a series of major wars, profound social changes, and other disturbances.[18]

If systematically studied, a similar uniformity would be found in the history of the fine arts of Spain, Germany, Austria, the Netherlands, and other countries. The situation may be summed up (with important reservations) by the extravagant statement of J. de Maistre:

"The arts and sciences and the outstanding enterprises and conceptions of the human race . . . prosper especially in time of war. . . . Nations reach the peak of their greatness only after long and bloody wars. The climax of Greek civilization was attained in the terrible epoch of the Peloponnesian War; the brilliant period of Augustus followed the Roman civil wars and proscriptions. The French genius was bred by the wars of the League and further refined by that of the Fronde. All the eminent men of the time of Queen Anne . . . were born amidst intense political commotion. In brief, . . . blood is a fertilizer of the plant called Genius. . . . I cannot conceive of anything less pacifistic than the periods of Alexander the Great and Pericles, Augustus, Leo X, Francis I, Louis XIV, or Queen Anne."[19]

Stated in these terms, the proposition is, of course, decidedly one-sided and calls for a threefold qualification. First, not all wars and revolutions *are* followed by a renaissance of the fine arts. Secondly, such revivals ordinarily occur not during the crisis but after it has passed its most acute and destructive phase. Thirdly, minor wars and revolutions seldom exert any notable positive or negative effect upon the fine arts.

3. General Summary of the Effects of Calamities upon Cultural Creativeness

Thus we see that the effects of calamities—particularly those of war and revolution—upon creativeness in the arts and sciences, ethics and religion, are not so simple as we are prone to think. The consequences are neither purely positive nor purely negative. They are two-sided—both constructive and destructive, stimulating and depressing. In this sense the most general uniformity is that which I have chosen to call the law of polarization.

This law of polarization, in its destructive and constructive aspects, constitutes a sort of caesura in cultural evolution—at once a death knell and the signal of rebirth, marking the termination of an outmoded social order, style, philosophy, dogma and the release of new creative forces. Profound and enduring calamities accordingly represent the collapse of one fundamental form of culture (either sensate, ideational, or idealistic) and the inception of a more vigorous system of thought and conduct.[20]

Chapter Fifteen

DYNAMICS OF IDEOLOGIES IN CALAMITY

1. *Introductory Remarks*

Preceding chapters have dealt with the typical transformations of religious beliefs, moral norms, scientific theories, and aesthetic forms under the impact of calamities.
This chapter will present characteristic changes in other
types of ideologies during and immediately after a calamity.
More specifically it will inquire how various ideologies
gain and lose popularity in relation to the calamities of
famine, war, and revolution. To answer this question, a
limited number of ideologies will be studied under the
concrete conditions of these calamities. Examples to be included are: the *Communist-Socialist-Totalitarian* ideologies, considered under the contrasting conditions of famine and prosperity; *pacifistic and militaristic* ideologies in
war and peace; ideologies of *freedom and restraint* in relation to social order and social revolution.

The conclusions reached by the study of these ideologies in calamity can, with slight variations, be applied to
the rise and decline of many other ideologies.

2. *Impoverishment and Socialist-Communist Ideology*

Do famine and impoverishment influence the ease of
diffusion and acceptance of Communist-Socialist Ideology?
They do, but only under quite definite conditions. First,
there must be no other ways of alleviating the increasing
impoverishment by war, colonization, migration, importation of food products, trade, development of new industries, and so on. Second, there must exist in the starving or
impoverished society a notable difference between the

non-starving and non-impoverished rich and the rest of the population.

Given these conditions, all ideologies that bless, urge, rationalize, approve and justify the partition and distribution of the property of the rich among the poor; that stimulate "equalization of property," "expropriation," "confiscation," "nationalization," "communization," "super-taxation;" that favor a more equal distribution of wealth among the mass of the starving or poverty-stricken population—all such ideologies become more infectious, diffuse more successfully, and are accepted more easily by a far larger part of the population than would ever subscribe to them in more normal times.

It is unimportant what specific form is assumed by such an ideology. It may be the Marxian theory of surplus value and the materialistic interpretation of history, or a Christian theory of evangelical poverty decrying riches as the source of perdition. Similarly, the redistribution of wealth may be attempted by the rulers, as in the cases of the Spartan kings, Agis IV and Cleomenes III; or it may be effected by a revolutionary dictator, a Spartacus, risen from the under-dogs. Sophisticated "rationalizations" and "theoretical justifications" are of secondary importance. What is essential is that the ideology directly urge the expropriation, partition, and distribution of the property of the rich among the poor, that it bless these acts and somehow justify such "equalization" and "socialization" either in the name of God, or "science," or "justice," or "the maximum of happiness for the maximum of human beings," or by some other form suited to the cultural conditions of the society. All such ideologies are called here, for the sake of economy, "Socialist-Communist ideologies."

On the other hand, *given the same abnormal conditions, all ideologies that directly or indirectly oppose, disapprove, or inhibit the acts of expropriation and partition of the property of the rich tend to become less popular, less infectious, less easily accepted by the population of the impoverished and starving society.*

Such is the main relationship between the factor of impoverishment and the success of the socialist-communist ideologies. By way of elaboration the following conclusions should be noted.

a) If the impoverishment occurs in a society in which all are poor or which has ways of alleviating its poverty other than by expropriating and partitioning wealth, the increase in the popularity of the "Socialist-Communist" and in the unpopularity of the anti-Socialist-Communist ideologies may not take place.

b) The greater the impoverishment, the more suddenly it occurs, and the greater the contrast between the rich and the poor—the more rapid is the success of the Socialist-Communist ideologies.

c) If the society becomes more prosperous, while the difference between the poor and the rich classes grows still faster than the general prosperity, then the increasing economic contrast favors the success of the Socialist-Communist ideologies in spite of the upgrade economic trend.

d) When in a starving and impoverished society the wealth is partitioned, poverty nevertheless continuing, the ground for a further success of Socialist-Communist ideologies disappears. There is nothing left to be partitioned that can alleviate the poverty and starvation. In these circumstances such ideologies do not help at all to alleviate the lack of necessities. Therefore, in this stage they lose their infectious power and are replaced by anti-Socialist and anti-Communist ideologies.

These propositions sum up the essential uniformities in the relationship between the calamity of impoverishment and the rise and fall of the Socialist-Communist ideology, so far as its success depends upon the factor of starvation and impoverishment.

Inductive Verification. Inductive verification of these propositions by the relevant facts of history well corroborates their validity.[1] The main series of the corroborating facts follow.

1. In an economically differentiated society, such ideologies have always found most of their followers among the poor rather than among the rich. 2. A flare-up of the success of these ideologies has always taken place under conditions of impoverishment and/or of increasing economic contrasts between the rich and the poor. 3. If, in times of increasing prosperity, the economic contrasts did not grow faster than the general prosperity, then these ideologies either lost their infectious power or did not gain any further successes. 4. An enormous number of previously poor persons and groups which actively participated in the partition of wealth or clamored for it, have changed their original Socialist-Communist ideologies for different, even opposite ones, once they became rich.

Historical Facts. A. Though most of the Socialist-Communist ideologies and movements have often been led by the members of the aristocracy, even by kings, or by those of the rich or middle classes, the rank and file of followers have always been recruited from the poor and impoverished classes. So it was in the "Communist" revolution in ancient Egypt (*ca.,* 2500 B. C.) described by Ipuwer and others, and in the Corcyrean revolution described by Thucydides. Thus it was in an enormous number of movements for the partition and redistribution of wealth in ancient Greece after the fourth century B. C. When Greece entered an economic decline, such partitions became chronic. The armies of all the equalizers and partitionists have been recruited from the impoverished masses,[2] whether in the movements of Agis IV, Cleomenes III, and Nabis or in a legion of other upheavals of those centuries.[2] Now bloody and violent, now comparatively peaceful, all these upheavals were directed toward economic equalization by expropriation of the rich.

The same is true of similar movements in Rome demanding the *aequatio bonorum* and *pecunias equare*, with and without proscription of the rich (*proscriptio locupletium*). The main army of such movements, whether led by Gracchi, Drusus, Catilina, Dolabella, Saturninus, Rullus, Spartacus, or by many others, was recruited from the poor peasants, slaves, soldiers, and proletariat. The same is true of the rank-and-file of the early Christians insofar as the equalizing and communizing tendencies were present in this movement, as indeed they were in the early stages.[3] The situation is no different in the later medieval movements and ideologies of this kind represented by the Christian sectarian movements of the Arnoldists, the Poors of Lyon, the Waldenses, the Humiliates, the Catarrens, the Diggers, the Bohemian and Moravian Brothers, the Fifth Monarchists, the Anabaptists, the Millenarians, the followers of Thomas Müntzer and of John of Leiden. There were numerous other medieval movements professing and seeking an equalization and communization of property.[4] The bulk of the followers of these ideologies and movements was recruited from the impoverished or underdog classes and groups. The same is true of the later Socialist, Communist, and other movements of the eighteenth, nineteenth, and twentieth centuries aiming at a more equable distribution, socialization, or advocating nationalization of property, preaching expropriation of the exploiters, and direct and indirect confiscation of wealth. The truth of this proposition is attested many times in modern history, beginning with the Jacobins, the Babouvists, and the Hebertists in the French Revolution, and ending with the different varieties of Anarchism, Socialism, Communism, and Totalitarianism. The mass of the adherents of these ideologies are drawn largely from the proletariat, from the impoverished groups of the urban and rural populations. Even among the leaders, drawn predominantly from the upper and middle classes, quite a large proportion belongs to the impoverished classes.

On the other hand, from the most remote past to our own time, the bulk of the rich and well-to-do classes has always opposed such ideologies and movements.

B. No less certain is the fact that these ideologies of partition, equalization, socialization, or nationalization of wealth have uniformly flared up during periods of impoverishment and famine in societies where the differentiation into poor and rich was acute, and where other ways of alleviating poverty were inaccessible.

In Greece, beginning with the late fifth century B. C., these movements flourished throughout the three subsequent centuries. During that epoch the cancellation of debts, the confiscation, redistribution, and equalization of wealth became habitual in most of the Greek states, not excepting even the very conservative Sparta. The respective ideologies assumed different forms: now an idealization of the ancient "Communist Sparta" of Lycurgus (by Ephorus, Isocrates, and others); now an idealization of "the natural Communist primitive society"; now the "Communist-totalitarian" ideology of the Platonian *Republic*. But most often they appeared as primitive revolutionary ideologies of expropriation, spoliation, partition, and redistribution of wealth to be carried out in any way from mass murder of the rich to super-taxation. The stream of these ideologies swelled into a great river in these centuries. The pressure manifested itself in the chronic re-distribution of economic possessions, sometimes violently and sometimes in more orderly fashion. The same centuries saw a fairly steady impoverishment of Greece paralleled by a concentration of wealth in fewer and fewer hands.

With variations the same is true of the Roman movements. They emerged in the centuries of the impoverishment of the Roman peasantry, soldiers, and other large classes of the population. They appeared with the growth of the Roman proletariat; which coincided with the concentration of wealth in the hands of the rich.

Starting on a large scale with the movement of the Gracchi (*ca.* 123 B. C., the date of the introduction of the frumentarian law), the respective ideologies and movements led to the introduction of many such measures as the dole for the Roman proletariat and other similar acts of a "socialist-equalitarian-totalitarian" nature. At the time of Julius Caesar the number of families supplied by the dole in Rome was about 320,000, and with the members of the families, it reached some 600,000 persons. They were furnished with bread, oil, meat, clothing, and on various occasions with wine, theater tickets, and even with "ration cards" for prostitutes (*lasciva numismata*). The ideologies assumed various forms. Now it was an idealization of the imagined simple and equal and collectivistic economy of the forefathers; now it was the utopian paradise of the society without private property and with common abundance for all. Sometimes it took the form of a sectarian or religious collectivism; and on other occasions it manifested the communistic and equalitarian tendencies of early Christianity. We must not forget that Christianity exalted the moral command for the rich to "go and sell that thou has and give to the poor" (*Matthew*, 19:21-23). "Verily I say unto you, that a rich man shall hardly enter into the kingdom of heaven." "Blessed be ye poor (and hungry) for yours is the kingdom of God." Christianity morally required one to share with others everything he had. In the early Christian communes—in Jerusalem, Corinth, Ephesus, "they had all things in common"; and when Ananias and Sapphira sold their property and kept a part of the money to themselves, Ananias was punished by God with death (*The Acts*, IV, V). In brief, Communist-equalitarian tendencies were strong in Christianity during the first centuries of its existence and they were often voiced by the Church Fathers. Christianity in its sociopolitical program was the spokesman of the poor and the downtrodden. In this sense, it was one of the noblest manifestations of the Socialist-Communist-equalitarian ideologies of those times.

When, after the eighth century, the Christian church became the richest organization in Europe, these tendencies progressively disappeared from its teachings and practices. After the eleventh century the general economic conditions began somewhat to improve, while the contrast between the rich and poor grew still more. Consequently the Socialist-Communist ideologies and movements appeared again, but this time in the numerous non-orthodox sects outside the official church: the Cattharreans, the Waldenses, the Arnoldists, the Humiliates, the Bohemian and Moravian Brothers, and so on. Most of them were communistic or collectivistic in their economic organization. *Omnem nostram possessionem cum omnibus hominibus communen habemus* could be said not only of the Cattharreans but of most of the other sects. Composed mainly of the impoverished or disfranchised groups of artisans, workers, and peasants, with a sprinkling of members from somewhat higher social groups,[5] these movements emerged and flourished.

As in other similar movements, their policies were directed toward the redistribution, partition, and communization of wealth and property. First of all, they wanted the rich official Christian Church to return to "primitive Christianity" and "pure evangelical poverty." As with the early Christians, their ideologies were based not upon the theory of surplus value, but upon the commands of Jesus and the apostles as they were interpreted by the leaders of the sects.

The same conditions—either impoverishment with a notable economic contrast between rich and poor, or a contrast growing faster than the general economic well-being—were present in subsequent flare-ups of socialist-communist ideologies and movements. 1) In a great revival of these in Bohemia in the fourteenth and fifteenth centuries (the Bohemian and Moravian Brothers, the Adamits, the beggars, the Anabaptists, the Nicolaits, and others): there was established the communist state of the Taborites with the communization of women as well as of property. 2) In several other movements in Europe in the sixteenth century, the same preconditions can be observed, especially in the cases of Thomas Münzer's commune in Mülhausen, and John of Leiden's in Münster. 3) Another instance was the revival of these ideologies and movements in England in the second part of the seventeenth century, the Diggers, the Millenarians, the Men of the Fifth Monarchy, the Anabaptists, the Brownists, and to a certain extent the Quakers. 4) There was another stirring of these ideologies in England during the early nineteenth century (R. Owen, the Chartist movement, and others). 5) We see a rapid growth of these ideologies in France in the second part of the eighteenth century (Morelli, Mably, and certain aspects of Rousseau, Brissot, and a few of the Encyclopedists). Their appeal was widest during the French Revolution (Saint Simon, Babeuf, the Hebertists, etc.). 6) There was a renewal of their popularity in Europe in the middle nineteenth century (P. Leroux, Enfantin, Furier, Lassale, Karl Marx, F. Engels, M. Bakunin, Louis Blanc, Proudhon, Cabet, and others). 7) The Paris Commune of 1871 is another case. 8) Finally, we can point to the enormous spread of these ideologies and movements in the late nineteenth and above all in the twentieth century. During and after the First World War there occurred the Russian Communist Revolution, other Communist revolutions in Bavaria and Hungary, and a great development of Socialist, National-Socialist, Fascist, and totalitarian movements throughout the world.

In all these revivals of Socialist-Communist ideologies and movements in their diverse forms we invariably find the conditions formulated above. This does not mean that only the factors of impoverishment and increasing economic contrast are operative in a resuscitation of these ideologies. Other factors, beginning with war, certainly play their rôles. But in nearly all the great flare-ups of the ideologies studied, the factors discussed have unquestionably played an important part.

C. Finally, the proposition is corroborated by the fact that many persons, groups, and classes that clamor for the socialization of property when they are impoverished, frequently discard their Socialist ideologies and Communist policies once they become rich. Such an about-face often occurs when the contrast between their previously poor economic status and that of the former rich class has disappeared. This tragi-comedy has repeated itself as generally as the uniformity in the flare-up of Communist-

Socialist movements discussed in the preceding section. R. Pöhlmann well sums up this common transformation in Greek and Roman socialist movements. When in the numerous socializations and re-distributions of wealth in Greece and Rome the most zealous leaders became rich:

"... they had every reason to fear the outburst of revolutionary speeches, for in a new revolution (or re-distribution) they could only lose without any gain; therefore they needed not to go about any more masquerading as proletarian-revolutionaries. Usually, in these conditions, they rapidly acquired the most reactionary ideology in economics as well as in politics. They turned into the partisans of the *Beati possidentes*. They worried little over the growth of a new inequality. They would not listen to the idea of a new division of property now that they themselves were the owners. Consequently their Socialist fraternity lasted only till the rich were conquered and the process of the spoliation accomplished."[8]

The same story repeated itself with most of the successful communizers in Rome. Even the Christian Church, as mentioned before, experienced it. Parallel with its enrichment, its earlier Communist-Socialist and similar tendencies passed from *forte* to *piano* and *pianissimo* in the official body of church authorities. A corresponding transformation occurred in several monasteries and monastic orders dedicated to Poverty, and in many sectarian movements like the Hiliats, the Taborites, and the Communes of T. Münzer and John of Leiden. Similar decommunization took place with the Waldenses and the Bohemian and Moravian Brothers after they became well-to-do. The Jacobins likewise, having robbed the aristocracy and the rich, became very bourgeois and ardent partisans of the sacredness of private property. Such also was the destiny of the several Communist and Socialist communities founded in America and Australia.

The story of desocialization and decommunization re-

peated itself in recent times with many *ci-devant* leaders
of Socialism, Communism, and related movements: with
Scheidemann, Renodel, Tomas, Viviani, Clemenceau,
Briand, Samba, MacDonald, Atlee, Bevins, Vandervelde,
Henderson, Noske, and with a legion of other leaders of
these movements. Having climbed to the top of the political and economic ladder they became increasingly tame,
and their Socialist and Communist colors faded accordingly. Even the Socialist movement and parties of the last
third of the nineteenth century when the economic situation of labor improved—became progressively more moderate and more bourgeois in England, France, and Germany. Their policies and practical ideologies tended to
become more and more like those of liberal capitalism and
"sensible progressivism." So it was in the past; and so it is
in the present.

The totality of these concisely summarized facts can
hardly leave any doubt as to the validity of our proposition. It means that famine, the extreme form of impoverishment, notably changes the character and the success
of the Socialist-Communist ideologies. The change is not
confined to these ideologies. It involves an enormous number of beliefs, convictions, ideas, tastes, norms, and
opinions, both simple and complex. The general direction
of the change is given by this analysis and by the references in Chapter Four.

Summing up, we can say that when a society passes from
a state of prosperity to one of impoverishment, especially
to mass famine, it experiences a shocking deformation of
many of its ideologies. What was accepted before is now
rejected, and vice versa. Likewise, when a given group
passes from poverty or starvation to prosperity and riches,
the opposite revision takes place. Ideologies popular in
times of famine now become unpopular. The rise and fall
of Socialist-Communist ideologies is only an illustrative case

of this eternal deformation and reformation of ideologies under conditions of starvation and prosperity.

3. *Transmutation of Ideologies in War*

President A. Lawrence Lowell has well shown how rapidly and deeply ideologies and attitudes are changed in war and peace.

"When civilians enlist in time of war their change of attitude takes place, not after long experience of army life and of battles, but almost at once; and it is due to a new orientation, a recognition of a different and paramount object, transcending in immediate importance the former ones. It is the result, in short, of a radical change in the focus of attention. . . . Moreover the change of sentiment is not confined to the army. The men and women who stay at home also assume a new attitude on the outbreak of a war that requires a great national effort. They are not less ready than soldiers to restrict liberty. They do not shudder at reports of the loss of thousands of lives of their fellow-citizens in a victorious battle, as they would at the loss of scores in an accident in time of peace. . . . They delight to work and deny themselves comforts in a way that they would otherwise think intolerable.[7]

A large mass of people who are militant pacifists in peace-time suddenly become super-patriots and supporters of war after the outbreak of hostilities; and many a war-time militarist turns into a pacifist in time of peace. This monotonous transmutation has repeated itself time and again with thousands of persons since the comedy of Aristophanes to this very day when, as in the days of the First World War, millions of socialists, communists, and pacifists are becoming super-patriots, soldiers, militarists, and nationalists.

The same is true of the evaluation of the army and the military profession. In time of peace many persons regard them as parasitic, useless, and socially harmful; in time of war the army and the military profession are glorified. During peaceful periods, war is regarded by a large proportion of the intellectuals as an unadulterated evil. In time of war it becomes the noblest and most necessary social duty. When peace prevails, a given nation is often glorified and praised. When this nation becomes an enemy it is denied almost every virtue: all the evils imaginable are ascribed to it.

Many ideologies popular in time of peace are branded "fifth-column propaganda" in war-time. A hero in time of peace may become a traitor in time of war, if he expresses opinions different from those prevalent in the government and the masses. "War-hysteria" is a term that includes an enormous number of these transmutations of ideologies and values in time of war.

This transmutation affects almost every ideology and value that is directly or indirectly connected with the war, from aesthetic, political, religious, scientific, and moral values to "patriotic" and "unpatriotic" foods, drinks, clothing, etc. It is enough to glance through the advertisements of any paper nowadays, or to listen to the radio advertising for a few minutes to see the truth of this statement. Even laxatives and cereals, chewing gums and soap are advertised as "patriotic" and necessary for defense and victory.

When war gives way to peace the opposite trend predominates. What was glorified during the war is now debunked, ridiculed, indignantly repudiated, socially ostracised, and heatedly condemned. This "comedy of transmutation" has occurred so many times and so regularly that there is no need to go into details. Verily blessed are those who do not see or do not remember the endless *corsi* and *ricorsi*.

4. *Transformation of Ideologies in Revolution*

A host of ideologies rise and fall when a society passes from the non-revolutionary period into the revolution and thence, finally, to the post-revolutionary era. Theoretically we can distinguish in any revolution two phases: first, destructive and "liberating," second, constructive and "restraining."

1. *Liberating Phase.* With the approach of the revolution all ideologies that attack the oppressing institutions and values from which the revolutionary group suffers gain rapidly in popularity and acceptance. All kinds of "liberating ideologies" become rife. The sought-after "liberation" may be freedom from tyrants, kings, aristocracies, Tories, slavery or serfdom. It may mean liberation from the payment of debts, royalties, corvée, rents, and similar duties. One may seek freedom from religion, the "opiate of the masses," from subordination to the upper class or to foreign subjugators, or freedom from the sacredness of property. In really radical revolutions, groups may strive for liberation from any "restraining" norm or value—moral commandments, religious prescriptions, juridical norms, even family ties. All such ideologies grow enormously in popularity and acceptance.

The purpose of these ideologists is to undermine the existing inhibitions, restraints, and taboos, and to rationalize and justify the destruction of these "oppressive" institutions. The ideologies are often marked by such characteristic slogans as "Down with . . . ", and "Long live liberty," i. e., freedom to act without inhibitions in the way the revolutionaries desire.

On the approach of a revolution these ideologies emerge to prepare the way for the upheaval. When this breaks out, they diffuse far and wide. If the revolution is mainly political, the ideologies are primarily political; if the revolution is also economic the ideologies have an economic character; and if the revolution is religious, the ideologies assume a religious nature. At the beginning of the revolutionary period in Greece (typified by Thrasymachus, Georgias, Protagoras and others) the destructive ideologies of the Sophists began to diffuse among the dissatisfied elements of the population. They assailed most of the currently accepted values of Greek society, especially those pertaining to God, the family, and property.

Similarly, when Rome approached its period of civil wars and chronic revolutions, the sophisticated Epicurean and the grossly materialistic ideologies working against property and religion, undermining almost the whole value-system of pre-revolutionary Rome, were enormously accentuated. They were diffused in a more sophisticated form among the high-brow group, while in the lower classes they necessarily appeared in cruder versions. Philosophers, rhetoricians, poets, scholars and politicians all began to manufacture such ideologies.

A few other samples of such ideologies are those of Huss and his followers before the Bohemian revolution; those of Wycliffe and the Lollards; of the Anabaptists before the Cromwellian revolution; of the Humanists and Profligate Libertines before the chronic revolutions of the Italian Renaissance. Similar also were the ideologies of Luther and Melanchton before the upheavals of the Reformation, and those of the Encyclopedists on the eve of the French Revolution. The Marxians and other modern revolutionaries are more recent examples of these ideologies with their characteristic "Down with . . ." and "Long live . . .", and "Give me liberty or give me death."

As a matter of fact, so long as the pre-revolutionary system of values is stable and strong, no important successful revolution is possible. The "liberating ideologies" act as underminers, destroyers, and de-moralizers of these values. Only when their work is considerably progressed so that the society's established system of values is conspicuously disintegrated—only then can the revolutionary explosion take place.

As specified above, if the revolution is only a political one, the "liberating" ideologies center mainly upon discrediting the existing political regime and idealising the projected system. Economic and other values are also factors in this situation, but only secondary and incidental ones. Concrete examples in this category are the French revolutions of 1830, 1848, and the 1851 *coup d'etat* of Napoleon III; the other European revolutions of 1848; and the Russian revolution of 1905.

If the revolution is nationalistic and is directed toward ending the political domination of a foreign country, the ideologies would tend to assail the values of the foreign nation and its government. They would exalt freedom from alien rule. Here we can point to the Greek and Serbian revolts against Turkey, the Italian revolt against Austria, and the American War for Independence.

If the revolution is centered around the religious values, the ideologies attack mainly the Church and its regime, against which hostility is directed. In that case the revolutionary ideologies have a pronounced theological character, and they focus primarily on religious problems. In this class were several revolutions in Italy, such as the uprising of the Arnoldists against the Papacy and many other revolts against the authority, dogma, wealth and vices of the Catholic Church. Such were also the revolutions of the Protestants, and many a civil war of the Reformation and the Counter-Reformation.

If the revolution is centered chiefly around the economic values, whether aiming for the re-distribution of wealth, restrictions on private property, or cancellation of debts, the revolutionary ideologies are coloured by economic preoccupations. Many Greek and Roman revolu-

tions seeking debt cancellation or the redistribution of land
and wealth had this character. However, since economic
revolutions are much deeper than political ones, they
hardly ever occur without having at the same time their
political, religious, or nationalistic aspects. Ordinarily the
greatest revolutions become economic. In that case they
assume the character of "Communist-Socialist" revolutions, like the Paris Commune, the Russian Revolution of
1917, and other similar revolutions of the past.[8]

2. *Restraining Phase.* Whether the revolution is abor-
tive and is suppressed by the counter-revolutionary forces
or whether it runs its full cycle unchecked, in both cases
it sooner or later enters its second phase. Then construction replaces destruction, and restraint is substituted for
the "liberation" of the first period.

The categorical "Down with . . ." ideologies of the
first stage are insufficient for the erection of a new social
structure. A constructive blueprint is needed before the
building plans can be executed. The mere liberation of the
masses from religious, political, sexual, economic, and
moral inhibitions to enable them to destroy "the old regime" is inadequate during the constructive phase. On the
contrary, such unrestraint now constitutes the greatest
danger for the reconstruction.

For construction needs discipline. It requires subordination to the new bosses and strict obedience on the part
of the masses of the population, regardless of whether their
circumstances have been improved by the revolution or
not. Such a construction needs economic resources which
can be taken only from the masses by taxes, by labour
duty, and by similar measures. Furthermore it needs at
least an elementary social order. If the masses "liberated"
in the first phase of the revolution remain as wild, wilful,
and anarchistic as they were in the first phase, no con-

struction is possible. Permanent anarchy is the only result of such a situation.

This explains why the second period of revolution is always a period of *restraint* as against the *liberation* of the first phase. As the latter stage of a great revolution is usually developed so exhaustively that the masses become very wild and unruly, the restraint and inhibition of the second phase of the revolution is always an exceedingly painful process for the people. It does not matter whether it is effected by the revolutionary government or by the counter-revolutionaries. The greater the liberation and anarchy of the first phase, the more rigid is the straight-jacket put upon the masses in the second period. The name of this straight-jacket is *Terror*. When it is impossible to bring the liberated masses to their senses by mild and peaceable methods, the revolution in its second phase uses firing squads, guillotines, prisons, concentration camps, torture, confiscations, and all kinds of the most cruel techniques to sober the intoxicated masses and to introduce discipline and order.

As a result, many activities stimulated in the first period of revolution are now prohibited under the severest penalties. Conversely, many an activity forbidden during the first phase is now encouraged or demanded. Murder, violation, and spoliation, directed in the first stage against the "old regime" and its representatives, now is prohibited because the old regime no longer exists. The newly rich aristocracy established by the revolution does not want to be murdered or robbed. Failure to obey authority is not tolerated. Non-fulfillment of their duties by the subordinate classes—serfs, peasants, soldiers, clerks, etc.—is now absolutely prohibited. The anarchy and wild destruction of the first phase are unreservedly banned. They are replaced by an iron discipline. The greater the loosening and the liberation of the first period, the more pitiless is the strait-jacket of restraint and inhibition in the second.

In the first period the liberating ideologies were paving the way to freedom from inhibitions. In the second stage the restraining ideologies reinculcate new norms of behavior. The reappearances of "Don't" and "Do," "Thou shall" and "Thou shall not" prepare the way for the actual restraining measures. They justify the new strait-jacket soon to be put upon the half-mad society. Most of the previously popular ideologies gradually fade out amidst widespread criticism of them. They are replaced by the radically different ideologies of the "new order" and the "new revolutionary discipline." Preceded by this shift in the ideologies, the revolution makes an about-face.

Although in a new form, these ideologies in their practical effects are very similar to those of the pre-revolutionary period. They reflect the ultimate living trends of the society, the basic, long-run developments which were temporarily stopped by the revolution. Only the ideologies which had outlived themselves, only those reflecting conditions permanently ended by the revolution are not regenerated. Others which rationalize and embody the living values of the society are now revived, but in new colours and new trimmings.

The old ideologies which demanded obedience to the Old Regime now reappear in new form to require unconditional subordination to the "New Revolutionary Government," to the "Government of the Masses," the "Government of the Proletarian and Peasant," "the Government of the People, for the People, and by the People" and so on. Old ideologies of the sacredness of the property now come back in the form of the sacredness of public property, of the property of labouring masses, of the "Proletarian Republic" or of the "Servants of the People."

Old ideologies of political and economic inequality re-appear in different form to justify the new stratification imposed by the Communist or Socialist or Fascist Party. They justify the inequality of the "lazy" and of the "industrious," of the Christian and non-Christian, of the Germans and the non-Germans, of the Proletarians and the non-Proletarians; of the Aryans and the non-Aryans; of the Brahmins and the Sudras.

Capital punishment and other severe penalties which were done away with in the first period of the revolution now return in more cruel forms.

And, similarly, in regard to war and peace, religion and irreligion, restrained and free sex life, and the forms of science and art. As A. de Tocqueville and H. Taine rightly noted, revolution in its constructive phase always resumes the work of continuing the pre-revolutionary living trends having rid society of the dead ones. Correspondingly, the ideologies of the second stage represent a revival of the living ideologies of the pre-revolutionary society in new dress and colours. The Revolution itself, when successful, inherently and necessarily consumes its earlier ideologies and resurrects the living pre-revolutionary ideologies.

This explains why in practically all great revolutions the ideologies of the first phase turned out to be unpopular in the second. In the second phase of the Greek revolutions of the Ten and Thirty tyrants the once popular Sophist ideologies became so unpopular that even Socrates suffered the death penalty, supposedly for "undermining the religion" but actually for having been a teacher of some of the tyrants. Likewise, the materialist, Epicurean, atheistic, and similar ideologies of the revolutionary period of the second and first centuries B. C. were very unpopular in the second stage of those revolutions; cf. the dictatorships of Julius Caesar and Augustus. Regardless of the policies of the government, the radically different ideologies of neo-Platonism, Neo-Pythagorianism, of the oriental religions, and of Christianity began to get the upper hand.

The same uniformity appears in the loss of popularity by the Hussite, Taborite, and other Communist-Socialist ideologies in the Bohemian, German, and English revolutions from the fifteenth to the seventeenth centuries. Everyone knows the refrain, "It was the fault of Rousseau and Voltaire," sung in the second period of the French Revolution, when the ideologies of the first phase were giving way to those of Chateaubriand, J. de Maistre, de Bonald, and others. The story repeated itself in the Russian revolution. In the first period bourgeois science, philosophy, Pushkin, Tschaikovsky and other representatives of the "degenerate aristocracy" and the "bourgeoisie" were assailed. Religion, the emperors and the great military generals of the past, the family, marriage, and sexual chastity were likewise attacked. In the second period, the Revolution banned the Marxian texts of history, restored the family, praised sexual chastity, and elevated Pushkin and Tschaikovsky to even higher positions than they had before. It idealized the great Russian Czars, the famous generals, and even the religious leaders of the past. It exalted patriotism, "Our Soviet Fatherland." The new phase of the Revolution saw the introduction of enormous economic and other inequalities with corresponding ideologies to justify them. Soviet Russia resumed exactly the same foreign policy as that of the Czarist regime. As a finishing touch, it prohibited or destroyed most of the writings of the Communist leaders themselves. These writings, produced in the first period of the Revolution, and including those of Stalin and some other contemporary leaders, were taken out of circulation and banned. Many of their authors were eliminated by purges.[9]

Such is the eternal "cycle" of ideologies in revolutions. The concrete forms in each revolution are different, but the pattern of the cycle is the same. In the second phase revolution burns what it deified in the first, and it exalts in the second period what it destroyed in the first. This tragic story continues in endless repetitions.

5. General Conclusion

The above shows that many ideologies undergo an enormous change in their popularity under conditions of calamity. Calamities make popular many ideologies normally unpopular. They cause many to be hated that are highly favored both before and after the disaster. Some of the calamities, like revolution, make an about-face and elevate in their second phase what was cast down in the first. What conditions determine these alternations of popularity and unpopularity have been indicated clearly in the text.

PART FIVE

CAUSES AND REMEDIES OF CALAMITIES

Chapter Sixteen

Causes of Calamities

1. *Mutual Association of Calamities*

Once in a while each of our four calamities occurs alone and spreads without the company of the others, but more often than not they ravage in various combinations. However, not every one of the four calamities mingles equally well with the others. Some are more solitary and run their courses alone, while the others are more "gregarious" and appear side by side.

Pestilence or plague seems to have better chances than any of the other three calamities to emerge alone. At least, we know of many epidemics which occurred without being followed by famine or revolution or war. This calamity thus is more solitary than the others.

Next to pestilence comes *famine and impoverishment*. Occasionally, when not too severe, a famine has come and gone alone. But as a rule any great famine has almost invariably been followed by pestilence, and not infrequently by war or revolution. It is a less solitary calamity than pestilence. Its regular association with pestilence, especially in the past, is well stressed by the historian of the English epidemics.

"The history of English epidemics, previous to the Black Death, is almost wholly a history of famine sicknesses; and the list of such famines, with attendant sickness, is a considerable one."[1]

The same can be said of epidemics in other countries in the past. At the present time, because of the progress of medical science in its struggle with the infectious diseases, the tie may appear to be somewhat less close than before.

Nevertheless, it continues to exist. All the recent great famines—in Russia, Poland, Greece and other countries—have been followed by several epidemics, including the spotted typhus and sometimes involving plagues whose real nature has remained, at least in the case of Russia in 1918-1922, unknown to medical science.

The relationships of *famine and impoverishment* to *revolution and war* are far less close than the association with pestilence. Famine and impoverishment may facilitate revolution or war only when certain conditions are present; they do not necessarily cause such conflicts. The popular idea that revolutions always occur in periods of intense poverty is not accurate. Nor is war a necessary result of impoverishment. Many a famine did not produce either revolution or war.[2] And many a war and revolution have occurred in prosperous societies.

What are the conditions under which famine and impoverishment may lead to riot, revolution, or war? First, for a given society there must be no other means except revolution or war to alleviate its impoverishment. The possibility of imports, emigration, migration, or a peaceful colonization of other regions should be non-existent. The orderly distribution of surpluses of food and wealth, or the discovery of new food resources on a sufficient scale must be out of the question.

Secondly, in a famishing society there must be a notable contrast between the starving and the non-starving groups. The same comparison can be made between several societies; a sharp economic cleavage among them may set the stage for war. If such a contrast does not exist neither revolution nor war can solve the dilemma. Thirdly, the rich and the ruling classes (or the rich societies) must be poorly organized and poorly armed. If they have lost their vigor, or if they doubt the justice and right of their defending the existing order and themselves by all possible means against the impoverished classes or societies, then their doom may well be imminent.

A revolution rarely conquers any strong class or group. It usually takes "the empty place" occupied by the softened, demoralized, and parasitical posterity of the great forefathers who established the aristocratic, governing stratum of society. This poor posterity of great fathers does not serve the society, nor is it able—even willing—to protect itself and the existing order vigorously. Only such hollow regimes as these are conquered by revolution. Conversely, if the rich society is strong, its very strength is a sufficient protection against attack by a weaker society. It is a rare phenomenon for a weak society to start a hopeless war against a stronger one. In times of desperation such a thing may happen, but very seldom. On its part, the rich society may and sometimes does start a war against a poor society in order to forestall attacks against itself. But since the other society is impoverished and starving, and promises no booty, the wealthy society does not ordinarily have any reason for a preventive war.

Fourth, the most important condition for a causal relationship between impoverishment and war or revolution is the disintegration of the system of norms and values—moral, juridical, religious, and others—in a considerable part of the starving masses or the poverty-stricken society. In Chapter Four we saw that under the influence of starvation a part of the population becomes so demoralized as to commit all kinds of crimes and antisocial actions. However, in most famines this happens only in a fraction of the population. Those whose moral, religious, juridical, aesthetic, and social values and norms are not disintegrated do not break these restraints. They often suffer and may even die from starvation, yet they do not resort to murder, theft, cannibalism, bloodshed or other such anti-social actions. If the system of values and norms in a starving society remains strong, a revolution will not take place, no matter how terrible the famine. If the same is true on an international scale, war will not break out. Other means will be found to alleviate the sufferings. If no adequate resources are found, the population will die from starvation, but it will not revolt. The number of famines that have occurred in the history of any great nation has been much greater than the number of wars and revolutions caused by famine.

These four conditions, not to mention others of less importance, must be present if famine and impoverishment are to produce war or revolution. In many famines some or all of these prerequisites were absent, and consequently they were not attended by either war or revolution. This gives a concise answer to the question, why some famines have been followed by war or revolution, while others have not.

Finally, *war and revolution* are the least solitary calamities of the four studied. Any great war or revolution nearly always has been attended by famine and pestilence. In addition, war has often (but not always) generated revolution; and revolution, war.[3] In other words, war-famine-pestilence, and revolution-famine-pestilence—these trios of calamities are typically associated together. Quite frequently (but again, not always) war appears in the quadruple combination of calamities: war-famine-pestilence-revolution; and the same is true of revolution. War and revolution are thus the most fruitful parents of calamities. They generate pestilence and famine more often than pestilence and famine generate war and revolution.

This analysis means that among the causes of each calamity is to be included one of the other calamities. One calamity becomes a cause of another. This is especially true of war and revolution. We have thus made a first step in the study of the causation of calamities. Let us now proceed to the core of this problem.

2. Causes of Calamities

By causes of a calamity are meant two kinds of conditions. First, there is *the necessary condition* or cause, without which the calamity cannot occur. Second, there are *supplementary conditions*, that do not hinder or neutralize but rather facilitate the realization of the consequences of the necessary condition, thus making *the necessary cause a sufficient cause*. The necessary cause of an infectious disease, say diphtheria, is infection. But if a person is innoculated against it, he may be in the closest contact with the germs and yet remain uninfected. Innoculation is an *adverse* supplementary condition neutralizing the results of the necessary cause of diphtheria. This is the reason why, besides the necessary cause, an absence of adverse, and the presence of favoring supplementary conditions also are elements of the causation of such a calamity.

From this standpoint, the following factors are the necessary causes and supplementary conditions of each type of calamity studied.

Causes of Pestilence. Necessary cause: infection. Supplementary conditions: A. A concurrence of various cosmic and biological conditions such as weather, climate, and other circumstances favorable for the breeding and increase of the respective germs and their bearers. A random example is the multiplication of animals, such as mice and rats, which are the carriers of certain germs. B. A constellation of sociocultural conditions not hindering, but facilitating the infection. A few of these are: a lack of sanitary precautions and quarantine; ignorance of the real cause of the illness; an undeveloped medical science; intensive commercial or political contact with the places that are the focal points of the infection; general dirtiness and filth; war, revolution and famine; and many other sociocultural conditions.

Causes of Famine. Necessary cause: inability of a given society to procure the food required by all its members. Supplementary conditions: A. The unfavorable play of natural forces such as drought, flood, fire, earthquakes, invasion of locusts or similar pests, epidemics, and other cosmic and biological processes. B. A disastrous constellation of sociocultural forces, e. g., invasion, war, revolution, dislocation of trade and commerce, breakdown of transportation and distribution of food, lack of organization for a possible food emergency; carelessness, laziness, ignorance, etc.

As soon as enough of these supplementary conditions make real the potential inability of the society to procure food for its members, famine emerges. Its necessary cause remains this inability, but it is actualized by different combinations of supplementary conditions. To take a parallel case—the cause of diphtheria is infection, but infection can be acquired in many different ways; by direct touch of the infected person, by contact with different infected objects, even through the air in some disease, and in a dozen other ways.

This means that a mass famine is never a product of purely cosmic or biological factors. It is chiefly the result of sociocultural circumstances that make the society unable to cope with the food problem under current conditions.

Causes of War and Revolution. Necessary cause: disintegration of the system of religious, moral, juridical, and other values of a given society (in revolution) or societies (in war). This collapse manifests itself, among other ways, in a widening gap between the value-systems of the upper, privileged, governing groups and those of the lower, middle, underprivileged groups (in revolution); and between the value-systems of two or more societies (in war). Without this necessary cause no combination of supplementary conditions can generate revolution or war.[4] Supplementary conditions: A. Cosmic and biological circumstances such as famine, pestilence, flood, and others that facilitate the disintegration of values and norms. B. More important are sociocultural conditions like the great economic and social contrasts between the upper and lower classes. Parallel contrasts may exist between societies, some being weak and softened, with incapable governments and parasitic upper classes, while others are vigorous and stable with resourceful ruling classes. The factor of war is an important supplementary condition for revolution and revolution, in turn, for war. Other examples are new inventions that sometimes strengthen the disfranchised and subordinated classes or societies, while weakening the privileged classes or nations. We can also mention changes in economic and social conditions, and the influence of other societies through propaganda and the engineering of international disturbances by financial aid to neighboring revolutionaries. By their mere existence foreign nations serve as catalytic agents. Needless to say there are hundreds of other supplementary sociocultural conditions. In war and revolution these play a much greater rôle than do the cosmic and biological factors, in contrast to the importance of the latter in famine and pestilence.

The necessary cause (the disintegration of the system of values and norms) can be generated immanently in a given society by the spontaneous development of the society and its culture. In this process no specific condition plays a predominant rôle. Rather, the whole sociocultural life imperceptibly undermines and then disintegrates the existing value-system of the society. Like a human being, who, by the very process of his living becomes imperceptibly older until one day he finds himself senile and fragile and on the brink of death—like this immanent process of aging, the system of values and norms of a society changes in the process of its functioning and, without any specific supplementary factor, comes to its disintegration.

Such in a brief and concise form are the causes, necessary and supplementary, of calamities. When we study any example of the four calamities, we invariably find that the indicated necessary cause, and some of the supplementary factors mentioned above, are always present.

Chapter Seventeen

THE WAY OUT OF CALAMITIES

1. *Rational and "Natural Death" Ways*

All calamities come to an end sooner or later. Some terminate only after the costliest toll of death and suffering on the part of their victims. For these unfortunates there is no relief till the forces of the calamity have exhausted themselves in the most torturing and painful ways. Other calamities, however, run less disastrous courses because of the application of rational counter-measures which serve to combat and to minimize the enormous human toll. Let us now glance more closely at these possibilities, keeping in mind the contrast between *the way in which many calamities have actually ended and the way in which they could have been ended if the societies involved had used the best, most efficient, and least costly techniques of counteracting the disasters.*

2. *Termination of Famines*

All famines have been terminated either *by the removal of their necessary and supplementary causes or by the catastrophic exhaustion of the famine after it has taken its full toll of suffering and death.* The removal of the necessary cause means the restoration of society's ability to procure the required minimum of food for its members. This restoration is possible only in societies with discipline and resourcefulness, reinforced by many favorable supplementary conditions. Among the latter are climatic and biological conditions making for a good harvest, the disappearance of all the supplementary factors of a given famine, the importing of food supplies from other regions, and

THE WAY OUT OF CALAMITIES

migration of the population to more prosperous regions where they can live comfortably, at the same time relieving those left behind. Still others are: the voluntary or obligatory distribution of the food surpluses in the society, the discovery of new sources and forms of food, and in chronic famines, the reduction of the birth and marriage rates.

These measures are comparatively rational, not especially painful, and they tend to prevent an enormous toll of human lives. Their application presupposes, however, a society well disciplined and integrated in all respects. It presupposes leadership, willingness on the part of prosperous groups to share their resources with the starving classes, and the possibilities either of buying food from other countries or of emigrating to other regions. The society must be capable of making new adaptations and inventions to alleviate the famine. In brief, these measures can be and have been carried through only by well integrated societies with a strong system of values and social discipline. These permit the society to remove the necessary cause of famine and to shorten or terminate the ordeal.

Unfortunately not all impoverished societies have been able to meet these conditions. Many of these advantages have been lacking in such societies. Therefore, their famines have often ended in different—and much more tragic —ways. First, they have resulted in internal disturbances and conflicts which, except in mild and superficial revolutions, have hardly ever alleviated the famine. Instead, practically all the great revolutions have enormously aggravated starvation, to say nothing of generating various epidemics, civil wars, and revolutionary terrors. By these means, revolutions have greatly increased the death toll and the death rate in the society. If after months or years of revolution the famine ended, it did so mainly because of the decrease of huge numbers of victims claimed by famine, pestilence, and civil strife.

The same is true of war. At least for the vanquished party war does not end but intensifies the famine and death toll. In this sense war also terminates famine mainly by elevating the death toll to appalling levels.

Finally, famines have been brought to a close in many societies by the terrible mortality of the population, not only from starvation, but also from epidemics and other satellites of extreme poverty. The great losses from death and from frequent reductions in the birth rate bring the surviving part of the population into an equilibrium with the available food supply.

In general, most famines have been ended by a mixture of all these more or less fatal ways and measures. Only a small proportion of severe famines has been dealt with by comparatively rational and painless methods. A much larger proportion has been liquidated by the scythe of death disguised in the form of riots, revolutions, wars, pestilence, and starvation.

The practical lesson of history is this: the orderly ways of an integrated society are always more successful and less costly in dealing with famine than are the various disorderly modes resulting in huge mortality. If the starving society is wise, if its governing and well-to-do classes are unselfish, it will always seek a combination of the rational and less painful ways out of the famine, never would it turn to revolutions, war, and other similar "medicines" which cure the sickness by killing the patient. Unfortunately, many a society does not possess this wisdom of temporary sacrifice. They turn to pseudo-measures and pay the terrible penalty for their foolishness and egotism, their lack of sociality and mutual help.

3. *Termination of Pestilence*

With slight modification, what has been said of the modes of escaping from famine can be applied to the termination of epidemics. Some of the latter have been ended by the removal of their necessary cause, infection, either by timely elimination of the source or by stopping its spread. Application of scientific means—medical, sanitary, and others—successfully combats the source of infection or its spread by numerous methods—by preventive inoculation, by quarantines, by severance of contact and communication with the infected regions, and by extermination of various carriers of the disease, such as lice, rats, mice, and others. Other measures involve the removal of filth, dirt, and other conditions favoring the diffusion of the disease; and the elimination of famine or war or revolution that originally gave rise to the epidemics.

These are samples of the rational and least costly measures. They presuppose a society already possessing scientific knowledge of the nature and causes of disease, and of the measures effective against it. It presupposes also a well disciplined society with an understanding of the necessity of these measures and of the value of temporary sacrifice and inconvenience. It assumes that the society has the necessary minimum of medical facilities and personnel, and so on.[1]

Unfortunately many societies in the past, and even in the present, have not met these conditions necessary for the successful termination or prevention of epidemics. The scientific knowledge of the nature of disease and of the efficient means against it is a comparatively recent discovery. Likewise, many other prerequisites, such as adequate sanitation and hygienic conditions in cities and villages, were and still are absent in numerous regions. Famine, revolution, and war often could not and cannot be stopped. Therefore most of the epidemics in the past, and a part of those in the present, have been terminated not in easy and comparatively painless ways, but through the much more costly ways discussed above.

The only important variation has been in the rate or toll of death. Depending upon the specific disease and other conditions the death toll of some pestilences has been terrific (as we have seen in Chapter Five). In others, the toll has been less, but still large. Occasionally, societies have been completely at the mercy of the pestilence, which ravaged and killed until it had run its course, and then, having lost its virulence, subsided and disappeared. Others have offered a degree of resistance and, when this was efficient, have somewhat decreased their death toll. But they have still paid a high price. Only in comparatively recent times, however, as mentioned earlier, have societies been able to fight epidemics successfully. Even now it cannot be said that any society is entirely capable of forestalling or stopping all epidemics by the rational methods of scientific prevention and therapy. The outbreak of influenza at the end of the First World War took an enormous toll throughout the world.[2] On a smaller scale influenza and other diseases are still active enough to afflict seriously almost all societies. Further, we still seem to be unable to eliminate famines, revolutions, wars, and other calamities that breed and spread epidemics. Even with the knowledge of the efficient means of combating them we remain helpless to fight them successfully as long as revolutions, famines, and wars remain. This is the reason why at the present moment epidemics of typhus, etc. are ravaging Greece, the Balkans, Poland, Russia, Rumania, and other countries suffering from starvation, war, and revolution. As long as these "supplementary" causes of epidemics exist, medical science is incapable of removing pestilence from the list of the great calamities of mankind. Such an elimination requires not only medical techniques but above all social measures. Until these are effected, pestilence will, to some extent, remain with us.

Again this means that side by side with the biological and medical questions, the problem of alleviation and elimination of epidemics has its no less important social and cultural aspects. A wise society, desirous of being free from pestilence, would eliminate not only its biological roots but also the social causes of epidemics; famine, ignorance, revolution, and war. Such a goal requires a society supremely well integrated in scientific, religious, moral and social respects. Unfortunately, many societies have been, are, and probably will be lacking in this integration and wisdom. Hence, they have been paying the penalty of the visitation of pestilence with its death toll and will probably so continue.

4. *Termination of Revolution and War*

Some revolutions and wars are ended quickly, before they grow and deepen. Others run their full course, spread, and reach their zenith sometimes becoming chronic for decades, occasionally lasting even more than a century. Those that were short-lived, and generally slight, were terminated mainly because their causes—both necessary and supplementary—were superficial and easily removable. This means that their necessary cause, a disintegration of the prevailing religious, moral, juridical, and social values, was only superficially developed. It means that the difference between the values of the upper and lower classes, of the governing and the governed groups in the same society (for revolution) was only slight. It indicates that the cleavage between the value systems of two or more societies (for war) was small, involving a disintegration of only unimportant portions of their value systems.

Likewise the supplementary causes of minor wars and revolutions are far from formidable and overwhelming. The ruling groups being only partially degenerate, the masses become but slightly demoralized. Poverty, famine, and economic conflicts are easily handled or adjusted; and so on.

The superficiality of these necessary and supplementary causes is the real reason why so many revolutions have been suppressed at their initial stage by the forces of order or by the counter-revolution. This explains why some turned out to be "palace revolutions" replacing one group of ruler by another of the same class, family, or group; why many other revolutions were mere rearrangements of the political *status quo*, or slight modifications of economic or other existing social systems, a mere change of one dynasty for another. The liquidation of minor revolutions is due primarily not to some mythical ability of the leaders of the revolutions and counter-revolutions, but mainly to the superficiality of their necessary and supplementary causes. Ordinary persons with ordinary common sense can and do cope easily with these, restoring social order through slight modifications of the sociopolitical, economic, and other conditions.

The situation has been quite different with the revolutions whose causes—necessary and supplementary—have been deep and formidable. If the disintegration of the value-system of a given society is universal, embracing all the main classes of the values, (religious, moral, juridical, economic, aesthetic, social, etc.); if all these values are relativized and atomized, no longer binding all the groups of the society; if the gulf between the values of the governing, rich, and privileged groups and the governed, poor, and disfranchised groups is unbridgeable; if there are no universal norms uniting most of the members of the society—then such a disintegration of the values cannot be cured by any superficial measures. The revolution cannot be ended until a new system of universally binding values is created. For the emergence of a new system of values a long time is necessary, and in real historical conditions, it has never been achieved without the bloodshed and ravages of a violent revolution. Such a deep and universal disintegration of the values is itself sufficient to make the revolution destructive, beastly, and either long-lasting or chronic.

When the necessary cause of revolution is reinforced by a series of supplementary factors in the form of a degenerated—religiously, morally, intellectually, socially—rich class; if there is an enormous contrast between their privileges and the disfranchisements of the subordinated class; if there are various famines, impoverishments, and other calamities—in these conditions it would be a miracle if the revolution were liquidated easily and quickly. No matter how great or talented the leaders of the society are, they find themselves helpless to stop the rush of events even if they want to—which they, the revolutionary leaders, at least, do not.

Under such circumstances revolutions run their full course with all their devastation, destruction, and death, until they burn everything to ashes and figuratively present the society with an ultimatum: Either perish, or begin to build a new system of values binding firmly the members and groups, with a new distribution of rights and duties. In brief, these events proceed until the necessary cause is removed, and the disintegrated values replaced by a new reintegrated value system.

With a slight change the same can be said of war. Short and easily terminated wars presuppose superficiality in the disintegration of values. They indicate that the contrasts in the value systems of one or both of the belligerent societies are only slight. For this reason the break can easily be repaired and the bloody conflict quickly terminated by slight modifications of the international situation in its political, economic, religious, moral, or other aspects. When the disintegration of the value systems is enormous in one or both of the belligerent societies; when their governing groups become nihilistic and unrestrained by any religious, moral, or juridical, norms; when in addition the supplementary causes of war are serious—in such circumstances the conflict cannot easily be solved. This holds true regardless of the number of Leagues of Nations, Sacred Alliances, International Arbitration Bodies, International Conferences, or Hague Courts. It is true, no matter how many schemes they conceive or how numerous the machinations they perform. It remains valid, no matter how capable the leaders of the conflicting countries.

Such wars are bound to be long, devastating, and often chronic. Despite short armistices and even "peace" treaties they flare up again and again until their necessary cause and the most important supplementary factors are removed. The removal means a rebuilding of a new international system of values. Until this is done all the palliative measures can help but little. Otherwise, the parties are sure to double cross one another repeatedly. As soon as any one of them feels the situation is advantageous, it will break its pledges and start a war in the vain hope of profiting from it. Here again a long time is necessary to rebuild a system of values in the actual presence of the demoralized societies.

If human beings and societies were entirely rational and

truly wise, the rebuilding of the new system of national or international values could be accomplished in a short time. Even more, under these conditions wars and revolutions would be avoidable. As soon as such societies saw their systems of values beginning to disintegrate, they would immediately pay attention to this most important issue. They would start a systematic revaluation of values, discarding the outlived ones and introducing new ones. In this way they could make the necessary reconstruction comparatively peaceably and without endless bloodshed and destruction.

Unfortunately, human beings and societies rarely exhibit this wisdom. They are so rash and foolish as not to understand, even now after thousands of years of historical experience, that revolutions and wars can hardly cure the evils they want them to cure; that they are the destructive measures of despair rather than the fruitful tools of construction. The foolishness of societies and their leaders manifests itself also in the fact that they do not understand either the real causes of war and revolution or the best means of their prevention. Most of our leaders still believe that by tinkering with the purely economic or political conditions they can prevent revolutions and wars or minimize their destructiveness without touching the system of values, however disintegrated it may be.

The activities of the statesmen, of the League of Nations, and of all the innumerable "ousters of war and revolution" after the First World War is an illustration of this. They were busy with everything except the system of values. That was entirely forgotten. Scarcely any of these busy-bodies paid any attention to its status; hardly any of these shepherds of nations ever indicated its disintegrated and hopeless state. Only a very few thinkers, daubed by these "realists" as "idealists" and "utopians" and "arm-chair philosophers," once in a while raised their warning voices. In vain: Their voices were crying in the wilderness of the pseudo-realists. The latter were feverishly busy with one session of the League of Nations after another. Their "scientific" advisers—all those "practical" economists, political scientists, bankers, and politicians were likewise terribly busy "researching" and recommending an endless number of practical measures concerning money and finance, inflation and deflation, tariff and currency, prices and civil service, and so on and so forth. They had their hey-day. The result was terrible and horrible—a complete fiasco. They not only failed to eliminate war and revolution, poverty and injustice, and other calamities; they not only failed to reduce their destructive force, but they rather increased the catastrophe by making wars more appalling and world-wide; by brewing revolutions on a scale never seen before in history. Miseries and calamities have piled one upon another over ever increasing millions of victims and derelicts.

Even now when all the Horses of the Apocalypse are rampaging on the planet as never before, these leaders still remain blind and foolish in their pseudo-practicality and pseudo-realism. They still talk of anything but the system of values; they still plan the future society on any basis but that of a reintegrated normative pattern system. No wonder they have led mankind from bad to worse. And mankind has paid and is paying for their foolishness and its own, a higher and higher price in life, sorrow, suffering, and tragedy.

This explains why the theoretically simple task of building a new system of values is not actually so easy, with human beings and societies as they are. It indicates why a long time and severe ordeals are inevitable for the solution of the problem under such conditions.

This concise analysis gives the essential causes and cures of the calamities studied. It outlines the remedies that have been used in history, whether they were real or ineffective, and the remedies that should be used, if the afflicted societies possessed the necessary wisdom, knowledge, and conscience.

Chapter Eighteen

A GLANCE INTO THE FUTURE

We live amidst one of the greatest crises in human history. Not only war, famine, pestilence and revolution, but a legion of other calamities are rampant over the whole world. All values are unsettled; all norms are broken. Mental, moral, aesthetic, and social anarchy reigns supreme. Millions of human beings are killed annually. Many other millions are turned into the maimed victims and derelicts of humanity. Humanity has become a distorted image of its own noble self. The crisis is omnipresent and involves almost the whole of culture and society from top to bottom. It is manifest in the fine arts and science, in philosophy and religion, in ethics and law. It permeates the forms of social, economic, and political organization and the entire way of living and thinking.[1] Since much smaller calamities are regularly followed by the effects studied in the preceding chapters, there is every reason to expect that they will fall upon us in a much more intensive and extensive scale during this catastrophic age of ours. Therefore, as long as the calamities of war, famine, revolution and pestilence continue; and as long as the still deeper crisis of our culture and society lasts, the following trends can be expected to grow in all the contemporary societies involved in the crisis.

1. In part of the population there will be an increase of emotional and affective instability, irritability, depressive moods, and other such aforementioned painful experiences that accompany each and all of these calamities. The proportion of the population thus affected is going to

be considerably larger than in normal times. However, a majority of the population will remain free from these emotional and affective marks of calamities.

2. There will also be an increase of various mental disturbances, psychoneuroses and psychic diseases. The minds of these victims of calamities will generally be unable to function as satisfactorily as before the calamity. A considerable portion will be in need of hospitalization and of society's help, financial and other. Various mental epidemics will afflict many persons. But again, such mental derangements will by no means spread over the whole population of the societies in crisis.

3. In all these societies the death-rate will grow, even in the civilian population. The death-toll will be enormous for all societies, but more so for some than for others. Their birth-rate will decline, except in those populations which are only lightly exposed to the calamities. This does not exclude a temporary increase of the birth-rate during the next year in those societies which, like the United States, witnessed a flare-up of hasty marriages on the eve or at the beginning of active entrance into the war. The marriage rate will decrease in all societies having large draft armies fighting outside their country, provided that the family remains intact in such societies. If the familial and marital patterns become disorganized, then the marriage-rate may not decrease. But such marriages would be mere shadows of the real "unions for life," and they would not differ greatly from unsanctioned and incidental sexual relationships between males and females.

4. As to the biological or inherited quality of the population that will result, all in all it probably will not differ greatly from what it was before the calamities. If some of the calamities kill more of the superior elements—those more healthy, more intelligent, more integrated in per-

sonality—others exterminate mainly the inferior elements. In the end, these positive and negative influences are likely to neutralize each other, leaving the quality of the surviving population about the same as it was before. This does not exclude a preponderance of either positive or negative selection in this or that particular society.

5. Voluntary and compulsory migration from place to place will enormously increase. Thousands and millions will be uprooted from their permanent habitat and will be moved to other regions, often far distant from their former homes. Mankind will resemble a disturbed ant-hill with masses of human ants thrown hither and thither by the tornado of the crisis. A very large part of the population will become nomadic, without any permanent place of living. A growing proportion will become "refugees" and human "flotsam" drifting over the lands of this planet.

6. Likewise vertical mobility, social climbing and falling, promotion and demotion will enormously increase. Today's millionaires will suddenly become beggars; and today's beggars, millionaires. Many of the mighty will be dragged down and trampled upon, while many an underdog will become strong and powerful. Formerly privileged classes will be stripped of their riches, and the disfranchised will inherit their places. In this social "earthquake" not only will separate individuals be transposed *en masse* from one social stratum to another, sometimes over an enormous vertical distance, but whole social classes will bodily fall or rise. Furthermore, the pyramid of social stratification itself will be damaged and mutilated. It will be changed in its structure, height, form, inner mechanism selecting and distributing its members on the social ladder, and in the number of strata which it has. The existing "ranks," and "hierarchies" of groups and classes will be smashed, to a considerable degree, and replaced by different systems of

superiorities and inferiorities, and by new "upper and lower " classes.

7. First in the series of changes outlined in #6, the height and the profile of the pyramid of social stratification will be flattened. The existing contrasts between the rich and the poor, the privileged and the underdogs, aristocracy and common plebeians will diminish. The pyramid will become a kind of trapezium. This levelling of the pyramid will not prevent a few human hyenas from becoming the *nouveaux riches*, the new bosses of force and fraud. These few, however, will not constitute a permanent class or stratum to replace the previous rulers of the economic, political and social pyramids. They will remain but discreet individuals, most of whom will be thrown down as quickly as they climbed up.

The removal of class inequalities will assume diverse forms. One of these is a lessening contrast in the planes of living of the top and bottom groups. The extravagant luxury of the "big monkey monks" will tend to slip down to a less luxurious standard of living. This will adversely affect such material values as the number of servants, cars, palaces, mansions and estates, to say nothing of wines, food, and clothing. The leisure class will tend to become extinct. Likewise, the unbridgeable gap between the "aristocracies" of royalty, of wealth, and of "society" on the one hand and the underdog classes on the other will narrow and become more passable. The same thing will happen to the contrasts between the other forms of "superior" and "inferior" ranks. This does not mean the complete disappearance of inequality, but only a decrease in its range.

8. Second, the inner mechanism of selection and distribution of individuals among various social positions will temporarily be damaged and modified. As a result of the changes in this "social sifter," different types of individuals

will be promoted to the upper social levels. If, before the crisis, family position, inherited titles, and honesty or integrity were the factors in promotion, in the short-run future they will hardly play a very important rôle. Their place will be taken by different qualities, such as devotion to the dominant party, cynical manipulative ability, brutality in dealing with the opponents, impressive smartness, disregard of the sufferings of one's fellowmen, or a lack of scruples against fattening like a vulture on the tragedy and sacrifice of others. With slight modification we can say of this transitory period what was said of revolutions: "they are initiated by idealists, carried through by brutal murderers, and profiteered upon by scoundrels."

In the beginning of the transitory phase these brutal executioners and clever scoundrels will be climbing up the social ladder in larger numbers than in normal times. Many other changes will occur in the types of individuals promoted and demoted by the deranged mechanism of social selection and distribution of persons.

This applies not only to the economic or political groups, but also to the "cultural and educational" systems. In the pyramid of scientific, philosophical and artistic hierarchies the upper strata will be occupied in a much larger proportion than before by so-called "specialists," who perceive clearly an infinitesimal point in a picture but remain blind to its whole character. To an increasing extent the choice seats will be filled by "smart Alecs," by mediocre and uncreative "managers" of science, arts, philosophy, and the press—by people who sit on the directorates of scientific councils, of influential artistic institutions, of well-endowed foundations and of powerful press syndicates. The new ruling class will contain many lobbyists, politicians, and manipulators.

And similarly, in other pyramids and social hierarchies.

As a result, the dwellers in the various strata will consist of a mixture of former members of each class with "newcomers" from other strata.

9. The whole pyramid of social inequalities will remain in a fluid and muddled state during this transitional period, all the time crumbling here and there, and being incessantly remodelled. Only after the end of the calamities and the crisis will it resume a definite and comparatively durable form. But this form will again be very different from that of the period of calamities.

10. All the basic social institutions will also be disorganized and greatly remodelled.

A. The proportion of broken families will be notably greater; the sacredness of marriage will decline for many in the population; divorces will increase. This partial disintegration of marriage and the family will be counteracted eventually in other parts of the population by a stronger integration of the family and by a more favorable view of the sacredness of the marriage bonds. Later, in the post-calamity period this counteraction will gain sufficient headway to terminate the *anomie* in marriage and the family.

B. Private educational institutions will tend to disappear in favor of public or state-controlled institutions. Their autonomy from government control will decrease. The aims, ideals, and curricula of the schools and colleges will be drastically changed during the transitional period. Ever-increasing emphasis will be given to the training of practical technicians of war and revolution (or counter-revolution), of hygiene and medicine, and of industry and farming. Greater stress will be given to the education of dieticians, home-economists, financiers, practical educators, and practical researchers, to say nothing of "fiction-makers," "verse-makers," "picture-makers," "show-makers," "music-makers," "science-makers," "money-makers," and "robot-makers." The educational curricula and policies will necessarily change with each replacement of one governmental faction by another. As the factions will be shifting fairly rapidly, and at the same time sharply differing from one another, the programs and curricula will be perpetually upset and increasingly chaotic.

Later on, after the end of the calamities, this practical philistinism will be powerfully counteracted by the opposite trend towards deeper, more thoughtful, and more adequate systems for the cultivation of creative human genius in various fields, and especially in those of religion, ethics, humanities, and in the social sciences. All this will be of a less clerical, less superficial, and less specialized nature than in the transitory period.

11. As to the central trend in most of the social institutions and organizations, this will manifest itself mainly in the increasing control, regimentation, and regulation by the State, and in the decreasing autonomy of the private persons and groups in the management of their own affairs and relationships. Insofar as totalitarianism is a social régime in which the government controls everything and private persons or groups control nothing, all societies will continue to move toward more autocratic and more universal totalitarian Leviathans. In some societies it will assume the form of Communism or Socialism; in others of National-Socialism, Fascism, Nationalism, Militarism, Totalitarian Pseudo-Democracy, or some other version of totalitarianism.

Insofar as Democracy means the self-management and control of affairs and relationships by individuals and groups, this totalitarian trend means a diminishing of true democracy and of genuinely democratic political régimes. Insofar as private property and capitalism involve the regu-

lation and control of economic affairs by private individuals and groups, the State-operated totalitarian economy means a decline of private property and of the
capitalistic economy.

Insofar as freedom is the regulation of conduct and relationships by individuals and groups, the triumph of totalitarianism means a decline of freedom in all the main spheres
of social life. People will be turned more and more into
puppets manipulated, and controlled by the central Power
Station of the Leviathan Government. All the chief areas
of life and activities, of thoughts and speeches of individuals
will be prescribed by the Leviathan. The population must
either obey its orders or else bear the penalty. In this sense
the transitory period of the crisis and the calamities will be
the Age of Totalitarian Autocracy, the era of the excessive
centralization, of extreme regimentation by an army of
commanding bureaucrats. Freedom and self-regulation
vanish. In the post-calamity period the opposite movement
will prevail so as to liquidate the totalitarian development
and its monstrous Leviathan.

12. The economic well-being of societies involved in
the crisis will generally suffer with the exception of a few
nouveaux riches feathering their nests during the tragedy
of almost all mankind. The aforementioned trend toward
less contrast between the rich and the poor will occur not
so much by an elevation of the poor as by the collapse of
the rich and the impoverishment of the whole society.
More and more millions of human beings will be miserable
and destitute, deprived even of the minimum of economic
goods necessary for survival.

13. On the cultural side, all the compartments of culture will be permeated by the atmosphere of calamities,
which will become the central topic of science and philosophy, of painting and sculpture, of music and the the-

ater, of literature and architecture, of ethics and law, and of religion and technology. Calamities will occupy an ever-expanding place among the focal points of cultural activities. Science and technology, the humanities, the social sciences and philosophy will be increasingly busy with activities and projects pertaining to calamities. So also will other compartments of culture. Public opinion and the press will focus on the problems of calamity, which will become a front-page topic in the written and oral speech-reactions of the society. Society will become "calamity-minded." In brief the mentality and culture will be stamped by calamities in thousands of ways. Calamities will drive out from the focal points of the public mind most of the other unrelated topics. They will push them to the back-stage of culture.

14. Besides this impregnation by calamities, the fine arts will be marked by a spreading atmosphere of somberness, dolour, melancholy, and pessimism, sometimes becoming sadistic, macabre, and pathetique. Similar pessimism will invade science, philosophy, and other compartments of culture.

15. The life of millions will be characterized by incessant suspense, accompanied by uncertainty and insecurity.

16. In these conditions, an apocalyptic mentality in diverse forms will grow within a considerable part of the population. Various psychical epidemics will rapidly diffuse. The belief in various portents and omens, from astrological soothsaying to the queerest fantasmagorias, will also sweep over a considerable part of the population.

17. The bulk of the population will divide increasingly into sinners, libertines, profligates, downright criminals, atheists, and cynicists on the one hand, and into Stoics, saints, moral heroes, sublime altruists, intensely religious prophets, martyrs, ascetics, mystics, gnostics, and the like on the other hand. Militant atheism will be countered by

religiosity of the greatest intensity, and utter moral depravity by sublime moral heroism. Likewise, egotism will be counterbalanced by altruism, anti-sociality by supreme sacrifice, militant materialism by fearless idealism. Scepticism will be met by unquestioning fanaticism; and criticism, by dogmatism. Opposite the materialistic and utilitarian City of Man will be built the City of God. Earthly utopians will contend with God's Messiahs.

During the early stages of calamities, the movement of irreligiosity and moral cynicism will be dominant; but with the continuation of the crisis the movement toward religion and moral heroism will increasingly prevail, progressively curbing atheism and depravity. The struggle between these polarized movements will be multifarious, arduous and long, and sealed by the blood of martyrs, the inspiration of prophets, and the enthusiasm of apostles. These will be laying the cornerstone of the new system of values on which—in the post-calamity period—a new creative culture and society can be built.

18. Calamities and the crisis will influence science and art, philosophy and ethics, and other cultural phenomena in the same polarized modes. On the one hand, they will greatly impede and even destroy many creative activities in these fields. On the other, they will stimulate, reinforce, and facilitate creative work. Since they serve as a crucial test of prevailing ideas, calamities will kill many a theory accepted today, and will sustain many a theory rejected now. Having caused a revolution in the whole social system, calamities will call forth a true revolution in science and philosophy, fine arts, and other cultural activities. In the post-calamity period these all will be very different from what they are now.

Such are some of the developments which we must be prepared to meet as observers, actors, and victims of the age of calamities and crisis. Since the trends are already in operation they cannot be prevented or averted. They can be shortened and alleviated, however, by the individual as well as by societies.

The best way for an individual to meet them is by integrating his values and rooting them—not so much in the values of the sensory world—but rather in the moral duty and the transcendental values of the Kingdom of God. Persons with such a system of values deeply ingrained will bear any calamity with fortitude. And they will endure it much more easily than persons either entirely lacking any integrated value-system, or having a system rooted chiefly in earthly values, from "Wine, Women and Song" to wealth, fame, and power. Such values crumble under the impact of calamity, and their devotees become complete bankrupts, ruined wrecks, and helpless derelicts who have nothing to live for and nothing to fall back upon for support. Persons with a transcendental system of values and a deep sense of moral duty are the possessors of the values which no man and no catastrophe can take from them. Under all circumstances they can maintain their peace of mind, their conviction of human dignity, their self-respect, and their sense of duty. With these inviolate, they can weather any trial, no matter how severe.

For societies, the shortest, the most efficient, and the only practical way of really alleviating and shortening the crisis is by reintegrating its religious, moral, scientific, philosophical and other values. This reintegration must be effected in such a way that the new system of values is rooted not only in the noblest values of this sensory world, but primarily in the values of moral duty and the kingdom of God. Until this is done, all the wars, revolutions, political and economic machinations, "scientific advise," and "technological devices" will help but little. Such things, as we have seen, are not the necessary cause of war, of revolution, or of the great crisis we now confront. Without a reintegrated system of sensory and transcendental values, other measures are not helpful, and they may even be harmful, serving the Dark Angel of Destruction. With the system of values rooted in the sense of moral duty and the Kingdom of God, rational devices can help to solve many a practical problem of cultural and social reconstruction. But only under the conditions just stated is this statement true:

This, the best way out of the crisis, was marvelously formulated a long time ago.

"Therefore, I say unto you, Take no thought for your life, what ye shall eat, or what ye shall drink; nor yet for your body, what ye shall put on. But seek ye first the kingdom of God, and his righteousness; and all these things shall be added unto you. . . ."

Given the values of the kingdom of God, the worldly problems of food and drink can be solved in passing. Then great calamities become unnecessary and *meaningless* in human history. But without the Kingdom of God we are doomed to a weary and torturing pilgrimage from calamity to calamity, from crisis to crisis, with only brief moments of transitory improvement for regaining our breath. In that case the way out will always be the "way of death," ordeal, and destruction, discussed in the preceding chapter. Then the presence of calamities in human history becomes inevitable and above all *meaningful*. For they become a part of Theodicy, the only educative instrument that by pitiless ordeal can restore the demoralized human animal and remind him of his Divine mission on this planet.

It is up to us which of the ways out we select.

NOTES

Chapter One

How Calamities Influence our Affective and Emotional Life

1. The term *emotion* is used in the sense of L. Petrajitzky's definition as a simultaneously active-passive experience, in contradistinction to one-sided passive sensation and feeling and active volition. Appetite and hunger are emotions in this sense. Cf. L. Petrajitzky's *Introduction to the Theory of Law and Morals* (St. Petersburg, 1907) (Russian).

2. For an excellent analysis of appetite, cf. L. Petrajitzky's *Introduction to the Theory of Law and Ethics* (St. Petersburg, 1907) (Russian), pp. 223ff., and I. Pavlov's *The Work of the Digestive Glands* (London, 1902). For a general summary of the main theories and their literature, cf. Edwin G. Boring's *Sensation and Perception in the History of Experimental Psychology* (New York, 1942), pp. 551-61, 573. Cf. also W. B. Cannon's *Bodily Changes in Pain, Hunger, Fear and Rage* (New York, 1927), pp. 232ff., and the works of Luciani and Boring, quoted in next foot-note. Among literary works, A. Chekhov's *Syrena* gives a remarkable description of appetite and of the technique of its stimulation.

3. Cf. the detailed description of the experience of hunger in E. G. Boring's "Processes Referred to Alimentary and Urinary Tracts," *Psychological Review*, 1915; H. D. Marsh's "Individual and Sex Differences Brought out by Fasting," *Psychological Review*, 1916; Luciani's *Das Hungern* (Hamburg and Leipzig, 1890); and B. Pashutin's *General and Experimental Pathology* (St. Petersburg, 1902 (Russian), Vol. II. A still better description of the psychology of hunger is given in such works as K. Hamsun's *Hunger* (passim), B. Lesskoff's *Udol* (Russian), Maupassant's *Vagabond* or *Tramp*, and in the works of many an Arctic explorer, such as F. Nansen's *Farthest North* (New York, 1897), E. Mikkelsen's *Lost in the Arctic* (London, 1913), R. Peary's *Northward Over the Great Ice* (New York, 1898), and his wife's *My Arctic Journal* (New York, 1894).

4. Boring, op. cit., pp. 311-317. Pashutin, op. cit., pp. 573ff.

5. E. Mikkelsen, op. cit., pp. 265, 300.

6. E. Mikkelsen, op. cit., p. 299.
7. Cf. K. Hamsun's *Hunger* (London, 1926), passim.
8. F. Curschmann, *Hungersnöte* in *Mittelalter* (Leipzig, 1900), pp. 53 et passim.
9. Cf. for instance, W. Digby's *The Famine Campaign in Southern India* (London, 1878; 2 vols.), passim, and Soloview's *History of Russia* (3d ed.) (Russian), Vol. III, p. 1447.
10. N. Lesskoff, *Udol, Works* (St. Petersburg, 1909), Vol. XXXII, pp. 12ff.
11. Dr. Aronovitch, "Children's Hunger Defectiveness," *Medical Journal of Viatka Scientific Committee of Department of Public Health*, No. 2, Part II, pp. 3-4.
12. Pashutin, op. cit., pp. 562ff.
13. Marsh, op. cit., pp. 43ff.
14. F. Nansen, op. cit., p. 221.
15. E. Mikkelsen, op. cit., p. 279, et passim through chaps. 11, 12.
16. D. Obolensky, "Sketches of the Past," *Historical Messenger* (Istorichesky Vestnik, January, 1895), p. 105.
17. Cf. Bessières's *Le Chemin des Dames*.
18. Cf. Ardan du Pic's *Études sur le combat* (Paris, 1880).
19. Cf. J. Norton-Cru's *Témoins. Essais d'analyse et de critique des souvenirs de combattants* (Paris, 1929).
20. General N. N. Golovine, *The Science of War* (Paris, 1938) (Russian), p. 86. Chapters 2 and 3 give an admirable analysis of the problem, with facts and references.
21. Cf. the cases and facts cited by General N. N. Golovin, op. cit., pp. 107ff.
22. E. Wittkower and J. P. Spillane, "Neuroses in War," *British Medical Journal*, Vol. I, p. 223, 1940. See other details in R. D. Gillespie's *Psychological Effects of War On Citizen and Soldier* (New York, 1942), chaps. 4, 5.

Chapter Two

How Calamities Affect Our Cognitive Processes, Desires, and Volition

1. W. Firey in an unpublished *Experimental Study of the Limits to Social Variability* demonstrated the validity of the proposition experimentally. Cf. Marsh, "Individual and Sex Differences Brought Out by Fasting," *Psychological Review*, 1916, pp. 438ff.; Luciani, op. cit., pp. 67ff.; and L. Taracevitch's *Concerning Hunger* (Kiev, 1907) (Russian), pp. 14ff.

2. Cf. L. Petrajitzky, op. cit., p. 233.
3. L. Petrajitzky, op. cit., pp. 231-232.
4. Mikkelsen, op. cit., pp. 125-126.
5. Cf. I. Pavlov's *The Work of the Digestive Glands*, pp. 105-106, in its Russian edition. During the latest stages of starvation of dogs, the sensitivity of their nervous system generally decreases and a state of semicoma occurs shortly before death. Cf. also I. Rosental's "Influence of Starvation upon the Conditioned Reflexes," *Archiv Biologicheskich nauk*, 1922; N. Frolov's "Influence of a Sharp Change in Food," ibid.; and Pashutin, op. cit., pp. 608ff.
6. Aronovitch, op. cit., p. 33.
7. For the details, cf. Boring, op. cit., pp. 307-310, 315. Cf. also Marsh, op. cit.
8. Mikkelsen, op. cit., pp. 291, 303-304.
9. Ibid., pp. 276-277.
10. Ibid., pp. 303-304. Cf. also F. Nansen, op. cit., Vol. II, chaps. v, vi. For the hallucinations of the unfortunate sailors from the wrecked *Medusa*, cf. Pashutin, op. cit., p. 562.
11. Mikkelsen, op. cit., p. 270. Mrs. Marsh dreamed of cucumbers and olives (Marsh, op. cit., pp. 43-45.) In K. Hamsun's *Hunger* are given many an accurate description of the changes of that kind. Guy de Maupassant, in his *Tramp*, excellently describes the increased sensitivity of the hungry tramp toward the smell of a meat soup.
12. Cf. A. Böckh's *Die Staatshaushaltung der Athener* (Berlin, 1851), Vol. I, pp. 125ff., and Novosadsky's "The Struggle against Dearth in Ancient Greece," *The Journal of the Ministry of Public Education* (St. Petersburg, 1917) (in Russian), pp. 78-80.
13. G. Dumas, *Troubles Mentaux et Troubles Nerveux de Guerre* (Paris, 1919), pp. 3-5. Among other details the author gives the concrete cases and letters of the patients.
14. Cf. G. Dumas, op. cit., pp. 25ff., 44ff., 62, 88, et passim. Cf. also other works in the field of the psychoneuroses of war cited below.
15. Marsh, op. cit., pp. 444-445.
16. K. Hamsun, *Hunger* (London, 1926), pp. 100-104.
17. Rosenbach, *The Influence of Starvation upon the Nervous Centers* (Moscow, 1922) (Russian), pp. 84-85. Cf. also Waldman's "The Problem of the Clinic of Starvation," *Volume in Honor of Grekoff* (Leningrad, 1921) (Russian), pp. 43-44, and Pashutin, op. cit., pp. 565-566, 608.

18. Hamsun, op. cit., pp. 28 et passim.
19. Boring, op. cit., pp. 312-316. Cf. also W. Cannon, op. cit., p. 236.
20. Cf. *Red Moscow* (1921) (Russian), pp. 494-496.
21. Aronovitch, op. cit., p. 31.
22. Frolov, op. cit., pp. 169-170.
23. Gorovoi-Shaltan, "The Problem of Mental Disease under Contemporary Conditions," *Psychology, Neurology, and Experimental Psychology* (Leningrad, 1922) (Russian), p. 34ff. Cf. also the same author's article in *Vrachebnoie Delo*, February 1, 1921, and Ossipoff's "Mental Disease in Petrograd," *Isvestia Kommissariata Zdravookhranenia*, 1919, Nos. 7-12.
24. *Isvestia*, February 12, 1922.
25. *Petrograd Pravda*, March 10, 1922.
26. *Krasnaia Gazetta*, January 31, 1922. For other facts, cf. L. Vassilievsky's *Horrible Chronicle of Famine* (Ufa, 1922) (Russian).
27. G. Dumas, op. cit., pp. 3-4, passim. Cf. also J. T. MacCurdy's *War Neuroses* (Cambridge, 1918), passim; G. Roussy and J. Lhermitte's *The Psychoneuroses of War* (London and Paris, 1918); A. Kardiner's *The Traumatic Neuroses of War* (New York and London, 1941); K. Bonhoeffer's "Geistes- und Nervenkrankheiten," *Handbuch der ärtzlichen Erfahrung im Weltkriege, 1914-18* (Leipzig, 1922); F. Dillon's "Neuroses among Combatant Troops in the Great War," *British Medical Journal*, Vol. II, pp. 63-66, 1939; and E. Wittkower and J. P. Spillane's "Neuroses in War," *British Medical Journal*, Vol. I, pp. 223-225, 1940; R. D. Gillespie's *Psychological Effects of War on Citizen and Soldier* (New York, 1942).
28. Wittkower and Spilane, op. cit., pp. 223-224.
29. F. Dillon, op. cit., p. 63. *Official History of the Great War: Medical Services* (London, 1931), final volume, p. 116.
30. Wittkower and Spillane, op. cit., pp. 224-225.
31. N. Golovin, op. cit., pp. 102-104. For self-observations by the combatants, cf. J. Norton-Cru, op. cit.
32. In Leo Tolstoi's *War and Peace* and in Stendhal's *La Chartreuse de Parme* these phenomena are excellently depicted.
33. Cf. the statistical data given in the works of Ossipoff and Gorovoi-Shaltan cited above.
34. For the statistics, cf. F. Prinzing's *Handbuch der medizinischen Statistik* (Jena, 1906); also K. Bohnhoeffer, op. cit., and A. Oettingen's *Die Moralstatistik* (Leipzig, 1882). The at-

tempt of C. Landis and J. D. Page in their *Modern Society and Mental Disease* (New York, 1938), pp. 145ff.), to show that war and depression do not increase mental disease, as measured by the statistics of admission into hospitals, is unconvincing. Their evidence is based on hospital statistics for New York State and Massachusetts for the years immediately preceding and following the First World War and the depression of 1929. The participation of the United States in the First World War was too short to exert any notable influence; and the depression of 1929 did not end in 1932. Moreover, statistics of hospital admissions are hardly an accurate index of lesser mental diseases. For these and similar reasons their conclusions in no way invalidate the fact of the increase of mental disorders among the civil population in periods of major wars.

35. Wittkower and Spillane, op. cit., p. 223. Gillespie, op. cit., chaps. 4, 5.

36. Wittkower and Spillane, op. cit., p. 229. Cf. other data in Gillespie's quoted work, pp. 106ff.

37. Wittkower and Spillane, op. cit., p. 223.

38. Cf. A. Oettingin's *Die Moralstatistik* (Leipzig, 1882), pp. 68ff.

39. Cf. the quoted studies of Ossipoff and Gorovoi-Shaltan; also such Soviet newspapers as *Isvestia* (February 15, 1922, and May 30, 1924), the *Petrograd Pravda* (March 10, 1920), and the *Red Gazette* (*Krasnaia Gazeta*) (January 31, 1920).

40. Cf. P. Sorokin's *Sociology of Revolution*, pp. 221-228.

41. Wittkower and Spillane, op. cit., p. 223.

42. For the details, cf. P. Sorokin's *Sociology of Revolution*, chap. x.

Chapter Three

How Famine Influences Our Behavior

1. Cf. K. Bücher's *Die Entstehung der Volkswirtschaft* (Leipzig, 1893), chaps. 1, 2; R. Steinmetz's, *Rechtsverhältnisse von eingeborenen Völkern in Afrika und Ozeanien* (Leipzig, 1903), pp. 15ff.; and R. Thurnwald's *Die menschliche Gesellschaft* (Berlin and Leipzig, 1932), Vol. III, pp. 27ff.

2. Cf. the above works; also E. Westermarck's *The Origin and Development of Moral Ideas* (London, 1908), pp. 268ff., and B. Spencer and F. Gillen, *The Northern Tribes of Central Australia* (London, 1904), chap. 10.

3. Cf. E. Mikkelsen, op. cit., chaps. 11-13, and F. Nansen, *Farthest North*, Vol. II, chap. 6 et passim.

4. For detailed data, cf. P. Sorokin and C. Berger's *Time-Budgets of Human Behavior* (Harvard University Press, 1939), p. 35 et passim.
5. Cf. C. C. Zimmerman's *Consumption and Standards of Living* (New York, 1936), chaps. 4-6.
6. For concrete examples of this kind of behavior on the part of polar bears, foxes, and other animals fatally attracted by food near the ship and the huts of Nansen or Mikkelsen, cf. Nansen, op. cit., Vol. I, pp. 171, 197ff., 283ff., et passim; Vol. II, pp. 20, 217, 335ff., et passim.
7. E. Mikkelsen, op. cit., p. 324.
8. Mikkelsen gives a classical description of such a case. He and Iversen decided to eat the liver of a dead dog, which, they knew, was poisonous and which even their dogs would not touch. They simply could not withstand the temptation, and they paid for their recklessness with severe sickness. Cf. Mikkelsen, op. cit., pp. 267ff.
9. For this experience, including his narrow escape from capture at the hands of the Communists, cf. the author's *Leaves from a Russian Diary* (New York, 1924), chap. 12.
10. Cf. Vassilievsky's *The Appalling Chronicle of Famine* (Ufa, 1922) (Russian), p. 4 et passim; *The Red Gazette*, 1922, No. 172; *Isvestia*, February 12, 1922; and *Artelnoie Delo*, 1922, Nos. 1-4, p. 64.
11. Cf. Okinchitz's "Vlianie voiny i revolutzii na polovuiy spheru jenschiny" (The Influence of War and Revolution upon the Sex Life of Women), *Vrachebnaia gasetta*, 1922, No. 1 (Russian); and V. Shervinsky's "Sovremennoie pitanie" (Contemporary Nutrition), *Priroda*, 1919, Nos. 4-6 (Russian). A series of experiments upon animals conducted by Morgulis, Poiarkoff, Loisel, Grandis, Stoppenbrink, and others show a similar weakening of sex functions (the decline of spermatogenesis, the atrophy of sex organs, etc.) engendered by starvation. Cf. I. Poiarkoff's "L'Influence du jeûne sur le travail des glandes sexuelles du chien," *Comptes rendus hebdomadaires des séances de la société biologique*, Tome 74, 1913, p. 141-143; S. Morgulis's "Studies of Inanition," in *Archiv für Entwicklungsmechanismus der Organismen*, Band XXXII, Heft 2, and Band XXXVI, Heft 4; and Loisel's "Influence dejûne sur la spermatogenèse," *Comptes rendus et memoires de la société biologique*, Tome 53.
12. L. Petrajitsky, *Introduction to the Theory of Law and Morals*, pp. 241-242. In K. Hamsun's *Hunger* the hero re-

marks, after declining the advances of a street girl, "Girls became for me about the same as men: starvation dried me up." On the other hand, in Maupassant's *Tramp* the vagabond ravishes the girl after having eaten; when he was hungry such an idea did not occur to him.

13. Cf. E. Westermarck, op. cit., Vol. II, pp. 292-295; also the chapters on the restriction of diet, asceticism, and celibacy.

14. Cf. Westermarck's *History of Human Marriage* (London, 1925), Vol. I, ch. 2; N. Kharusin's *Etnographia* (Moscow, 1904) (Russian), the volume on *The Family and Clan*, pp. 50ff.; J. W. Mannhardt's *Wald- und Feldkulte* (Berlin, 1904-1905), Vol. I, chap. 5; B. Spencer and F. J. Gillen's *The Northern Tribes of Central Australia* (London, 1904), pp. 20ff. and chap. 4; the same authors' *Native Tribes of Central Australia* (London, 1899), chapter on corroboree; R. Thurnwald's "Saturnalien" in the *Reallexikon der Vorgeschichte* (1924-1929); and W. I. Thomas's *Primitive Behavior* (New York, 1937), pp. 264ff.

15. For statistical data, cf. M. Gernet's *Crime and Its Prevention* (Moscow, 1922) (Russian), pp. 392ff.

16. F. Curschmann, op. cit., p. 213. Curschmann cites the statements of several other chroniclers, as well.

17. N. Lesskoff, op. cit., pp. 52-55.

18. Vassilievsky, op. cit., p. 17.

19. Cf. Pilniak's *Golyi God* (Naked or Starvation Year) (Moscow, 1922).

20. Cf. Parent-Duchatelet's *De la prostitution dans la ville de Paris* (Paris, 1857), Vol. II, p. 78, and Vol. I, p. 10; Elistratoff's *Struggle with Prostitution* (Moscow, 1909) (Russian); *Prostitutes: Their Early Lives*, by the Advisory Committee of Social Questions of the League of Nations (Geneva, 1938).

21. Not all cannibalism, of course, is due to starvation. We are concerned here with only those persons who become cannibals through the pressure of hunger.

22. R. Steinmetz and others greatly exaggerate when they say that primitive man regularly practiced cannibalism, without any inhibitions. Such a statement is factually wrong; for many primitive groups are not cannibalistic, and most peoples at least refrain from eating members of their own groups. Even among animal species, only a few are cannibalistic. Most of them, in normal conditions, do not devour members of their own species. Only in extreme starvation do some of them, such as dogs, eat their own kind. (Cf. Steinmetz's

Endokannibalismus (Vienna, 1896), pp. 25ff. For cannibalism among famished dogs, cf. E. Mikkelsen, op. cit., pp. 45 et passim.

23. Cf. E. Westermarck's *The Origin and Development of the Moral Ideas*, Vol. I, pp. 390ff., and Vol. II, pp. 555ff.; also R. Steinmetz's *Endokannibalismus*, pp. 25ff.

24. *Deuteronomy*, xxviii, 53ff.

25. F. Curschmann, op. cit., pp. 59-60, 90-99, 112-114 et passim. Curschmann gives many other citations from medieval chroniclers.

26. Cf. Curschmann's quoted work; Tzitovitch's "Famines in Europe," in *Famines in Russia and Europe* (Kiev, 1892) (Russian); Hazzi's *Betrachtungen über Theuerung und Noth* (München, 1818); Bonnemère's *Histoire des paysans* (Paris, 1874), Vol. II, pp. 235ff.; A. Issaieff's *Poor Crops and Famine* (St. Petersburg, 1892) (Russian); A. Romanovitch-Slavatinsky's *Famines in Russia* (Kiev, 1892) (Russian); Creighton, op. cit., Vol. I, pp. 27-48; and L. Kawan's *Gli esodi e le carestie in Europa* (Rome, 1932).

27. Cf. E. Westermarck's *Origin and Development*, Vol. I, pp. 285ff., and Vol. II, p. 570; Oetker's "Notwehr und Notstand," in the *Vergleichende Darstellung* of the German Criminal Law, Allgemeiner Teil, Vol. II, pp. 328ff.; and Pashutin, op. cit., p. 562.

28. Cf. *The Red Gazette*, December 31, 1921; the *Petrograd Pravda*, January 5, February 10, March 26, and May 12, 1922; *Isvestia*, January 29, 1922; and other issues of Soviet newspapers for 1921-1922. Cf. also Vassilievsky's quoted work; K. Georgievsky's *O golode* (Kharkov, 1922); F. Nansen's *Rapport sur la famine en Russie* (Genève, 1922); P. Mühlems's *Die Russische Hunger- und Seuchenkatastrophe in den Jahren 1921-22* (Berlin, 1923). There are no statistics for cannibalism in Russia, but their number may be computed by hundreds, if not thousands.

29. Cf. E. Westermarck, op. cit., Vol. I, pp. 387ff.

30. Leshkóff, *Russian People and the State* (Moscow, 1858) (Russian), p. 454.

31. Westermarck, op. cit., Vol. I, pp. 399-401.

32. Cf. Westermarck, Curschmann, Leshkoff, Tzitovitch, and Digby. See also R. Smith's, *Kinship and Marriage in Early Arabia* (London, 1903), pp. 293ff.; and Clavigero's *History of Mexico* (London, 1807), Vol. I, p. 360.

33. *Petrograd Pravda*, No. 215, 1921. See also *Village Pravda*, No. 162, 1921, and the *Red Gazette*, November 11, 1921.

Later on, such reports became so common that they can be found in almost any issue of Soviet newspapers for the end of 1921 and for 1922.

34. *Petrograd Pravda*, No. 192, 1921; *Isvestia*, February 12, 1922; *Samara Communa*, December 1, 1921; *Red Gazette*, December 31, 1921. In 1922 these and similar facts were reported in almost every issue of the Soviet newspapers.

35. For further quotations, cf. Curschmann, op. cit., p. 213.

36. For similar testimony, cf. Leshkoff, op. cit.

37. Cf. Westermarck, op. cit., Vol. I, pp. 412ff., and N. Leshkoff, op. cit., pp. 39-44.

38. Aronovitch, op. cit., p. 31. During these years I had at my disposal the records of several court cases relating to the killing of a chum or of a brother or sister by famished children.

39. Cf. Curschmann, op. cit., pp. 56-57, 213ff.

40. Curschmann, op. cit., pp. 56-57.

41. For a general juridical analysis of the emergency, cf. N. Rosin's *Extreme Emergency* (O krainey neobkhodimosti) (St. Petersburg, 1899) and E. Westermarck, op. cit., Vol. I, p. 285ff., Vol. II, pp. 14-15.

42. For food taboos and their violation, cf. E. Westermarck, op. cit., Vol. II, chap. 38; Solovieff's *History of Russia*, Vol. I, p. 1220; Digby, op. cit., passim; Tzitovitch, op. cit., pp. 4-6; Romanovitch-Slavatinsky, op. cit., pp. 35, 55; Leontovitch, op. cit., pp. 9ff.; and Ermoloff, op. cit., Part I.

43. Cf. Curschmann, p. 215; Leshkoff, pp. 460-465; Digby, Vol. I, pp. 104, 106, 194, et passim; Creighton, Vol. I, pp. 36, 49, 117, 151, et passim.

44. K. Hamsun, *Hunger*, pp. 67-68.

45. Ibid., pp. 170ff.

46. For the statistics, cf. M. Gernet's *Crime, and the Struggle against It*, pp. 386ff.; A. Jijilenko's *Criminality and Its Factors* (Leningrad, 1922); W. A. Bonger's *Criminalité et les conditions économiques* (Bruxelles, 1905; E. Roesner's *Der Einfluss von Wirtschaftslage, Alkohol und Jahreszeit auf die Kriminalität* (Leipzig, 1930); E. Rosengart's *Le Crime comme produit social et économique* (1929); and the relevant chapters in the works on criminology by E. Sutherland, J. Gillen, W. Reckless, et al. Many of the economic interpreters of criminality assign too important a rôle to the economic factors in general, though they give valuable data showing the direct influence of hunger upon criminality.

47. Official *Red Moscow* (1920), chapter on criminality.

48. *Isvestia*, October 2, 1921.
49. Cf. P. Sorokin's *Sociology of Revolution*, pp. 62ff.
50. Cf. N. Rosin and F. Oetker, and Harburger's "Diebstahl und Unterschlagung," in the *Vergleichende Darstellung* of the German Criminal law, Besonderer Teil, Vol. VI.
51. Hamsun's hero illustrates the point: his pride finally gives way, and he is prepared to endure any insult for the sake of a mere sandwich.
52. Curschmann, op. cit., p. 55.
53. Ermoloff, op. cit., pp. 8 and 415ff.
54. Mendicabant etiam infiniti artifices et diversarum artium operatii, ex quibus nonnuli habuere de facultatibus rerum suarum ad valorem centun marcarum argenti.—Curschmann, op. cit., pp. 55ff. Cf. Also Leshkoff, op. cit., p. 18.
55. For example, during a famine in Prague the poor and the rich alike undertook to sell everything they had. "Et hiis omnibus alii expoliati, aliqui in familia sua consumptis vendevant de uxoribus suis armillas, inaures, monalia et omnem ornatum qui cultui femineo competebat in vestitu, cupientes salutem vitae depulsa esurie conservare."—Curschmann, op. cit., p. 56.
56. Mikkelsen, op. cit., p. 268.

Chapter Four

How Pestilence, War, and Revolution Influence Our Behavior

1. For a detailed description, cf. P. Sorokin's *Sociology of Revolution*, chaps. iii-ix.

Chapter Five

How Calamities Influence the Vital Processes— Death, Birth, and Marriage Rates and Social Selection

1. Cf. Charles Creighton's *History of Epidemics in England* (Cambridge, 1891), Vol. I, pp. 2, 123ff., and J. Nohl's *The Black Death* (tr. by C. H. Clarke) (London, 1926), p. 2.
2. Cf. Charles Creighton, op. cit.
3. Ibid., Vol. I, p. 15.
4. *Isvestia*, 5, XI, 1922, No. 214.
5. Cf. P. Sorokin's *Sociology of Revolution* (Philadelphia and London, 1925), pp. 195-228.

6. Ibid., pp. 196-200. Cf. also P. Sorokin's *Social and Cultural Dynamics* (New York, 1937), Vol. III, chaps. 12-14.

7. For the size of the armies and for the casualties of all the wars of Greece, Rome, and other European countries from 500 B.C. to A.D. 1925, cf. P. Sorokin's *Social and Cultural Dynamics*, Vol. III, chaps. 9-11.

8. J. Nohl, op. cit., p. 262. The statement "Marriages were *everywhere* so numerous . . ." is an overgeneralization. This was true in only certain localities.

9. Charles Creighton, op. cit., Vol. I, p. 200.

10. Cf. P. Sorokin's *Social and Cultural Dynamics*, Vol. III, pp. 351ff. and 473ff.

11. Cf. P. Sorokin's *Contemporary Sociological Theories*, pp. 329ff., and *Sociology of Revolution*, pp. 212ff. (The latter work presents a somewhat one-sided conclusion, overstressing the negative selective rôle of revolution.) Cf. also Sorokin's *Social and Cultural Dynamics*, Vol. III, chaps. 9-14.

12. Cf. P. Sorokin's *Social Mobility* (New York, 1927), chaps. 10-13, and *Contemporary Sociological Theories*, chap. 5.

Chapter Six

MIGRATION, MOBILITY, AND DISRUPTION OF SOCIAL INSTITUTIONS

1. Cf. P. Sorokin's *Social Mobility* (New York, 1927).

2. J. P. Waltzing, *Étude historique sur les corporations professionnelles chez les Romains* (Louvain, 1896), Vol. II, p. 102.

3. Cf. F. Curschmann, op. cit., pp. 62-68.

4. *Red Moscow* (Official Soviet edition), 1917-1920, p. 54; *Materials on Petrograd Statistics*, 1920-1921, No. III, pp. 3, 4, 23.

5. I have at my disposal many data on migration and exodus in times of famine. Cf. L. Kawan's *Gli esodi e le carestia in Europa* (Rome, 1932), passim.

6. Cf. L. Kawan, op. cit., pp. 21ff.

7. Cf. Nohl, op. cit., pp. 19, 24, 43, 87ff., et passim; also C. Creighton, op. cit., Vol. I, pp. 7, 27, 36, 49, 177, 181, 195.

8. Cf. L. Kawan, op. cit., pp. 250ff.

9. Cf. L. Kawan, op. cit., pp. 138ff.

10. C. Creighton, op. cit., Vol. I, p. 9.

11. C. Creighton, op. cit., Vol. I, pp. 182ff.

12. Ibid., p. 186.

13. Ibid., p. 132.

14. Nohl, op. cit., p. 162.
15. Cf. P. Sorokin's *Social Mobility*, especially chapters 7-9, 17-19.
16. Cf. P. Sorokin's *Sociology of Revolution*, chap. 12 et passim.
17. Cf. P. Sorokin's *Sociology of Revolution*, chap. 12; and *Social Mobility*, chaps. 17-19.
18. Cf. P. Sorokin's *Social Mobility*, chap. 15.

Chapter Seven

THE INFLUENCE OF CALAMITIES UPON POLITICAL, ECONOMIC,
AND SOCIAL ORGANIZATION

1. This lack of understanding is clearly evidenced in the present war, with its slogan "Democracy vs. totalitarianism"; for Stalin's régime is even more totalitarian than Hitler's, and the war government of the "democracies" has become about as totalitarian as those of the Axis powers. In a word, the struggle is by no means one of totalitarianism versus democracy: it is, rather, a struggle of rival totalitarianisms for values that have little to do with either of the two ideologies—a contest for the preservation or increase of the independence, power, prestige, and well-being of the several nations involved, regardless of their respective ideologies and régimes.
2. Cf. S. H. Prince's *Catastrophe and Social Change*, pp. 100ff.
3. Cf. Nohl, op. cit., pp. 108ff.
4. Creighton, op. cit., Vol. I, pp. 151-152.
5. Ibid., pp. 49-50.
6. Ibid., pp. 180ff.
7. See Genesis xlvii, 12-20.
8. J. H. Breasted, *Ancient Records of Egypt*, Vol. I, sects. 189, 281, 459, 523, et al.
9. Cf. M. Rostovtzeff's *State and Personality in the Economic Life of the Ptolemaic Egypt* (Russian, *Sovremennya Zapiski*), No. 10; also his *Social and Economic History of the Hellenistic World*, Vol. I, pp. 267ff.
10. Chen Huan Chang, *The Economic Principles of Confucius*, Columbia University Studies, Vol. XLIV, (1911) No. I, pp. 168ff.; No. II, pp. 497ff.
11. Cf. Mabel P. H. Lee's *The Economic History of China* (New York, 1921), pp. 40, 46, 58-60, 63, 77-80, 83, 92, 99, 101-104, 110, 122, 140, 155, et passim.
12. R. Pöhlmann, *Geschichte des antiken Communismus und Sozialismus* (Russian translation), pp. 32ff., 430ff.

13. Cf. A. Böckh's *Die Staatshaushaltung der Athener I* (Berlin, 1851), 125ff., and Novosadsky's "The Struggle against Dearth in Ancient Greece," *The Journal of the Ministry of Public Education* (Russian), 1917, pp. 78-80.

14. Novosadsky, op. cit., pp. 80-82; Pöhlmann, op. cit., pp. 235-236; Böckh, op. cit., pp. 116-125; Francotte, "Le pain à bon marché et le pain gratuit dans les cités grecques," in *Mélanges du droit publique grec* (1910), pp. 291ff.

15. Cf. P. Giraud's *Études economiques sur l'antiquité* (Paris, 1905), pp. 68ff.; G. Buzold's *Griechische Geschichte*, Teil III, (Gotha, 1902-1903), pp. 1456, 1614, 1628; B. Niese, *Geschichte der griechischen und macedonischen Staaten* (Gotha, 1893-1903), Teil II, pp. 296ff.; and Teil III, pp. 42ff.; M. Rostovtzeff's *Social and Economic History of the Hellenistic World*, pp. 208ff.; and W. W. Tarn's *The Hellenistic Age* (Cambridge, 1925).

16. Cf. O. Hirschfeld's *Die kaiserlichen Verwaltungsbeamten* (Berlin, 1905), pp. 231ff.; Waltzing's *Étude historique sur les corporations professionnelles chez les Romains*, Vol. I (1896), pp. 26-103; and M. Rostovtzeff's *The Roman Leaden Tessera* (Russian), 1903, pp. 111-113, and his *Social and Economic History of the Roman Empire*.

17. Waltzing, op. cit., Vol. II, pp. 383-384; Duruy, *Histoire des Romains*, Vol. VIII (1885), pp. 550ff.

18. F. Curschmann, *Hungersnöte im Mittelalter*, pp. 71-75 et passim.

19. G. E. Afanassieff, *The Conditions of the Food Trade* (Russian, 1892), pp. 1-3, 8, 17, 144-148, 155, 158. A. Araskranianz, "Die französische Getreidehandelspolitik bis zum Jahre 1789," *Schmollers Staats- und Sozialwissenschaftliche Forschungen* (1882), Vol. 4, pp. 3, 10-14. C. Creighton, op. cit., Vol. I, pp. 49-50, 151, 178ff. It is curious to note that the phenomenon in question regularly occurred even when the heads of the French government were persons who were inimical to an expansion of governmental control of economic affairs. An example is given by Turgot. In 1774 he decreed complete freedom of trade. In 1775, under the influence of the famine of 1774-1775, he was forced to annul his decree. The same happened with Necker, Dupont de Nemure, and the National Assembly (see Afanassieff, op. cit., pp. 299ff., 370-371). All these governments decreed free trade in food supplies (cf. the National Assembly's edicts of 1789, 1790, and 1791). Yet all these laws remained impotent: owing to the increase of

famine and poverty, governmental control grew until in the Jacobin dictatorship it became totalitarian.
20. Cf. P. Sorokin's "The Influence of Famine upon Social Organization," *Russian Economist* (in Russian), 1922, No. 2.
21. Cf. Herbert Spencer's *Principles of Sociology*, Vol. II, chaps. 17, 18; also W. G. Sumner's *War and Other Essays* (New Haven, 1911), and R. Pöhlmann, op. cit.
22. Cf. P. Sorokin's *Sociology of Revolution*, chap. 13 et passim.

Chapter Eight

THE INFLUENCE OF CALAMITIES UPON THE ECONOMIC
STANDARD OF LIVING

1. Cf. P. Sorokin's *Sociology of Revolution*, pp. 321ff., with special reference to the Russian and other revolutions.
2. For the history of totalitarian experiments, cf. the following works: Aristotle, *Politics;* M. I. Rostovtzeff, *The Social and Economic History of the Roman Empire* (Oxford, 1926), chaps. ix-x; his *"Ptolemaic Egypt,"* in the *Cambridge Ancient History* (Cambridge, 1924), Vol. VII; and his *Social and Economic History of the Hellenistic World* (Oxford, 1941) (3 vols., passim); J. H. Breasted, "The Foundation and Expansion of the Egyptian Empire," in the *Cambridge Ancient History*, Vol. II; J. Baikie, op. cit.; R. Pöhlmann, *Geschichte der sozialen Frage und des Sozialismus in der antiken Welt* (München, 1912); J. P. Waltzing, *Étude historique sur les corporations professionelles chez les Romains* (Louvain, 1896), Vol. II, pp. 480ff.; C. Diehl, *Byzance, grandeur et décadence* (Paris, 1928); A. A. Vasilieff, *Histoire de l'empire byzantine* (Paris, 1932); L. Brentano, "Die byzantinische Volkswirtschaft," *Schmollers Jahrbuch*, Vol. XLI (1917); J. Brissant, *Le Régime de la terre dans la société étatiste du Bas-Empire* (Paris, 1927); P. A. Means, *Ancient Civilizations of the Andes* (New York, 1931); L. Baudin, "Agrarian Communities of Pre-Columbian Peru," *Revue d'histoire économique et sociale*, 1927, No. 3; R. Grousset, *Histoire de l'Asie* (Paris, 1922), Vol. II, pp. 325ff.; P. Ivanov, *Wang-an Shih* (St. Petersburg, 1909) (Russian); Chen Huan Chang, *The Economic Principles of Confucius* (New York, 1911), Vol. II, pp. 497ff.; M. P. Lee, *Economic History of China* (New York, 1921); T. Ono, *Peasant Movements in the Period of Tokugawa* (1927); H. R. Williamson, *Wang-an Shih* (London, 1935-1936); K. Kautsky, *Vorläufer des neuren sozialismus* (Stuttgart, 1909); E. Denis, *Huss et la guerre des*

Hussites (Paris, 1878); T. Arnold, *The Caliphate* (Oxford, 1924); M. Hartmann, *Die Islamische Verfassung und Verwaltung* (Leipzig, 1911); Herbert Spencer, *Principles of Sociology* (New York, 1910), Vol. II, pp. 547-582; P. Sorokin, *The Sociology of Revolution,* chaps. 13 and 14; V. Pareto, *Les Systèmes socialistes* (Paris, 1902-1903).
3. For the details of the Russian and other revolutions, cf. P. Sorokin's *Sociology of Revolution,* chaps. 5 and 14.
4. Cf. P. Sorokin's *Social Mobility,* pp. 466ff.

Chapter Nine

TWO GENERAL EFFECTS OF CALAMITIES UPON SOCIOCULTURAL LIFE

1. The polarity and diversity of these effects is somewhat analogous to "the wisdom of the body" in which various processes counterbalance one another and thus maintain its equilibrium. (Cf. W. Cannon's *Wisdom of the Body* (New York, 1933).)

Chapter Ten

HOW CALAMITIES AFFECT THE RELIGIOUS AND ETHICAL LIFE OF SOCIETY

1. *Boston Traveler,* February 9, 1942.
2. Ibid., February 27, 1942.
3. Ibid., January 17, 1942.
4. J. Burckhardt, *The Civilization of the Renaissance in Italy* (translated by S. G. C. Middlemore) (London, 1898), p. 501.
5. Ibid., p. 541.
6. Ibid., pp. 542-543.
7. St. Augustine, *Confessions,* Bk. IV.
8. C. Creighton, op. cit., Vol. I, p. 6.
9. Sidney G. Dimond, *The Psychology of the Methodist Revival* (Oxford University Press, 1926), p. 91.
10. Cf. *Beethoven's Letters* (translated by Lady Wallace) (New York, 1867), Vol. II, Nos. 235, 238, 249, 473, et passim.
11. Letter No. 249. Such notes are very rare in the letters of his earlier (happier) period and quite common in those of his later period.
12. S. H. Prince, *Catastrophe and Social Change (Based upon a Sociological Study of the Halifax Disaster)* (New York, 1920), p. 51.

13. Ibid., pp. 38, 76.
14. Ibid., pp. 47-48.
15. Ibid., pp. 53-55.
16. Ibid., pp. 53-57, 63. See also pages 76, 81, 114.
17. Ibid., pp. 40ff.
18. Ibid., pp. 50-51.
19. Ibid., pp. 96-97.
20. E. T. Glueck, "Juvenile Delinquency in Wartime," *The Survey*, March, 1942.
21. Harry S. Sullivan, "Psychiatric Aspects of Morale," *American Journal of Sociology*, November, 1941, p. 288.
22. *New York Times*, April 5, 1942.
23. *Boston Globe*, January 13, 1942.
24. Ibid., January 1, 1942.
25. *New York Times*, January 4, 1942.
26. *Boston Globe*, March 5, 1942.
27. Here is a comparatively modest sample. "Good Grooming Now. To the Editor.—Many of your readers are wondering how they can help in the far-reaching defense program. . . . It is possible for us to keep and build up the morale of the country by appearing well-groomed at all times. . . . The psychological effects of a happy, healthy, well-appearing populace is something that will help us not only win the war but win the peace that follows.—Andre H. Behns, Director, Wilfred Academy of Hair and Beauty Culture, Boston." (*The Boston Globe.*) In the *Boston Traveler* we have a picture of a scantily clad lady with the inscription "Winning the War.—This patriotic young lady . . . is doing her bit to win the war by conserving the material in her bathing suit."
28. Thucydides, *History of the Peloponnesian War* (Everyman's Library), pp. 132-133.
29. These and subsequent quotations are taken from A. M. Campbell's *The Black Death and Men of Learning* (New York, 1931), p. 3.
30. Ibid., p. 138. For the full text, cf. the *Chronicon Johannis de Reading* (J. Tait, editor) (Manchester, 1914), pp. 109-110.
31. Campbell, op. cit., p. 138. For the full text, cf. D. Wilkins' *Concilia Magnae Britanniae et Hiberniae* (London, 1737), Vol. 3, pp. 1-2, 50-51, 135-136.
32. Campbell, op. cit., p. 142. For the full text, cf. Felix Fabri's *Historia Suevorum* (c. 1480), Book II, pp. 309-310.
33. Campbell, op. cit., pp. 129, 134.
34. Cf. the reproduction of the 1625 English translation of

Boccaccio's description in J. Nohl's *The Black Death*, pp. 21-29.
35. Ibid., p. 168.
36. Ibid., p. 44.
37. Ibid., pp. 165-166.
38. Ibid., pp. 162ff.
39. Cf. the description of demoralization in various European plagues in Nohl's work, pp. 18, 23-26, 28, 89, 118, 161ff., 263, et passim; for the growth of irreligiousness, cf. pages 19, 20, 26, 37, 51-52, 165-168, et passim. For these phenomena in connection with English epidemics, cf. C. Creighton's *History of Epidemics in Britain*, Vol. I, pp. 5, 11-12, 26-27, 32-42, 50-51, 140, 151-152, 182, 186ff., et passim.
40. Thucydides, op. cit., pp. 131-132.
41. Creighton, op. cit., Vol. I, p. 42.
42. Nohl, op. cit., pp. 18-21.
43. Ibid., p. 21.
44. Ibid., p. 32.
45. Ibid., p. 47.
46. Ibid., p. 51.
47. Ibid., p. 114.
48. Ibid., pp. 115ff.
49. Ibid., p. 123.
50. Ibid., p. 128.
51. Ibid., p. 129.
52. Ibid., p. 109ff.
53. Ibid., pp. 121ff.
54. Ibid., p. 132.
55. Wittkower and Spillane, op. cit., p. 223.
56. J. Novicow, *War and Its Alleged Benefits* (New York, 1911), pp. 72ff.
57. R. Steinmetz, *Soziologie des Krieges* (Leipzig, 1929), chap. 2. For the literature of the question, cf. P. Sorokin's *Contemporary Sociological Theories*, pp. 340ff.
58. P. Sorokin, *Social and Cultural Dynamics* (New York, 1937), p. 352. If we take all the small wars and military expeditions of the United States, beginning with 1775 and ending with 1932, the percentage of war years is more than 50. Cf. the list of such wars in L. Dennis's *The Dynamics of War and Revolution* (New York, 1940), pp. 107-108.
59. Cf. the literature and data in P. Sorokin's *Contemporary Sociological Theories*, pp. 341ff. Cf. Also H. Mannheim's *War and Crime* (London, 1941).
60. From the admonitions of Ipuwer, quoted from James H.

Breasted's *The Dawn of Conscience* (New York, 1933),
pp. 194ff. The full text is given in Alan H. Gardiner's *The
Admonitions of an Egyptian Sage* (Leipzig, 1909). In a
similar way other Egyptian revolutions are described in such
Egyptian documents as "The Complaint of Khekheperre-
sonbu" and "The Prophecy of Neferrohu" (cf. A. Erman's
The Literature of the Ancient Egyptians (London, 1927),
pp. 92-116.

61. Thucydides, op. cit., pp. 223ff.
62. D. Greer, *The Incidence of the Terror during the French
Revolution* (Harvard University Press, 1935), pp. 26, 37.
63. M. Gernet, *Capital Punishment* (Moscow, 1915) (Russian),
pp. 57-76. P. Sorokin, *Sociology of Revolution*, pp. 142ff.
64. Cf. P. Sorokin's *Sociology of Revolution*, pp. 163ff.
65. James H. Breasted, *Dawn of Conscience* (New York, 1933),
p. 153.
66. J. Baikie, *A History of Egypt* (New York, 1929), Vol. I,
p. 217.
67. Breasted, op. cit., pp. 163-164. J. Baikie, op. cit., Vol. I,
pp. 364ff.
68. Breasted, op. cit., 165ff.
69. Breasted, op. cit., pp. 166-174. J. Baikie, op. cit., Vol. I,
pp. 248ff.
70. Ibid., pp. 178-181.
71. For the literature and indices of these trends, together with
a detailed analysis of the situation, cf. P. Sorokin's *Social and
Cultural Dynamics* (New York, 1937), Vol. II, chaps. 1,
2, 13.
72. M. Rostovtzeff, *Social and Economic History of the Hellenistic World* (Oxford University Press, 1941), Vol. II, pp.
610-612.
73. Ibid., Vol. I, pp. 200-202.
74. Cf. P. Sorokin's, *Social Dynamics*, Vol. II, chaps. 1, 2, 13.
75. F. Cumont, *L'Egypte des astrologues* (Bruxelles, 1937), pp.
178-184.
76. Ibid., p. 204.
77. P. Sorokin, *Social and Cultural Dynamics*, Vol. II, p. 76.
For the evidences and the literature on the topic, cf. chaps.
1, 2, 13, et passim.
78. F. Cumont, *The After-life in Roman Paganism* (New
Haven, 1922), pp. 11-12.
79. *The Cambridge Modern History* (New York, 1934), Vol. II,
p. 3. P. Villari, *The Life and Times of Niccolo Machiavelli*
(London, T. Fisher Union, no date), pp. 2ff. A. V. Martin,

Die Soziologie der Renaissance (Stuttgart, 1932), pp. 1-5, 17-21, 27, 45, et passim.
80. N. Machiavelli, *Discorsi*, Vol. I, chaps. 12 and 55.
81. For the data and indices, together with other evidence, cf. P. Sorokin's *Social Dynamics*, Vol. II, chaps. 1, 2, and 13, and Vol. I, pp. 334ff.
82. J. Burckhardt, *The Civilization of the Renaissance in Italy* (London, 1898), p. 272.
83. Ibid., p. 435.
84. Ibid., pp. 433ff., 441ff.
85. Ibid., p. 453.
86. J. Nohl, op. cit., p. 162.
87. J. Burckhardt, op. cit., p. 454.
88. *The Cambridge Modern History*, Vol. II, p. 3.

Chapter Eleven

CALAMITIES AND ETHICO-RELIGIOUS PROGRESS

1. J. Burckhardt, op. cit., pp. 485-489.
2. Ibid., p. 487.
3. *The Cambridge Modern History*, Vol. II, p. 3.
4. J. Burckhardt, op. cit., pp. 468-473.
5. Cf. P. Villari's work on Savouarola.
6. J. Huizinga, *The Waning of the Middle Ages* (London, 1927), chap. i, pp. 15ff. The thirteenth and fourteenth centuries were the most turbulent ones so far as internal disturbances and revolutions are concerned. (Cf. P. Sorokin's *Social and Cultural Dynamics*, Vol. III, chaps. 12-14.)
7. J. Huizinga, op. cit., pp. 18, 19, 127.
8. Cf. Sydney G. Dimond's *The Psychology of the Methodist Revival* (Oxford University Press, 1926), chap. 2.
9. S. G. Dimond, op. cit., p. 251-252.
10. John Wesley, *Journals* (edited by M. Curnoch) (London, 1909-1916), Vol. II, p. 322.
11. S. G. Dimond, op. cit., p. 252.
12. E. K. Nottingham, *Methodism and the Frontier* (New York, Columbia University Press, 1941), pp. 19-22.
13. Ibid., pp. 22-23.
14. Ibid., passim. Cf. also C. Cleveland's *Great Revivals in the West, 1797-1805* (Chicago, 1916).
15. E. K. Nottingham, op. cit., pp. 197ff.
16. Cf. James H. Breasted, op. cit., pp. 29-32 and (for the text), pp. 35ff.
17. Ibid., pp. 37, 38, 34, and 32.

18. "That this unification [of Egypt] had been by no means a peaceful one is evidenced by that fact that the [predynastic] mace-head records 'captives 120,000'; and of captive animals, 'oxen 400,000, goats 1,422,000.' "—J. Baikie, *A History of Egypt*, Vol. I, p. 64.
19. For the full texts, cf. A. Erman's *The Literature of the Ancient Egyptians* (translated by A. M. Blackman) (London, 1927), pp. 54ff.
20. Cf. J. Baikie, op. cit., Vol. I, chaps. 9 and 10.
21. Such is the title of Breasted's Chapter Ten dealing with this subject.
22. For the full text, cf. Erman, op. cit., pp. 75ff. "We meet with religious conceptions in this composition that are practically nonexistent in the other works of the same class," observes Erman.
23. Breasted, op. cit., pp. 154ff. Baikie, op. cit., Vol. I, pp. 226ff.
24. Baikie, Vol. I, p. 233.
25. Ibid., pp. 157-159.
26. Breasted, op. cit., p. 153.
27. Ibid., p. 161.
28. For the text, cf. Erman, op. cit., pp. 86ff.
29. Breasted, op. cit., p. 169.
30. Ibid., p. 176.
31. Erman, op. cit., p. 92.
32. For the text, cf. Erman, op. cit., pp. 108ff.
33. For the text, cf. Erman, op. cit., pp. 116ff.
34. Breasted, op. cit., pp. 182-193.
35. For the texts, cf. Erman, op. cit., pp. 92ff.
36. Breasted, op. cit., pp. 194-204.
37. Ibid., chap. 12.
38. Ibid., p. 212.
39. Ibid., pp. 213-214.
40. For the text, cf. Erman, op. cit., pp. 67ff.
41. Baikie, op. cit., Vol. I, pp. 357ff.
42. Ibid., p. 358.
43. Ibid., pp. 369ff. For the texts, cf. Erman, op. cit., pp. 29ff.
44. Cf. Baikie, op. cit., Vol. I, pp. 389-399.
45. Ibid., Vol. II, p. 10.
46. Ibid., Vol. II, p. 172. Cf. also chap. 27.
47. Cf. Baikie, op. cit., Vol. II, chap. 28, and Breasted, op. cit., chap. 15.
48. Cf. Breasted, op. cit., pp. 310-313.
49. For this period, cf. especially "The Advice of Ani" and

"The Wisdom of Amenomope," Baikie, op. cit., Vol. II, pp. 32ff., and Erman, op. cit., pp. 214ff. (for the foregoing texts and also for religious hymns).

50. Ibid., p. 330, and Baikie, Vol. II, chaps. 30 and 31.

51. Cf. James Legge's *The Life and Teachings of Confucius* (London, 1895), pp. 6off.

52. James Legge, *The Life and Works of Mencius* (Philadelphia, 1875), pp. 19ff.

53. Ibid., pp. 77ff.; G. F. Moore's *History of Religion* (New York, 1913), pp. 37ff.; M. Granet's *La Pensée Chinoise* (Paris, 1934), chapters on Confucianism, Taoism, Postivism, and Moh-tih; and H. A. Giles' *Confucianism and Its Rivals* (London, 1915).

54. In addition to the standard histories of China, cf. the account of internecine and other wars and disturbances in J. S. Lee's "The Periodic Recurrence of Internecine Wars in China," *China Journal*, March-April, 1931. Lee presents a statistical investigation of all the internecine wars from 221 B.C. to 1900, plotted by five-year periods. See his diagram in P. Sorokin's *Social and Cultural Dynamics*, Vol. III, pp. 357-359.

55. Cf. René Grousset's *Histoire de l'Asie, II, L'Inde et la Chine* (Paris, 1922), pp. 170ff.

56. Cf. Grousset, op. cit., pp. 188ff.; Mrs. Rhys Davies' *Buddhism* (London, 1912); and E. J. Thomas' *The History of Buddhist Thought* (London, 1933).

57. H. A. Giles, op. cit., p. 180.

58. For the data and the diagram of the internecine wars for these centuries, cf. Lee, op. cit. The curve of civil wars and similar disturbances shows a sharp upward trend.

59. Cf. Grousset, op. cit., pp. 200ff.

60. O. Sirén, *A History of Early Chinese Painting* (London, 1933), Vol. I, pp. 37ff.

61. Cf. Grousset, op. cit., pp. 26off.; also H. A. Giles' *History of Chinese Literature* (London, 1901), pp. 160ff., and *Confucianism and Its Rivals*, pp. 212ff.

62. Religious, because the attempts to depict Confucius as a mere agnostic are hardly accurate. (Cf. H. A. Giles' *Confucianism*, chaps. 3-4.)

63. Hu Shih, "The Establishment of Confucianism as a State Religion during the Han Dynasty," *The Journal of the North China Branch of the Royal Asiatic Society*, Vol. LX (1929), pp. 34-40.

64. Ibid., p. 22.

65. For the difference between these *Vedas*, cf. E. J. Rapson's *Ancient India* (Cambridge, 1914), pp. 47-48.
66. A. K. Mazumdar, *The Hindu History, B.C. 3000 to 1200 A.D.* (Faribadad, 1920), pp. 409ff.; R. C. Majumdar, "Evolution of Religio-Philosophic Culture in India," *The Cultural Heritage of India* (Belur Math, Calcutta, n.d.), Vol. III, pp. 2ff.; E. J. Rapson (editor), *The Cambridge History of India* (New York, 1922), chaps. 3, 4.
67. Mazumdar, op. cit., p. 550.
68. Majumdar, op. cit., p. 13.
69. Cf. Rapson's *Ancient India*, pp. 52-63; *Cambridge History of India*, Vol. I, pp. 120-122, 141; and Mazumdar, op. cit., pp. 494-534.
70. S. K. Aiyangar, *Ancient India* (London, 1911), p. 27; also pp. 54ff. For similar statements, cf. Rapson's *Ancient India*, p. 113.
71. E. B. Havell, *The History of Aryan Rule in India* (New York, n.d.), p. 172.
72. Besides the quoted works, cf. S. K. Das' *The Economic History of Ancient India* (Howrah, 1925), pp. 138-178; Havell, op. cit., pp. 66-88.
73. For the division of the day into 16 periods of 1.5 hours each, cf. Havell, op. cit., pp. 66-88.
74. V. A. Smith, *The Early History of India* (Oxford, 1924), p. 137.
75. Ibid., p. 149.
76. V. A. Smith, *The History of India from the Earliest Times to the End of 1911* (Oxford, 1911), p. 480.
77. E. B. Havell, *The History of Aryan Rule in India*, pp. 89-103; V. A. Smith, *The History of India from the Earliest Times to the End of 1911*, pp. 93-116; also his *Early History of India*, pp. 162-200.
78. Majumdar, op. cit., p. 4.
79. Majumdar, op. cit., pp. 23, 29. Cf. also V. A. Smith's *History of India*, pp. 119ff., and *Early History of India*, pp. 219-262; Havell, op. cit., pp. 119-146; and A. K. Mazumdar's *Hindu History*, pp. 632-646.
80. Cf. S. K. Das, op. cit., pp. 231-279; A. K. Mazumdar, op. cit., pp. 662-679; E. B. Havell, op. cit., pp. 147-170; V. A. Smith's *Early History of India*, pp. 295-347.
81. V. A. Smith, op. cit., pp. 379-389.
82. I. Prasad, *History of Mediaeval India* (Allahabad, 1925), p. 21.

83. Ibid., pp. xix-xxxix and 1-36. For a general characterization of the period, cf. A. K. Mazumdar, op. cit., pp. 688ff. and 702-871; V. A. Smith's *Early History of India*, pp. 376-438; and Havell, op. cit. pp. 247-275.
84. W. F. Albright, *From the Stone Age to Christianity* (Baltimore, 1940), p. 310.
85. Ibid., p. 252.
86. B. A. Turaieff, *A History of the Ancient Orient* (Russian) (Leningrad, 1935), Vol. II, p. 280.
87. Cf. Albright, op. cit., pp. 184-189, 196, 205, 207, and Breasted, op. cit., pp. 350-351.
88. Cf. Albright, op. cit., pp. 222ff.
89. Written in the sixth or fifth century B.C. Cf. Albright, op. cit., p. 253.
90. For the prophetic movements of the period and other points, cf. Turaieff, op. cit., Vol. II, pp. 67-75, 184-193, 276-283; Albright, op. cit., pp. 228-255; F. Jones' *Personalities of the Old Testament* (New York, 1939), pp. 210-269; and L. Finkelstein's *The Pharisees* (2 vols.) (Philadelphia, 1940).
91. Turaieff, op. cit., Vol. II, p. 266.
92. Albright, op. cit., pp. 269-271.
93. Cf. M. J. Lagrange's *Le Messianisme chez les Juifs* (Paris, 1909).
94. Cf. Breasted, op. cit., p. 343.
95. Cf. Albright, op. cit., pp. 148-149.
96. Ibid., p. 253.
97. E. Renan, *L'Antéchrist* (Paris, 1873), pp. 325-339.
98. Cf. M. I. Rostovtzeff's *Social and Economic History of the Roman Empire* (Oxford, 1926); S. Dill's *Roman Society from Nero to Marcus Aurelius* (London, 1925) and *Roman Society in the Last Century of the Western Empire* (London, 1929); F. Cumont's *Les Religions orientales dans le paganisme romain* (Paris, 1929); and P. Sorokin's *Social and Cultural Dynamics*, Vol. I, pp. 305ff., and Vol. II, pp. 69ff.

Chapter Twelve

SINNERS AND SAINTS IN CALAMITY

1. For the meaning of "integration of values," cf. P. Sorokin's *Social and Cultural Dynamics*, Vol. I, chap. 1, and Vol. IV, chaps. 1-3. Cf. also P. Sorokin's *The Crisis of Our Age*, chaps. 1, 7, 9.
2. Cf. P. Sorokin's *Crisis of Our Age*, chaps. 2-4.

3. Pareto's emphasis on the dependence of derivations and ideologies upon sentiments and various biological drives is applicable precisely to this type of person and finds scant application to other groups.
4. Cf. P. Sorokin's *The Crisis of Our Age*, chaps. 2-6.
5. For an adequate conception of the sensate, ideational, and idealistic dominant forms of culture, cf. P. Sorokin's *Social and Cultural Dynamics*, Vol. I, chaps. 2, 3, and Vols. I-IV, passim. An abridged treatment is presented in P. Sorokin's *The Crisis of Our Age*, chap. 1.
6. Cf. P. Sorokin's *Social and Cultural Dynamics* and *The Crisis of Our Age*.
7. For the revolutions, war, and other calamities that prevailed during these centuries, together with the concomitant transformation of cultural phenomena (arts and sciences, philosophy and ethics, forms of social organization, etc.), cf. P. Sorokin's *Social and Cultural Dynamics* and *The Crisis of Our Age*.
8. Cf. the indices and list of revolutions for these and other centuries of European history in P. Sorokin's *Social and Cultural Dynamics*, Vol. III, chaps. 12-14.
9. Cf. P. Sorokin's *Social and Cultural Dynamics* and *The Crisis of Our Age*.

Chapter Thirteen

THE INFLUENCE OF CALAMITIES UPON SCIENCE AND TECHNOLOGY

1. Cf. P. Sorokin's *Sociology of Revolution*, pp. 212ff.
2. Cf. P. Sorokin's *Social and Cultural Dynamics*, Vol. II, p. 164. For revolutions, cf. his *Sociology of Revolution*, chap. 15.
3. For the data and literature cf. R. K. Merton's "Science, Technology and Society in Seventeenth-Century England," *Osiris*, Vol. IV (1938).
4. For the monotonous repetition of this uniformity, cf. the works of Curschmann, Tzitovitch, Romanovitch-Slavatinsky, Kawan, Issaieff, Ermoloff, Digby, *et al.*
5. Cf. K. Bücher's *Arbért und Rhythmus* (Leipzig, 1902); Westermarck's *The Origin*, Vol. II, pp. 268ff., and the chapter entitled "Industry"; and A. J. Toynbee's *A Study of History* (Oxford, 1936), Vols. I-III.
6. Cf. the *Shû King*, in *The Sacred Books of the East*, Vol. III, pp. 51ff.

7. Cf. Leshkoff, op. cit., pp. 486ff.; Ermoloff, op. cit., Vol. I, pp. 16ff.; Romanovitch-Slavatinsky, op. cit., pp. 57ff.; and N. Novombergsky's *Ocherki vnutrenniago upravlennia Mos. Russy XVII stoletia* (Tomsk, 1914), Vol. I, Documents Nos. 7, 208, and 215, et passim.
8. Nohl, op. cit., pp. 110-113. For the sanitary ordinances issued after the plagues and epidemics in England, cf. Creighton, op. cit., Vol. I, pp. 322ff. For the medical progress in connection with epidemics, cf. Vol. I, pp. 51ff., 252ff., and 402ff., and Vol. II, passim.
9. Cf. Creighton, op. cit., Vols. I and II, passim.
10. Cf. B. K. Sarkar's *The Positive Background of Hindu Sociology* (Allahabad, 1937).

Chapter Fourteen

INFLUENCE OF CALAMITIES UPON THE FINE ARTS

1. E. Mâle, *Art et Artistes* (Paris, 1928), pp. 20ff.
2. Cf. L. Brehier's *L'Art chrétien* (Paris, 1918), pp. 335ff. For other data and for the literature, cf. P. Sorokin's *Social and Cultural Dynamics*, Vol. I, pp. 328ff., which gives also pictures of Death and the *danse macabre*.
3. J. Huizinga, *The Waning of the Middle Ages* (London, 1927), pp. 23ff.
4. Cf. Nohl, op. cit., p. 257.
5. For data on the wars and revolutions of the sixteenth and seventeenth centuries, cf. P. Sorokin's *Social and Cultural Dynamics*, Vol. III, chaps. 9-14.
6. Ibid., Vol. I, p. 341.
7. E. Mâle, *L'Art religieux après le concile de Trente* (Paris, 1932), pp. 148ff. Cf. also P. Sorokin's *Dynamics*, Vol. I, pp. 342ff.
8. Cf. Max Eastman's *Artists in Uniform* (New York, 1934), M. Josephson's *Nazi Culture* (New York, 1933), H. and W. Scheider and S. Clough's *Making Fascists* (Chicago, 1929).
9. For the literature on this subject, cf. P. Sorokin's *Contemporary Sociological Theories*, pp. 349ff.
10. For the detailed figures, cf. P. Sorokin's *Dynamics*, Vol. I, table 31.
11. For the indices of war and revolution in Greece, cf. P. Sorokin's *Dynamics*, Vol. III, chaps. 9-14 and p. 297 (diagram).
12. Ibid., Vol. III, chaps. 9-14.
13. Ibid., pp. 325, 447.

14. Cf. Cooley's "Genius, Fame, and Comparison of Races," *Annals of the American Academy*, Vol. IX, May, 1897, p. 31.
15. Cf. A. Odin's *Genèse des grands hommes* (Lausanne, 1895), Vol. II, table 2. For the indices of war and revolution during these periods, cf. P. Sorokin's *Dynamics*, Vol. III, pp. 307, 425.
16. Cf. E. L. Clarke's *American Men of Letters* (Columbia University Press, 1916), pp. 38-39.
17. For the indices of war and revolution in English history, cf. P. Sorokin's *Dynamics*, Vol. III, pp. 315, 435ff.
18. For the indices of war and revolution in Russia, cf. P. Sorokin's *Dynamics*, Vol. III, pp. 311, 462ff.
19. Cf. J. de Maistre's *Oeuvres complètes* (Lyon, 1891-1892), Vol. I, pp. 36-37.
20. Cf. P. Sorokin's *Dynamics* (all four volumes) and *The Crisis of Our Age*.

Chapter Fifteen

DYNAMICS OF IDEOLOGIES IN CALAMITY

1. Among the best of the enormous literature is G. Isambert's *Les idées socialistes en France de 1815 à 1848* (Paris, 1905), pp. 20-22, and passim.
2. See the facts and literature in Sorokin's "Famine and Ideology of Society," *Russian Ekonomist*, 1922, Nos. 4-5 (Russian). For Greek and Roman Socialist and Communist movements and ideologies the best source is still R. Pöhlmann's *Geschichte der Sozialen Frage und des Sozialismus in der antiken Welt* (München, 1912); cf. the analysis of the underlying economic situation in M. I. Rostovtzeff's *Social and Economic History of the Hellenistic World*, pp. 605-617, 722-757, 933ff., and passim. See there also the special literature on some of the socialist movements and ideologies, pp. 1367-1368.
3. Cf. *Matthew*, xix: 23-24; *Mark*, iv: 19; *Luke*, xviii: 22-25; vi: 20-25, 29-34; the *Acts*, iv: 32-35, etc. Concerning the Roman and early Christian movements, see Pöhlmann's quoted work.
4. See the sources in P. Sorokin's "Famine and Ideology of Society," *Russian Ekonomist*, 1922, Nos. 4-5 (Russian).
5. Cf. L. Karsavin's *Studies of Religious Life in Italy of the Twelfth and the Thirteenth Centuries* (St. Petersburg, 1912) (Russian); K. Kautsky's *Vorlaufer des neuren Sozialismus*

(Stuttgart, 1909), 2 vols. See other literature and facts in P. Sorokin's "Famine and Ideology of Society."

6. R. Pöhlmann, op. cit. (Russian translation of 1912), pp. 469-470, et passim.
7. A. Lawrence Lowell's *Public Opinion in War and Peace*, pp. 223-234. See passim.
8. See a detailed analysis of this whole problem of the dynamics of ideologies in revolutions in P. Sorokin's *Sociology of Revolution*, Part I.
9. See facts and details in P. Sorokin's *Sociology of Revolution* quoted.

Chapter Sixteen

CAUSES OF CALAMITIES

1. Creighton, op. cit., Vol. I, p. 15; see there his list of the famine attended by various epidemics.
2. See about that in P. Sorokin's *Dynamics*, Vol. III, chaps. 9-14.
3. Cf. detailed analysis of the relationship between war and revolution in P. Sorokin's *Dynamics*, Vol. III, pp. 487ff.
4. Cf. P. Sorokin's *Dynamics*, Vol. III, chaps. 11, 14. Also Sorokin's "A Neglected Factor of War," *American Sociological Review*, August, 1938.

Chapter Seventeen

THE WAY OUT OF CALAMITIES

1. Cf. the etiology, factors, and means of combating epidemics in Creighton's work. Cf. also, Mr. Greenwood's "On Some Factors which Influence the Prevalence of Plague," *Journal of Hygiene*, Plague Supplement, 1911, No. II, Vol. I; also M. Greenwood's "Factors that Determine the Rise, Spread, and Degree of Severity of Epidemic Diseases," the *XVII International Congress of Medicine* (1913), Sec. 18, pp. 49-80.
2. Cf. W. H. Davis' "The Influenza Epidemics," *American Journal of Public Health*, No. 9, 1919, pp. 50-61.

Chapter Eighteen

A GLANCE INTO THE FUTURE

1. See for a detailed analysis of the nature of the contemporary social and cultural crisis P. Sorokin's *The Crisis of Our Age*, and *Dynamics* (all four volumes).

INDEX*

---

* The list of quoted authors is given in the *Notes* at the end of the book. Their names are not included in the Index.

Communist-socialist ideologies, dynamics of, in calamity, 263-66
Communist-socialist movements, 266-75
Communization of property in calamity, 122-43, 150-53, 273, 310
Conditioned reflexes, order of extinction in starvation of, 39-40
Confiscation of property. See Communization of property
Conflict. See Antagonism
Confucianism, 207-14
Confucius, 207
Control governmental in calamity, 121-44, 314-15
Creative role of calamity, 10, 161-64, 194, 226, 243-51, 256-62
Criminality in, calamity, 160-63, 170, 188-93; famine, 59-82; pestilence, 174-79; revolution, 183-88; war, 180-83
Crises, ethics and religion in great, 188-93, 200-226
Culture, effects of calamities upon, 156-57
Death-rate in calamity, 92-93
Deaths, 90-91
Decrease of contrast in standard of living, 150-52
Delirium of inanition, 29, 38
Democracy, and calamity, 121-44, 314-15
Demoralization in calamity, 59-82, 161-66, 174-77, 181-93, 207, 215, 235
Desires in calamity, 45-46
Destructive role of calamities, 35-44, 57-89, 90-93, 106, 119-20, 144-45, 159-61, 185-86, 188-89, 241-43, 252-56
Dictatorship. See Absolutism, Control governmental
Discoveries and inventions, and calamities, 243-46. See also Creative role
Disease mental, and calamities, 35-42, 44-45
Disintegration of unity of mind, 35-45
Disintegration of values, as cause of demoralization, 227-33; of revolution and war, 293-95
Disruption of social institutions in calamity, 119-21
Diversification. See Polarization
Divorce, 313
Domination of hunger factor, 51-54, 57-82
Dostoevsky, Th., 231
Dreams in hunger, 29, 33
Dynamics of ideologies in, famine, 76-79, 263-75; revolution, 276-85; war, 275-76
Economic conditions, and Socialist-Communist ideology, 76-79, 263-75
Economic life in calamity, decrease of contrast between rich and poor, 150-52, 310-13; impoverishment, 146-50; inflation, 147-49; reallocation of wealth, 111-19, 152-53
Economic organization in calamity, 122, 127-44
Education, trend in, 313-14

Egypt ancient, government control, 128
Egyptian crises, ethics and religion in, 188-91, 201-07
Emotions in, famine, 15-21; pestilence, 21-22; revolution and war, 22-26
End-values, as factor of behavior, 229-33, 318-19
Epidemics. See Pestilence
Epidemics psychical, 316
Equality, and calamities, 150-52, 272-73, 310-13
Ethical conduct in calamities, demoralization of, 59-82, 161-66, 174-77, 181-93, 207, 215, 235; polarization of, 78-82, 158-64, 169-70; progress of, 166-67, 169, 171, 194-226
Executions in revolutions, 185-86
Exodus. See Migration
Expansion of government control in, calamities, 121-25, 139-40, 314-15; famine, 127-34; pestilence, 126-27; revolution, 142-44; war, 134-41
Explosion in Halifax, 169-71
Factors of, behavior, 55-57; integrity of personality, 229-33, 318-19. See also Causes
Family, and famine, 62-63; disorganization of, 313. See also Marriage
Famine, and aesthetic activity, 74-75; and cannibalism, 66-67; and change in behavior, 51-82; and criminality, 66-74; and prostitution, 62-63; and socialist-communist ideologies, 263-66; association with other calamities, 288-89; causes of, 293; stimulating role of, 247; termination of, 297-99
Famine's effects upon: association of ideas, 28; attention, 28, 31; birthrate, 92-94; death-rate, 90-91; economic life, 122, 145-46, 150-52; economic organization, 127-44; emotions, 16-21; ethics, 66-74, 161-64; fine arts, 153-56; marriage-rate, 94-95; memory, 29; mental disease, 40; migration, 106-7; mobility, 111; political organization, 122-24; 127-44; religion, 70-74, 81-82, 161-64; science and technology, 240-45; sensation and perception, 28; sex-life, 59-64; speech-reactions, 29-33, 156-57; volition and wishes, 45-46
Fear, and war, 22-25
Females, positive selection of, 98
Fine arts. See Arts fine
Fit and unfit, survival of, 96-104
Freedom, and hunger, 64-65; and revolution, 142-43; decrease of, in calamities, 121-44, 314-15
God, values of the kingdom of, 229-31. See also Religion
Golovin, N., 24, 42, 43
Government control, expansion of, contemporary, 139-40, 314-15; in famine, 127-34; in pestilence, 126-27; in revolution, 142-44; in war, 134-41

Greco-Roman crises, ethics and religion in, 184-85, 190-91, 224-26
Greece, government control in famines of, 129
Halifax explosion, effects of, 169-70
Hallucination in starvation, 29, 32-33, 38
Hamsun, K., 18, 37, 38, 39, 58, 72
Hedonism in calamities, 58-82, 161-66, 174-77, 181-93, 207, 215, 235
Hume, David, 249
Hunger, physiological and psychosocial, 15. See also Famine
Ideas, change in famine of, 76-79. See also Ideologies
Ideational culture, 237-40
Ideologies, dynamics of, in famine and impoverishment, 76-79, 263-75; revolution, 276-85; war, 275-76
Ideologies, socialist-communist. See Communist-socialist ideologies
Impoverishment. See Famine
Impregnation of culture, by calamities, 156-58, 241, 254-56
India, ethics and religion in crises of, 214-21
Insanity. See Disease mental
Integrated values, as a factor of conduct, 227-32. See also Factor
Ipuwer, 184, 204, 266
Irreligiosity. See Atheism
Inventions in calamities, 243-46
Irrational ways out of calamity, 296-306
Isolation, psychosocial in pestilence, 21-22, 84
Jainism, 215
Judaism, 222-24
Justice, progress of conception of, in China, 207-14; in Egypt, 201-07; in India, 214-21; in Judaism, 221-24
Lasciva numismata, 269
Law of Polarization. See Polarization
Lesskoff, N., 19
Libertines. See Hedonism
Liberating phase of revolution, 277-80
Liberty. See Freedom
Life, loss of, in calamities, 90-92
Literature, stimulated by war and revolution, 256-61
Lowell, A. L., 275
Loyola, Ignatius, 37, 167
Macabre, in fine arts, 253-54
Machiavelli, N., 240
Magnitude of polarized movements, 233-40
Mahavira, 37
Maistre, J. de, 261
Marriage, 309-313
Marriage-rate, in calamity, 94-95
Melancholia, in fine arts, 253-54
Mencius, 207
Messianic movements in calamities, 162-63
Methodism, 198-200
Migration in, famine, 106-08; pestilence, 109; revolution and war, 109-10, 310

Mikkelsen, E., 18, 20, 30, 32, 33
Mobility in, calamities, 111-12; famine and pestilence, 112-13; revolution, 113-16; war, 117-19; contemporary, 310-13
Mohammed, 37
Music, in revolution and war, 257-58. See also Arts fine
Nationalization of property, in calamity, 122-43, 150-53, 273, 310
Nihilism. See Atheism, Demoralization
Nobility, shift of, in calamity, 111-19, 310-13
Norms. See Value
Norton-Cru, J., 24
Ordeal of calamity, as educator, 10, 36, 319
Organization economic, political, social, changes in, 121-26
Ownership. See Property
Pathetique, in fine arts, 253-54
Pavlov, Ivan, 31, 64
pecunias equare, 267
Perception in hunger, 28
Pestilence, and demoralization, 174-77; and fine arts, 253-54; and moral heroism, 177-80; and religion, 178; and science, 244, 247-49; association with other calamities, 288-89; behavior in, 84-86; causes of, 293; government control in, 126-27; loss of life in, 90-91; psychosocial isolation in, 21-22, 84; selection by, 101-02; vital processes in, 92-94
Pöhlmann, R., 129, 273
Polarization of effects of calamity, 14-15, 158-64, 241-42, 256-57
Political regime, changes of, in calamities of, 121-25; in famine, 127-34; in pestilence, 126-27; in revolution, 142-44; in war, 134-41
Poverty. See Famine
Progress of ethics and religion in calamities, 161-63, 166-68, 169, 171, 194-96; 201-226
Propaganda-arts, 255
Property private, equalization of, 150-52; governmental control of, in calamities, 122-25; in famine, 127-34; in pestilence, 126-27; in revolution, 141-43; in redistribution of, 152-53; 273, 310; in war, 134-41
Proscriptio locupletium, 267
Prostitution in famine, 62-63
Psychoneuroses. See Disease mental
Rational ways out of calamity, 296-306
Redistribution of wealth, in calamities, 111-19, 150-53, 273, 310
Relationships social, disruption of, 119-20
Religion, change of, in calamities and famine, 70-71, 81-82, 157, 160-67, 169; in great crises, 188-93; in pestilence, 174-80; in revolution, 184-85; in war, 180-83
Religion, progress of in great crises, 200-26. See also Atheism, Polarization, Progress

352